THE COMPLETE
Live! Don't Diet!

Vicki Park

SWEET WATER PRESS

An Important Reminder:

This book is based on the author's personal experience and opinions. No diet program should be followed without first consulting a health care professional. If you have any special medical conditions you should consult with your health care professional regarding possible modification of the program contained in this book.

1998 Sweetwater Press Edition
Introduction and 40 additional recipes copyright © 1998 by PepperTree Press

This edition published by arrangement with Warner Books, Inc., New York, and with PepperTree Press. All rights reserved under International and Pan-American Copyright Conventions.
Published in the United States by Sweetwater Press, Birmingham, Alabama.

Library of Congress Cataloging-in-Publication Data

Park, Vicki.
The complete live! don't diet! / Vicki Park. –Sweetwater Press ed.
p.   cm.
Contains: Live! don't diet. Pleasant Grove, Ala. : PepperTree Press, c1995.
With a new introduction and 40 new recipes.
Contains: Exceed the feed limit. Pleasant Grove, Ala. : PepperTree Press, c1997.
Includes index.
ISBN 1-58173-046-9 (hbk.)
1. Low-fat diet—Recipes. 2. Reducing diets—Recipes. I. Park, Vicki. Live! don't diet. II. Park, Vicki. Exceed the feed limit. III. Title.
RM237.7P348   1998
641.5'638—dc21   98-29455
                                                                                      CIP

Manufactured in the United States of America

"Before" cover photograph by Lorene Whatley
"After" cover photograph by Spider Martin

Dedication

This book is dedicated to my terrific family and to all those wonderful friends and readers who have been so supportive. I love you all.

Special Thanks

While words can't fully express my gratitude for the love, assistance, and support I have received from so many people, I am especially grateful to all those readers who have written to share their success stories with me. I will treasure those letters forever. In addition, I would like to especially thank my husband, Ken; my daughter, Ashley; my Mom, Lorene Whatley; Elmer Park; Lou and Buddy Renfroe; Jan Moore; Mike Dulin; Irma and Joe Thomas; Kelli Agnew; Joe M. Thomas; Gina and Roy Bradley; Ressie and Thomas Grimes; Brian Weaver; Lisa Grubbs; Jo Ellen O'Hara; Gary Wright; Mel Parker; Julie Saltman; Edna Farley; Hallie Levine; Mark Mortensen; Gary Brown; Spider Martin; Christina Todd; Amy Gary; Helen Davis; Linda Mendel; Brenda Gill; Helen and Charles Horton; Lorraine Walker; Virginia Guthrie; Richard Manoske; Sam Granger; Doris Odom; Ann Isaac; Pam Rohr; Nadine Cochrum; Dr. Jimmy Bridges; Bruce Martin; Wanda Barton; Edith Harwell and the Homewood Library staff; Scott Moreland; Pat Pisanos; Randy West; Brenda Self; Kathryn Kaufman; Martha Chandler; Sue Harrison; Liz Parker; Gwen Maness; Archie and Sharon Phillips; Joan Colvert; Wanda Wheeler; Gerry Wheeler; Judy Clark; Margaret Glasscock; Joe Guin; Kate Cozart; Milt Kahn; Dot Gibson; Gil Gibson; Benny Wright; Amy Nolan; Laura Weathers; and Sandra Brown. All of you are simply the best!

Table Of Contents

Introduction

As we reach the dawn of a new millennium, it's just natural to take stock of our lives. Something about such a momentous event makes us feel vulnerable, makes us feel the need more than ever to take the best possible care of ourselves and of our families.

Many of us probably have pondered over the years what we would be doing at this point in time. Since I weighed 315 pounds for most of my life, and since my husband and daughter both weighed close to 250 pounds, I wondered if we would even be here to face the turn of the century.

I never guessed my family would be able to lose more than 355 pounds simply by learning to eat the meals we love in a healthier way. I never guessed my daughter Ashley would go from barely passing to making the Dean's List in college, due in no small part to her 85-pound weight loss and the sense of accomplishment it gave her.

I also never guessed I would sell more than 200,000 copies of my two cookbooks, weight-loss workbook, and video on healthy eating, or that I would be featured on more than 200 television and radio shows and in magazines in the United States, Europe, and Australia as a weight-loss expert.

I am as surprised by this as anyone. Some call me an expert, and I appreciate that they do, but I consider myself an average working mom who finally learned that you don't have to change your lifestyle or spend hours in the kitchen to eat healthier. You just learn how to fit healthy eating into your lifestyle–and it's as easy as pie.

What has happened to me and to my family is a vivid testimonial for the changes that can be made in your life by eating healthier. As a 315-pound couch potato I never expected too much out of life, but when you eat better you feel better and wonderful things can happen.

As we stand on the brink of a new century, our nation is increasingly overweight and unhealthy. Because the percentage of overweight adults and children grows larger each passing year, headlines warn that nutritionists fear an all-fat United States in the not-too-distant future. One wit said this might not be too bad. His reasoning was that if everyone were fat, then people would be too sluggish to go at the current hectic pace, and that as a result life would slow down. That's a clever rationale, but a more likely scenario is that an all-fat United States would eventually mean the death of our families and our country. You and I owe it not only to ourselves and to our families but also to future generations to see that this doesn't happen. The road to a better future for all of us starts in our kitchens today.

Since you are reading this, you are to be congratulated on your wisdom and foresight for wanting to eat better. It is an honor and a pleasure that you have chosen my recipes to help you do it. Whether you want to lose weight or just eat healthier, this book can help you do it. It can help change your life and the lives of those you love. Who knows, with all the progress medical science is making, if we take good care of ourselves we might even live to see the turn of another century!

Vicki Park
Birmingham, Alabama

Live! Don't Diet!

The Low-fat Cookbook That Can
Change Your Life!

Vicki Park

I dedicate this book to my family who has loved me and supported me through thick (and at 315 pounds, I do mean thick!) and thin, and to the memory of my Dad, Virgil Whatley.

A Special Thank You

My special thanks and deepest gratitude to my husband, Ken; my daughter, Ashley; my mom, Lorene Whatley; my in-laws, Elmer and Odell Park; my aunt, Lou Renfroe; my cousin, Jan Moore; and to Helen Davis, Steve Parker, Jim Lunsford, Lori Leath-Smith, Bill Stokes, Don Pippen, Spider Martin, Michael Dulin, Randy West, Cherie Kosak, Tom Moore, and Ann Isaac. Your hard work, guidance, faith, and encouragement are appreciated more than words can say.

Table of Contents

Preface

Isn't it an amazing coincidence that the word diet starts with die and has a cross at the end? It certainly is appropriate. If you diet, you feel as though you are starving to death. If you don't diet, your excess weight may eventually kill you. Even if you are not overweight, the dismal reports on the health dangers of many favorite foods make you wonder if you are killing yourself if you don't change to a healthier diet. It is an awful dilemma. I should know. I spent most of my life dieting, yet I ended up weighing 315 pounds. Conventional diets weren't working for me and my favorite non-diet foods were probably killing me. I was in a constant state of guilt, fear and frustration.

That was all before I learned about weight loss the low-fat way. As a last resort, I decided to give it a try. I figured that even if I didn't lose an ounce, I would at least be eating right. I never in my wildest dreams imagined that I would end up losing more than 165 pounds!

Many people ask me to tell them how I lost weight. I am the first to admit that I am no expert. I am not a doctor nor am I a nutritionist. I am just an average person. My life may be a lot like yours. I'm a working mother, with too much to do and too little time to spend hours in the kitchen. I love to eat. I have no willpower. I hate to exercise. Yet I lost 165 pounds by learning to prepare tasty, simple low-fat dishes that satisfied me and my family. No, I am not an expert, nor do I have miraculous solutions. I cannot guarantee that everyone will lose. However, I can share the benefit of my personal experience in losing 165 pounds through low-fat eating. That is one thing even most experts can't do. In addition I can offer you the low-fat recipes, cooking techniques and low-fat eating tips that I used to lose.

Low-fat eating literally saved my life. It is so easy and fulfilling to me that I cannot imagine ever going back to my old eating habits. Whether you want to lose weight, or just want to eat healthier, I hope you will find something in this book to help you. I also hope that you will find low-fat living as easy and as rewarding as I have.

How I Lost Weight the Low-fat Way

Why Try?

How I Lost More Than 165 Pounds

What The Low-fat Lifestyle Is Not

Some Additional Tips About Low-fat Weight Loss

Why Try?

In this day and time, it has become accepted wisdom that if you are satisfied with being overweight and are in reasonably good health, you should just forget about trying to lose. Perhaps that might work for some people, but it never worked for me. While I had tried just about every diet around and had finally given up trying, I was always nagged by the feeling that I should try again. However, I would never do anything about it. I just ate and ate and felt guilty. I worried about developing weight related health problems such as diabetes or heart trouble. I also worried about being an embarrassment to my family, although they are so sweet, they would never admit that I was. Unfortunately, worrying was all I did. It didn't motivate me to try to take the weight off.

In order to succeed at weight loss, most of us have to have a very personal reason. We all know that extra weight can cause health problems. In addition, society often discriminates against overweight people. However, that hasn't kept 50 million of us from holding on to those extra pounds. It isn't enough that someone else wants us to lose. We have to want to do it for ourselves. We have to find an intensely motivating personal reason to lose.

What pushed me into trying again? I simply realized that food had become the only exciting thing in my life. Once I came to this conclusion, I knew that I had to do something about it. I was missing out on so much! I was always tired and unhappy, because I was so fat. I didn't go a lot of places, such as the beach, because I was so fat. I avoided many social situations, because I was so fat. All I enjoyed and looked forward to was my next meal. I had allowed food to take center stage in my life.

Today, I love to get out and go. I have energy. I have rediscovered the excitement life can offer. I still love to eat, but now I control my food—it doesn't control me!

Find your own personal reason to want to lose. Keep that reason front and center in your mind at all times. It will be a motivating force that will lead you to weight loss success.

How I Lost More Than 165 Pounds

Who among us has not wished for a magic diet that would allow us to lose weight, while filling up on delicious, hearty food? The wishing is over. It is here now. However, it is not a diet in the conventional sense. It is simply a change to healthier eating habits. It has been referred to as a low-fat lifestyle. If you follow a low-fat lifestyle, you simply get rid of most of the fat in your food. You forget about deprivation, and eating "rabbit" food. You concentrate on filling up on delicious and hearty foods like vegetables, potatoes, pasta and bread in quantities that have always been taboo on conventional diets.

A friend once told me that when she joined a popular diet program, she was given a list of foods she could eat each day. "What can I do if I am still hungry when this is gone?" she asked the counselor. "Go to bed!" the counselor replied. That says it all. That is why I have never been able to stay on a conventional diet. Subconsciously, I can't handle any limit being placed on how much I can eat. Once the limit is imposed, I begin to feel deprived. I stay hungry and crave forbidden foods. That is why I could seldom stay on a conventional diet more than a few days.

The low-fat lifestyle changed all that for me. I am free to eat until I am full. I am able to handle cravings because I can fit almost any temptation into my daily fat allowance, or I can create low-fat variations, using the wonderful low-fat and fat-free substitutes now on the market.

Simply put, I lost the weight because I stopped eating fatty foods. Losing weight by reducing fat intake is certainly not a new concept. It has been widely studied and recommended by medical experts. Many feel that it is the best hope for successful long-term weight loss. There are a number of good books by physicians and nutritionists available on low-fat weight loss. While they all advise cutting fat intake to lose weight, they vary somewhat in their approach.

If you are thinking about reducing your fat intake in order to lose weight, go to the public library or bookstore and check out some books on the subject. Read them and come to your own conclusions about which plan is best for you. Of course, no one should ever make a change in eating habits without consulting a physician. Be sure to talk to your own physician before reducing your fat intake. Ask how many fat grams you should allow yourself. Also, ask if you need a vitamin supplement. Since all individuals are different, your physician's advice and consent is essential. I personally chose to limit my fat intake to a minimum of 25 grams and a maximum of 35 grams per day. Some doctors advise the elimination of meat in a low-fat eating plan, others do not. I chose not to exclude any foods. If I don't eat something, it is just because I don't want it, not that I can't have it. I feel that this approach is best for me because it is so similar to my old eating habits. I only had to modify my old, favorite recipes with low-fat ingredients. This is also why I feel confident that I won't go back to my old eating habits. As I said before, this is not really a diet. It is simply a change to healthier eating habits. It is amazing that something so easy could have such a profound effect on my life.

What The Low–Fat Lifestyle Is Not

"Please try just a little of this cake, it's low-fat," my well meaning friend said. "I'm watching my fat intake so I made it with only one stick of butter instead of two." Her misconception is not uncommon. Many people think they can lose weight by cutting out just a little fat. A low-fat lifestyle is not just dropping a few fat grams here and there. It is a commitment to low-fat eating as a way of life. It is also not a roller coaster ride of low-fat eating one day and high-fat the next. The media likes to point out that the 1990's are a time of contradictions food-wise. People will eat a prudent, healthy meal, then stuff themselves with an extravagant, fat-laden dessert. You can't lose much weight this way. Remember, this is a lifestyle, not one day on and one day off.

The low-fat lifestyle is also not a license to gorge. A friend of mine could not understand why she wasn't losing weight when she began watching her fat intake. It didn't take much detective work to discover why. She would habitually sit down and eat a whole bag of fat-free cookies while watching television at night. You need to stay away from too many sugary treats, even if they are low-fat. The low-fat lifestyle can allow you to lose weight because you fill up and stay full by eating a lot of complex carbohydrates and protein. Occasionally you might pig out on low-fat goodies, but, in general, moderation is the key to consistent weight loss. Eat only until you are comfortably full, not until you are ready to pop!

The low-fat lifestyle is not a quick fix. I lost at an average rate of about 10 pounds per month. It was not a constant 10 pounds. Some months I lost less and some months I lost more. You don't want to lose too fast. The more slowly it comes off, the more likely it will stay off. Don't get impatient!

When I first decided to see if low-fat eating would help me lose weight, I told myself I would just eat all I wanted, while staying within my allotted fat grams. I told myself that if I lost weight, it would be great, but if I didn't, I would at least be eating foods that were good for me. After all, every day new reports come out about the health benefits of a low-fat lifestyle. I didn't put myself under any pressure to lose. I just ate low-fat foods and the weight and inches started to come off. Everyone is different. There are no guarantees that everyone will lose, but it worked for me and may work for you. Don't put pressure on yourself. Just tell yourself that by eating plenty of delicious, low-fat foods, you will almost certainly be treating your body better. The weight you may lose will just be a wonderful dividend.

Some Additional Tips About Low-Fat Weight Loss

Since I have lived with a low-fat lifestyle for more than two years, I have learned quite a lot about what to expect in terms of weight loss. In addition to the personal experiences that I have already shared with you, I can add a few more things that I have learned.

1. Weigh seldom, if ever. It is really best to get rid of your bathroom scale. It is a seductive enemy. It lures you to weigh, then dashes your hopes if you haven't lost. Weight is not a stable thing. You may actually be losing, but due to normal fluid retention, may appear to be gaining. If you don't weigh, you won't worry. You won't be tempted to quit. I am sorry to say that I came to this realization only after I had lost the weight. I didn't know any better, so I did weigh. If I had not lost, I would get depressed. That is why I know it isn't a good thing to weigh. It is better to measure yourself around the chest, waist, hips, thighs and upper arms. Then measure again from time to time. Even when you are not losing pounds, you may be losing body fat. As strange as that sounds, that happened to me. You may even want to buy a caliper to measure body fat. That is what doctors use. You can also tell when

you are losing by the fit of your clothes.

2. I found that weight loss is a little different with a low-fat lifestyle than with a conventional diet. I lost in spurts. That is another reason it is important not to weigh. I would think I was never going to lose another ounce, then suddenly 10 pounds would drop off. I averaged losing 10 pounds per month. However, even when my weight loss slowed down, I would continue to lose inches. That is why it is important to measure periodically.

3. Be sure to eat plenty of high-fiber foods, including dry beans, whole grains, fruits and vegetables. They not only keep you full, they help prevent irregularity. Some people may experience bloating when they begin eating a lot of fiber. This can usually be avoided by increasing fiber intake gradually.

4. If you are still hungry at the end of a meal, wait a few minutes before eating more. Sometimes even a short break can make you realize that you are really full after all.

5. Remember this old saying, if you are tempted to stray from your low-fat lifestyle: **Nothing tastes as good as being thinner feels!**

The Voice of Experience

Useful Tips I've Learned About Low-fat Living

Substitute! Substitute! Substitute!

It's What's Up Front That Counts

How Important Is Exercise?

What About The Rest of the Family?

Are You Letting Fat Rob Your Life Of Romance?

Improve While You Lose

Dining Out

SUBSTITUTE! SUBSTITUTE! SUBSTITUTE!

Several years ago, I bought some fat-free cheese. After one bite, I threw it away. But then, several years ago, I weighed 315 pounds. Today I love fat-free cheese. I also weigh more than 165 pounds less than I did then. It's a trade off; fatty foods-fatty body, low-fat foods-low-fat body.

I recently read a cooking magazine in which there was a letter from an irate reader to the editor berating the magazine staff for saying that their low-fat version of tortilla chips was better tasting than fried, commercially prepared chips. There is a quality about fat that makes foods without it seem as though something is missing. Just think about it. If our foods do not naturally contain fat, we have to pile on the oil or butter, even though it provides little, if any additional taste.

Food experts call that something that fat adds to foods, "mouthfeel." This refers to the smooth, oily richness that fat imparts. It gives foods a full-bodied, satisfying taste that makes people naturally prefer them over low-fat foods. In a taste test, head to head, a low-fat or fat-free version of a food will probably seldom win over the original. The trick is to never let yourself make the comparison. It is the best thing you can possibly do for yourself if you want to be successful in following a low-fat lifestyle.

These are words to live by: I WILL NOT LET MYSELF COMPARE THE TASTE OF MY LOW-FAT FOODS TO THEIR HIGH-FAT COUNTERPARTS. I WILL SIMPLY ENJOY THEM, WITHOUT MAKING ANY COMPARISON. This statement is engraved on my brain. Engrave it on yours, too. It will allow you to prepare delicious, satisfying versions of your old favorites without missing the originals. You will also enjoy coming up with new ways to use substitutes in your cooking. Trips to the grocery store become an adventure. It is fun to see the new low-fat products that come out almost weekly. I especially enjoy finding new fat-free or reduced-fat dairy products. Fat-free cream cheese, sour cream, cottage cheese, and hard cheese have been mainstays in my low-fat cooking, and I anxiously await new dairy substitutes as they become available.

With my low-fat lifestyle, I am not tempted to stray back to my old eating habits because I know that I can either fit a serving of the original into my fat gram allowance, or better yet, create a reasonable facsimile of any dish that I might normally crave with low-fat substitutes. That knowledge is very liberating. On every diet that I tried before, I feared cravings. I knew that I would end up giving in to them and my diet would be history. I no longer have to fear them. They have lost their power over me. Want a hot fudge sundae? Fat-free fudge sauce and fat-free frozen yogurt with light whipped topping are so good no one would ever guess they are not the high-fat version. Crave a cheeseburger? No problem. A lower-fat version is not only possible, but delicious.

You may not believe it now, but in time you will probably come to prefer the low-fat versions of your favorites, just as the magazine staff did. You will find that you do not like the oily, greasy taste that the higher-fat originals leave in your mouth. You will become very sensitive to the unpleasant, slick sensation that fat imparts. Just think, would you eat a big spoonful of grease? Of course not. Yet when you eat a food that contains fat, you are coating your mouth with the same oily residue. This makes food taste good? I think not!!

It's What's Up Front That Counts

Have you noticed that when someone really wants you to see something, they stick it in front of you to get your attention? The same should be true with food. Often the most interesting ingredients in a dish get lost when they are mixed in with everything else. When I want to blow some of my fat grams on a teaspoon of nuts, a bit of real mayonnaise, or another special ingredient, I place it in the spotlight by putting it on top of my serving. Just a taste can seem like a lot.

An ingredient doesn't have to be high-fat to deserve to be front and center. Don't serve vegetables "topless" unless you just like them that way. Perk them up by adding a little something extra. A sprinkle of crunchy, minced dried onion, a bit of low-fat canned gravy, or a little catsup can do wonders for a plain, cooked vegetable. Even ultra-low-fat margarine can seem lavish when spread on top. It's fun to use your imagination to think up new toppings. The possibilities are endless.

HOW IMPORTANT IS EXERCISE?

I am not proud to admit that I hate to exercise. I have always hated to exercise. After all, I didn't come to weigh 315 pounds by being a fitness buff. I doubt that I will ever grow to like it, but I have come to recognize that it is an important part of weight management.

I lost more than 100 pounds through low-fat eating before I ever did any exercise. I say that mainly to let you know that it is often possible to lose weight this way even if you are not physically able to exercise, or if you do not feel that you are up to beginning both a new way of eating and a fitness regimen at the same time. Weight loss is likely to be faster with exercise. Quite frankly, I probably would have never begun my low-fat lifestyle if exercise was required for it to work. I simply changed my eating habits, not my exercise habits, which were nonexistent. However, when I had lost just over 100 pounds, I hit a lengthy plateau. My weight didn't budge for several months. Since adjustments in food intake and/or exercise have always been considered classic ways to get off a weight loss plateau, I decided that exercise might be the jump start I needed to begin losing again.

I decided to give aerobic exercise a try. Experts feel that aerobic exercise for 20 minutes to one hour, three times a week or more, increases the metabolic rate and thus the rate at which our bodies burn fat. Walking, bicycling and swimming are all great aerobic exercises, but I felt I would do better with an exercise program that provided a lot of variety. I found a great exercise video that consists of several segments of simple movements. Each segment lasts about 20 minutes. I do one segment every other day. I probably should do more, but I figure that I am doing good to make myself exercise at all. The aerobics did the trick. I got off the plateau and went on to lose over 65 more pounds. I plan to continue this simple exercise program.

I also try to get "non-exercise" exercise. I park my car as far from the mall as possible. I get up from my desk and move around more at work. I push my cart at a brisk pace down the uncrowded aisles in the discount store, instead of strolling at a leisurely pace. I even sprint up the stairs several times a day.

You will have to make your own decision about exercise. You should definitely consult your doctor before embarking on any exercise program, as well as any change in eating habits. Exercise is an important part of good health. It helps you gain energy and can help you lose weight faster. There are so many kinds that you should be able to find one, or more, that is right for you. I really regret that I did not start exercising sooner. Most experts agree that exercise is the true key to permanent weight loss.

What About the Rest of the Family?

Not long after we married, my husband Ken developed a major weight problem—me. In order to impress my new husband, I prepared rich, tempting dishes for every meal. I also kept the pantry stocked with his favorite goodies. While my weight zoomed immediately, he was more fortunate. Because he was more active, he was able to maintain a reasonable weight while eating a lot of fattening foods. As the years passed, however, his luck changed. By the time we celebrated our 20th wedding anniversary, he weighed almost 250 pounds, while I weighed more than 300. Needless to say, neither of us had ever had much luck with our attempts at conventional dieting.

When I made the decision to serve only low-fat meals, Ken supported me all the way. While he doesn't count fat grams, he did begin to watch his fat intake. He eats only my low-fat cooking at home, and tries to select lower-fat dishes in restaurants. As a result he now weighs 175 pounds. His doctor recently removed him from the blood pressure medication that he has taken for years.

Ken is often amazed that the dishes I prepare are low in fat. During a meal, he will sometimes look at me skeptically and say, "Are you sure we can have this?" Like myself, he doesn't really miss our old high-fat eating habits.

Our daughter, Ashley, grew up with an aversion to fresh vegetables, fruits and other nutritious foods. Despite my best efforts, she is a picky eater with a passion for fast food. She is now away at college, and is delighted that she is finally free to eat pizza three times a day. However, she does admit that some of the low-fat dishes at home were not bad at all.

Many experts feel that for the average person, no more than 30% of the calories consumed daily should come from fat. Therefore other family members should benefit from low-fat meals. Ask your physician how many fat grams each member of your household needs daily.

It may vary somewhat according to sex, age and physical condition. Of course, it also can depend upon whether an individual wants to lose weight or just wants to eat healthier. In general, the same low-fat meals should work for everyone, with only minor modifications necessary to fulfill the dietary requirements of those whose fat intake needs to be a bit higher.

ARE YOU LETTING FAT ROB YOUR LIFE OF ROMANCE?

It has been said that a day without wine is like a day without sunshine. The same could be said of romance. Even in this cynical day and time, romance is an important part of life. People are hungry for it. Witness the popularity of romantic books, movies, and television shows. We can't seem to get enough of them. We seek romance vicariously, through the lives of fictional characters, often because there is not enough of it in our real lives. Romance, even when experienced through the lives of others, adds a certain zest to life. When we have our own romance, it can really add excitement. It doesn't have to be a blazing, torrid love affair. It can be as simple as a little pleasant flirting with the one we love.

It is unfortunate that the amount of romance in real life generally decreases as the amount of body fat increases. Of course, we all know that romantic attraction should be based on the inner beauty of a person, not the exterior. However, that's not reality. Right or wrong, romantic attraction is usually based on appearance. If you don't believe it, ask yourself why sexy, thin actors always play the romantic leads in movies, while overweight actors end up in the funny, but loveless best friend roles. We may feel deep spiritual love for our beloved, but if he lets himself get fat, our romantic interest in him can fade.

One rainy afternoon, I picked up a deliciously romantic novel that was enthralling. I couldn't put it down. As I finished the final page, I wondered if real life couldn't be as romantic if I worked at making it that way. Since I had let myself get up to 315 pounds, I obviously, hadn't worked at it in a long time. Romance was one of the things my life was missing because I had let fat gain control. As Ken and I both lost weight through our low-fat lifestyles, the romance did come back. It is wonderful.

Perhaps you have also let fat rob your life of romance. You may not even think that it is important in your life. Maybe it's not. But give it a chance. If the spark of romance in your soul has gone out, read a romantic book, listen to seductive music, or fall under the spell of a movie love story. One of these may relight that spark. It may motivate you to want to lose weight and perhaps bring romance back to your personal life. While losing weight isn't guaranteed to do this, it certainly won't hurt the chances of it happening. After all, who could resist the new, thinner you?

Improve While You Lose

As you lose, you often begin to think about making other improvements in your appearance. I developed an image of how I wanted to look. I kept that image in mind every day. It helped me stay on track with my weight loss plan. I decided to make major changes in how I dressed. I had worn so many pastel prints while fat that I decided to wear more sophisticated solid color suits and dresses. I learned that good, striking jewelry will make even the plainest outfit look great, so I also began to purchase pieces that were unique. I previously bought make-up at the discount store. I decided to visit a professional and learn how to properly use the right makeup. I had never taken the least bit of care of my complexion, just leaving my face to fate, soap, and water. I visited the dermatologist and got a prescription for Retin-A, which has evened out my complexion. I also learned that daily use of sunscreen can help prevent some wrinkles.

I am no beauty now, but I do feel that the changes I made have vastly improved my appearance, as well as my self esteem. Most women would die if they heard that their husband had been seen with another woman. I was thrilled, because the other woman my husband was seen with was me! A friend gleefully related to me that a mutual acquaintance who had not seen me in a long time reported to her that my husband and I were apparently no longer together. He had been seen from a distance on several occasions with a much slimmer, more attractive woman! What a compliment!

You may find making some style and appearance changes as rewarding as I did. They can really perk up your life.

DINING OUT

I have seen books on low-fat living that devoted long, wordy chapters to dining out. Frankly, I don't have the patience to wade through all that. It is just not necessary.

Since I do not like to take my lunch to work, I have dined out almost every weekday since I began following a low-fat lifestyle. I carry a small fat gram counter in my purse. If the restaurant is one of a national chain, I can often look up the fat content of their dishes in the book.

Many full service and fast food restaurants now offer low-fat selections. If you are dining in a full service restaurant, you may also simply confide in your servers that you are watching your fat intake. They can be most helpful in making suggestions. Usually broiled entrées, such as chicken or fish, can easily be prepared without oil or butter. Other entrées may also be modified to your requirements. Order baked potatoes or vegetables plain and add catsup or lemon juice. Salads can be eaten with fat-free dressing or, if not available, with regular dressing on the side. Dip your fork into the dressing, then the greens. You get a taste of the dressing without too much fat.

I usually eat at fast food restaurants several days a week. Their grilled chicken sandwiches (without mayo), ultra-lean burgers or turkey sandwiches, along with a side salad with fat-free dressing, make a fine meal. Many of their meal-size salads are also quite low in fat.

Fat-free salad dressings are widely available in grocery stores in individual packets. I carry a supply of my favorites, as well as a shaker of fat-free butter-flavored granules, sour cream-flavored granules, and Cheddar cheese-flavored granules in a zipper top plastic bag in my car. When dining out, I can drop any or all of them into my purse and use them discreetly in the restaurant.

Tips For Cooking The Low-fat Way

REDUCING THE FAT IN YOUR RECIPES

It is really easy to lower the fat in your own favorite recipes. These are a few of the ingredients that will help you.

Original Ingredient:	Low-Fat Alternative:
Swiss or Cheddar cheese	Fat-free Swiss or Cheddar
Butter or Margarine	Ultra-light or fat-free margarine
	Butter-flavored granules
	Butter-flavored cooking spray
Eggs	Fat-free egg substitute
	Egg whites
Canned cream soup	99% fat-free canned cream soup
1 cup whole or low-fat milk	1 cup skim milk
1 cup cream or half and half	1 cup evaporated skim milk
Sour cream	Fat-free sour cream
Cream cheese	Fat-free cream cheese
Oil	No-stick cooking spray
	Applesauce (in baked goods)
	Baby food prunes
	(in baked goods)
Salad dressing	Fat-free salad dressing
Mayonnaise	Fat-free mayonnaise
	Fat-free salad dressing
Wieners	97% fat-free wieners
Baked ham	98% fat-free precooked ham
Ground beef	Ground top round

A Short Guide To Fat Grams

When I decided to limit my fat intake, I went to the bookstore and invested in several copies of a good fat gram guide. There are a number on the market. Most list the fat grams in thousands of foods. I keep one at home, one in the car, one at the office, and a very small one in my purse. Even after more than two years of low-fat eating, I still consult them when I need to determine the amount of fat grams in an unfamiliar food.

Counting fat grams is very easy. Just remember: plain vegetables and plain fruits (except avocado) have practically no fat. The following is a very short list of the fat grams in some other common foods. This is merely a sample. Buy at least one fat gram guide to use as a reference. You will be surprised to learn that some of your favorite foods are probably lower in fat than you think.

Breakfast Foods:

Bacon, fried	1 slice	3.1 grams
Bagel	1 whole	1.4 grams
Cornflakes	1 cup	.1 gram
Eggs	1 whole	5.0 grams

Dairy Products:

Buttermilk	1 cup	4.0 grams
Cheese, hard	1 oz.	4.9-9.4 grams
Milk, 1%	1 cup	2.6 grams
Milk, skim	1 cup	1.0 gram
Milk, whole	1 cup	8.2 grams
Sour cream	1 tablespoon	3.0 grams

Meats (trimmed of all fat):

Beef, eye of round	3 oz.	6.5 grams
Beef, ground	3 oz.	19.2 grams
Ham, extra-lean	3 oz.	4.1 grams
Lamb chop	3 oz.	32.0 grams
Pork tenderloin	3 oz.	4.1 grams

Poultry (skinless):

Chicken breast	4 oz.	5.1 grams
Turkey breast	4 oz.	1.0 grams

USING SUGAR AND SUGAR SUBSTITUTES

I have very little willpower, and when there is a dessert in the house, one piece is never enough for me. If you fill up on healthy grains, beans, vegetables and fruits, you won't really want or miss sugary desserts. When I do prepare a recipe that calls for sugar, I usually replace all or part of the sugar with sugar substitutes. You may prefer not to use them, but while I don't count calories I like to cut calories out of my recipes whenever and however possible. My recipes call for the use of saccharin-based granulated-style substitute, which replaces the sugar measure for measure. Aspartame-based substitutes are great in foods that don't require lengthy heating, but tend to lose their sweetness when used in foods that are cooked. Therefore it is best to use saccharin-based substitutes in cooked dishes. If you choose to use sugar substitutes, try these equivalents in your cooking:

Bulk granulated-style saccharin-based substitute: Measure the same as sugar.

Saccharin-based packets: ¼ cup = 3 packets, ⅓ cup = 4 packets ½ cup = 6 packets, 1 cup = 12 packets.

Bulk granulated-style aspartame-based substitute: Measure the same as sugar.

Aspartame-based packets: ¼ cup = 6 packets, ⅓ cup = 8 packets, ½ cup = 12 packets, ⅔ cup = 16 packets, 1 cup = 24 packets.

WHAT ABOUT SODIUM?

As a busy person who is not fond of spending a lot of time in the kitchen, I depend heavily on convenience foods and canned goods while preparing the meals for my low-fat lifestyle. Unfortunately, many such foods are quite high in sodium. In order to limit my family's sodium intake, I take the following steps:

1. I seldom add salt to any food. Most dishes are sufficiently salty from ingredients used in their preparation.

2. I buy only light salt. While it still has sodium, it has less than regular salt.

3. I buy a variety of the herb/spice salt replacement products that add interesting tastes to food in order to eliminate the need for salt. They come in many blends, such as onion/herb, garlic/herb and lemon/herb.

4. I drain and rinse canned vegetables. They are often high in sodium and rinsing can eliminate some of it.

5. I buy low-sodium products whenever possible. Just as new low-fat products come out almost daily, low-sodium varieties of our favorite foods are also becoming widely available. Low-sodium bouillon cubes, soy sauce, catsup, processed meats and canned goods are just a few of the products you can now find.

6. If I use a high-sodium processed meat in a recipe, I try to limit the amount used to the bare minimum.

Cooking With Ground Beef

The average ground beef sold in grocery stores can contain a lot of fat, so it has no place in a low-fat lifestyle. However, you don't have to throw out all of your old recipes that contain ground beef. There are low-fat alternatives.

One alternative is to use ground turkey instead of ground beef. If you choose to do this, make sure the ground turkey is 100 percent pure ground breast meat. The ground turkey sold in stores often contains fat or even skin. You may need to have the butcher grind turkey breast for you.

I prefer ground beef, so I buy several pounds of top round and have it trimmed of all fat and ground by the butcher. I brown it in my dutch oven, pat it with paper towels to absorb any grease, then rinse it under hot running water to remove any additional grease. The meat is so lean to start with that I have never had any problems with grease in my drain, but if you have a particularly sensitive plumbing system, you may want to skip the rinsing step. Finally, I place the meat on paper towels and pat dry. I then divide it into 6-ounce portions and freeze. When I make any casserole or sauce that calls for ground beef, I just use a 6-ounce portion of my frozen cooked ground round. Just a little does as well as a lot in most dishes and the amount of fat per serving is just about 4 grams, compared to around 30 grams in regular ground beef.

There are other alternatives. Many stores sell ultra-lean ground beef that has around 7 grams of fat per 4-ounce uncooked serving. There is also ground beef-style textured vegetable protein. This may not sound familiar to you, but anytime you eat imitation bacon bits, you are eating textured vegetable protein. It is a low-fat soy derivative that is indistinguishable from ground beef in sauces, soups and casseroles. Textured vegetable protein is sold in health food stores and mail order health related catalogs. It comes in other styles such as beef and chicken chunks, and the bacon bits we have all eaten. Unlike crunchy bacon bits, cooked textured vegetable protein develops the texture and taste of cooked meat, but with less fat and calories. You might want to give it a try.

You may notice that I don't include ground beef in many of my recipes that traditionally are made with it, for example, lasagna or tacos. I usually make these dishes without meat because we like them just as much without it. If you prefer it, by all means add some. Just be sure you use the ultra-lean kind and just a little of it.

Spice Is the Variety of Life

The title may be a corny twist on the old saying, but it is the truth. Spices do add variety to life by enhancing the taste of food. Along with herbs and condiments, they are particularly important in adding flavor to low-fat dishes. They replace some of the sensory satisfaction usually provided by fat. My spice cabinet is overflowing with just about every spice and herb available. I like nothing more than adding a lot of them to my food. The amounts shown in my recipes are only guidelines. Keep adding a little at a time until the dish is as spicy as you like. I normally double or even triple the amount.

It is now possible to find almost any spice or herb in discount stores, where they often cost less than $1 per bottle. At that price, you may be able to afford to experiment. It's fun to make up some tasty spice and herb blends.

I also love to keep a lot of condiments on hand. Many of the sauces and other condiments in the grocery store are fat-free. If a dish seems bland, just add a dollop of catsup, a splash of hot sauce, or a spoonful of spicy relish. If you season your foods well with herbs, spices and condiments, you'll find that you don't miss the fat at all.

A Guide To Basic Spices

Allspice has a delicate, spicy flavor that resembles a blend of cloves, cinnamon and nutmeg. It is used in baked goods, preserves, relishes and puddings.

Anise has a sweet, licorice flavor. It is used in cakes, cookies, and sweet breads.

Basil has a mild taste. It is often used in tomato dishes, but is also good with peas, squash, green beans, salads and chicken.

Bay leaves have a rather sweet taste. They are often used in soups and stews.

Caraway seeds have a pronounced zesty taste with hints of dill. They are often used in sauerkraut, noodles and rye bread, but are also good with potatoes, green beans and carrots.

Chervil has flavor similar to parsley but milder. It is very popular in France. It is used in salads, sauces and soups.

Curry is a blend of many spices, among them ginger, turmeric, and fenugreek. It is commonly used in Indian dishes.

Dill has a clean, aromatic taste. It is widely used in pickling, but also adds flavor to sauerkraut, potatoes and macaroni dishes.

Fennel has a licorice flavor. It is used in many dishes, from salads and soups to cookies and cakes.

Ginger has a fresh, spicy flavor. It is used in meat, vegetable and dessert dishes.

Mace is very similar to nutmeg in flavor, which is understandable since it is the outer covering of the nutmeg seed. It is used in baked goods and pickling.

Marjoram has a sweet, minty flavor. It is used with lamb, and in soups and stews.

Mint has a mild flavor in spearmint and a stronger, peppery flavor in peppermint. Spearmint is used in sauces. Peppermint is most commonly used in candies and desserts. Mint also goes well with a few vegetables, such as potatoes and peas.

Mustard has a sharp, spicy flavor. Ground mustard is used to make one of our most popular condiments. Mustard seeds are used in sauerkraut and cabbage dishes.

Oregano is an aromatic, spicy herb often used in tomato dishes.

Parsley is very mild in flavor, with curly leaves that make it a popular garnish. Italian parsley has a flatter leaf and stronger flavor. It is often used in soups, casseroles, and vegetable dishes.

Paprika has a sweet, mild flavor. It is used to give color to pale foods, and as a seasoning in chicken dishes and salad dressing.

Poppy seeds are tiny, nutty tasting seeds that are found in baked goods and noodle dishes.

Rosemary has a sweet, fresh taste. It is popular in lamb dishes, and with potatoes, chicken and peas.

Sage has a rather minty flavor. It is used in stuffing, meat dishes and in sausage.

Tarragon has a licorice flavor. It is used in sauces, salads, vegetable dishes and chicken dishes.

Thyme has a strong flavor. It is used with poultry, fish and vegetable dishes.

Turmeric has a peppery flavor. It is used as a coloring and flavoring agent in pickles and mustard.

OIL SUBSTITUTES IN BAKED GOODS

People are amazed when they ask for my corn bread recipe and I list applesauce as one of the ingredients. They cannot believe that it doesn't make the finished product taste like a dessert. You actually can't taste it at all. It simply imparts a moistness that usually takes oil to achieve. Try using applesauce in any baked goods that you prepare, measure for measure.

In addition, there are other oil substitutes available that you might want to try. Fat-free sour cream and fat-free cottage cheese can also add moistness to baked goods, as can baby food prunes. You might like to experiment and find the one that works best for you.

Serving Suggestions For Fresh Fruit

I keep a variety of fresh fruits in case I want something sweet. It is very filling and much better for you than most desserts or snack foods. Most traditional desserts and commercially prepared snack foods just leave you hungry for more. That old advertising slogan for potato chips—"Bet you can't eat just one"—has a lot of truth in it. Eat one apple and you are full. Eat one piece of cake and you'll want another. If plain fresh fruit becomes boring, try some of my ideas for pepping it up.

1. Slice the fruit into thin wedges. Arrange attractively around a small mound of granulated sugar substitute mixed with a bit of cinnamon or nutmeg. Dip each bite of fruit into the mixture. You can also make a dip for the fruit by combining a little fat-free sour cream or yogurt with a dash of vanilla, some sugar substitute and cinnamon.

2. Prepare a small box of sugar-free vanilla pudding mix with skim milk, using a bit more than the package directions suggest. The pudding should be the consistency of a fairly thick sauce. Pour a small amount of the sauce over fruit.

3. Crumble a cinnamon-sugar graham cracker. Sprinkle over a bowl of cooked or uncooked fresh fruit. The effect is a little like fruit cobbler.

4. Make fat-free frozen yogurt a topping for fruit. Place a very small scoop of vanilla frozen yogurt atop a bowl of cooked or uncooked fruit. Allow it to soften slightly.

Low-fat Cooking Methods

How To Fry And Sauté The Low-fat Way

Some Ideas For Oven Frying

Outdoor Cooking

Bountiful Beans: A Guide to Beans and Their Preparation

Glorious Grains: Some Old And New Grains to Enjoy

A Short Course In Cooking Grains

How To Can Homemade Condiments

Basic Vegetable Cooking

A Short Guide To Steaming

Quick And Healthy Cooking The Microwave Way

How To Fry and Saute Foods the Low-fat Way

I always loved fried foods, but I hated to prepare them at home since cleaning an oil spattered stove top was not my idea of fun. Years ago, when I learned about oven frying, I was thrilled. I could enjoy fried foods without the mess or the constant attention that stove top frying requires.

Fortunately, oven frying adapts well to low-fat cooking techniques. I generally place a sheet of aluminum foil on a baking sheet with low sides. I then coat the foil with no-stick cooking spray. I also coat the food with the cooking spray after it has been placed on the baking sheet. This aids in browning. The cooking spray is primarily oil, so don't saturate the baking sheet or the food with it.The main benefit of using the spray instead of bottled oil is that a 1¼ second spritz, which is a sufficient amount to coat a 10" skillet, has less than 1 fat gram and only 7 calories, compared to 12-14 fat grams and 120 calories per table-spoon for bottled oil. If you prefer to use some of your fat grams to oven fry with bottled oil or even reduced-fat mayonnaise, see more of my tips for oven frying in the section entitled "Some Ideas For Oven Frying." One more thing I like about oven frying is that when you finish, the foil can be discarded. The baking sheet will seldom need washing.

You will also find no-stick cooking spray a great help in preparing sautéed foods. Just spray your skillet or sauté pan and add the vegetables or meat. I sometimes add a little bit of extra spray after the food has been placed in the pan. The spray comes in plain, butter and olive oil flavors, so you can impart the taste you prefer.

It is also possible to conventionally fry foods on the stove top using low-fat cooking techniques. You can quite successfully fry both breaded and unbreaded foods using either the cooking spray or by using just a tablespoon of oil.

One additional frying technique is the use of chicken broth! Place a tablespoon or so of defatted chicken broth in your skillet. Place the skillet over medium heat. When the broth begins to simmer, add your food. Because chicken broth evaporates, you may need to add an additional amount during the cooking process. Believe it or not, the foods, including fried chicken, will brown somewhat, although they will not be very crisp. The skillet needs to be well coated with no-stick cooking spray before the broth is added. Otherwise the breading may stick to the skillet. Chicken broth can also be used to sauté or to stir-fry.

Some Ideas For Oven Frying

I normally don't use any oil to oven fry, since I think that no-stick cooking spray does an acceptable job. However, you might prefer to use oil, tahini or reduced-fat mayonnaise. Remember that both vegetable oil and tahini have considerable fat grams. Most oils have 12-14 grams per tablespoon. Tahini, a delicious sesame seed paste found in health food stores and larger grocery stores, has about 8 fat grams per tablespoon. Reduced-fat mayonnaise has around 3-5 grams per tablespoon, depending upon the brand.

Sliced vegetables, chicken and fish are all candidates for oven frying. You might like to prepare them in the following quick and easy manner:

Place the vegetables or chicken in a zipper top plastic bag. Add 1 tablespoon oil, tahini or reduced-fat mayonnaise. Zip the bag and work the vegetables around so that each piece gets coated. Add ½ cup fine, dry breadcrumbs. Garlic powder, salt and pepper, or other spices may be added, according to preference. Bake the vegetables or chicken on a shallow baking sheet that has been sprayed with no-stick cooking spray at 425° until browned to your taste.

Outdoor Cooking

Who doesn't love the aroma and taste of foods cooked on an outdoor grill? Don't think that living a low-fat lifestyle will put a damper on your enjoyment of foods cooked outdoors. Chicken, beef top round, turkey, fish, lean pork tenderloin and even low-fat wieners are wonderful when grilled, barbecued or smoked. Even if fatty ribs have always been your meat of choice when cooking outdoors, you can make a reasonable facsimile by slicing pork tenderloins into thick strips that resemble the boneless country style ribs sold in the grocery store. Since the meats that you will be cooking are not fatty, you will need to be careful not to let them dry out. Reduced cooking temperature, carefully watched cooking time and use of marinades, or basting sauces can take care of that possibility. Here's another use for good old no-stick cooking spray: Coat the food to be cooked outdoors with no-stick spray. It will keep it from sticking to the grill, and will add a tiny bit of oil to the food, which will keep it more moist. Perfectly delicious grilled chicken can be prepared by simply coating boneless breasts with the spray, then sprinkling them with garlic powder and/or herbs to taste. If you also spray your grill rack, it will be easier to clean.

Vegetables are also terrific cooked outdoors, either combined with meat in a kabob or grilled whole or in slices along with the entrée. They may be wrapped in foil first, if desired. I personally like the vegetables cooked directly on the grill, so that they absorb more of the outdoor flavor. No-stick cooking spray, as well as garlic, herbs or basting sauces that enhance flavor, are terrific helps when cooking vegetables on the grill. So is the accessory grill rack made with smaller grids. It prevents small items like vegetable slices or shrimp from falling through.

Many traditional accompaniments to outdoor meals can be easily prepared in a low-fat manner. Baked beans, coleslaw and potato salad are delicious made the low-fat way. You may have other side dishes that you like to serve with your outdoor meals. With your imagination and the low-fat substitutes on the market, there is virtually no dish that you can't adapt to the low-fat lifestyle. That is part of the beauty of it!

BOUNTIFUL BEANS:
A GUIDE TO BEANS AND THEIR PREPARATION

I cannot say enough good things about beans. They have become just about my favorite food. They are a large part of my success on the low-fat lifestyle. They are easy to prepare, versatile, nutritious, and best of all, filling. When you make a bean dish a large part of your meal, you fill up quickly and stay full. While it is possible to find fresh beans at times, most of the time I depend on the dried version. In a pinch, canned beans will do. However, it is very inexpensive and easy to prepare dried beans yourself. I like to soak them overnight, then cook them all day in the slow cooker. When I come home from work, they are ready to eat. There are two basic ways to soak dried beans. Choose the one that best suits your schedule:

Overnight Method: Wash and pick over the beans. Cover one pound of beans with 6-8 cups of water. There are disagreements about cooking beans in the soaking water. Some nutritionists feel that they should be, so that nutrients removed in the soaking process will not be lost. Others feel that the nutrients lost are negligible, and that the soaking water should be replaced with fresh water. You can make your own choice. I prefer to discard the soaking liquid.

Quick soaking method: Place the beans, along with 6-8 cups of water per pound, in a kettle over medium heat. Bring to a rapid boil, remove from the heat, and let stand one hour. Then cook as usual. Beans may be cooked on the stovetop over medium heat, according to package directions, for 45 minutes to three hours, depending on the bean. They may also be cooked in a slow cooker for 8-12 hours on low. My favorite way to season dried beans is to add 1-2 chicken bouillon cubes for each two cups of water.

While most of us are familiar with common types of dried beans, here is a short guide in case you need it:

Black beans: A small, black, kidney shaped bean that is heavily used in Caribbean-style dishes, such as Cuban black beans. They are also called turtle beans.

Blackeyed peas are small and cream colored with a small, black mark at the sprouting point. They are also called cow peas. Because they are thin-skinned, they can be cooked without soaking.

Butter beans come in two varieties, the large butter bean and the smaller lima bean. Both are popular and delicious.

Chickpeas are also called garbanzo beans. They are probably most familiar as an ingredient at salad bars, but they are used in a large number of Mediterranean-style dishes. They are very nutritious, with high amounts of protein and B vitamins.

Northern and navy beans are very popular all over the world. In this country the navy bean is probably best known as the bean used in baked beans.

Kidney beans are large red beans that are probably best known for their role in Mexican-style dishes.

Lentils are thought to be the first beans to be eaten by man. There are several varieties. The most common variety is the brown lentil. They are very high in protein.

Peas are thought to go back to the days of ancient Rome. The most common variety is the English pea.

Pintos are among the most popular beans in this country. They are an important ingredient in many Mexican-style dishes.

Soy beans are eaten all over the world, but in this country are often used to create other products.

GLORIOUS GRAINS:
SOME OLD AND NEW GRAINS TO ENJOY

It is entirely appropriate that the bread, cereal, rice and pasta group makes up the broad, strong base of the food pyramid. All of these foods are grains in one form or another. Just as they are the foundation on which the pyramid rests, they are the foundation of my low-fat lifestyle. Grains are versatile, full of nutrients and fiber, and are wonderfully filling. Use them as a mainstay in your meals and you will not get hungry. While the old standbys, wheat, rice, oats and corn are most familiar and popular, more unusual grains, such as millet and bulgur, can add variety to your meals. For the adventurous, some ancient grains are becoming a modern day delicacy. Amaranth, quinoa and Job's Tears may delight you as much as they delighted people a thousand years ago. You may choose to enjoy your grains in their natural state or ground into flour and made into bread or pasta. However you eat them, they are sure to become a favorite part of your low-fat lifestyle.

While we may be unfamiliar with a number of the more obscure grains on the market, we often don't know much about the ones we've eaten all our lives. The following pages will give you a brief description of a number of grains, both common and uncommon. In addition, there is a chart which gives you the cooking instructions for many of them.

Before beginning a description of various grains and grain products, you should know what makes up a kernel of grain. It is actually a seed of the plant. The outer layer of the seed is called the husk, and it is removed from grains that are prepared for humans to eat. Inside the husk is the bran layer, which is high in fiber. The germ is also a nutritious part of the seed, full of protein, vitamins and minerals. The endosperm is the starchy center of the seed, and is the only part left in highly processed grain products. Since much of the nutrition of the grain is in the bran and germ, it is easy to see that the less the grain is processed, the better it is for us. Therefore, select as many whole-grain products as possible.

Amaranth is the ancient grain staple of the Aztecs. Amaranth is very different and may not be to everyone's taste. Amaranth and amaranth flour are available in health food stores.

Barley is mainly available in a form called pearl barley, which has had the hull and bran removed. It is often added to soups and stews, but is also excellent as a side dish with meals.

Buckwheat is mainly available ground into flour which is used in pancakes and bread, or as kasha, which is toasted buckwheat.

Bulgur is made from wheat berries that have been degermed, steamed and dried. It is often sold in medium and finely ground forms.

Cornmeal is basically ground, dried corn. It is commonly available in both white and yellow forms. Blue cornmeal is popular in some areas. Dried corn is also used to create other products. Hominy is dried corn that has been treated with lye or slaked lime, while grits are made from finely ground hominy. Masa harina is hominy that has been very finely ground. It is used to make corn tortillas.

Couscous is a grain product. Many people think of it as a grain, but it is made from durum wheat and is actually similar to pasta. It is very popular in Middle Eastern cooking.

Job's Tears is an interesting name for a unique grain that is popular in Asian countries. It resembles barley in many ways.

Millet, while not eaten much in this country, is a staple in many parts of the world. It consists of round, crunchy, yellow seeds and can be eaten cooked as a side dish or added to breads for textural interest.

Oats are a staple on many breakfast tables in the form of oatmeal, which is actually the steamed and rolled form of whole-grain oat groats. Most oatmeal is either whole rolled oat grains or rolled oats that have been cut up to make them cook more quickly. Unprocessed whole oat groats are also good when cooked and served as a side dish or included as an ingredient is breads.

Quinoa is the grain of the ancient Inca Indians. It is becoming quite popular in modern times, in part due to the very high nutritional value. It is available in health food stores.

White rice is rice that has been highly processed. Only the endosperm of the kernel is left. It is one of the most widely eaten grains.

Brown rice is not as popular as white rice. However it is somewhat more nutritious since the germ and bran have not been removed. Because of this, it has a chewier texture than white rice.

Rye is most widely available in this country in the form of flour, which is used as an ingredient in several breads, such as rye bread and pumpernickel.

Triticale is actually a hybrid grain made by crossing wheat with rye. It looks a little like rice. The nutritional value of triticale is very high.

Wheat is of course the queen of grains. The whole-wheat kernel is often sold as wheat berries which are eaten cooked as a cereal or side dish. They are also added to whole-wheat breads. Wheat berries are also often sprouted. Cracked wheat and bulgur are also forms of wheat which are quite popular. However, most wheat is ground into flour which is used to make breads, pastas and numerous other food products. Most are made with white flour, which is highly processed. It consists of the bleached, ground endosperm of the wheat kernel. Whole-wheat flour is less processed than white flour and therefore has more nutritional value. Products made with whole-wheat flour are also generally more filling and have more textural interest than those made with white flour.

Wild rice has always been viewed as a gourmet food, partly because it is very expensive. It is not a rice but the seed of a grass that grows in water. In recent years, it has become more widely available and is probably most popular with consumers when teamed with white or brown rice in packaged mixes.

A SHORT COURSE IN COOKING GRAINS

The following chart is for preparation of one cup of uncooked grain. The grain should be added when the water has come to a rolling boil. Allow the water to boil again, reduce the heat, cover tightly, and simmer for the number of minutes shown on the chart. It is usually best to allow the cooked grain to stand for a few minutes before serving. I generally do not add salt before cooking. After cooking, I use just a bit of light salt. The amount of salt shown on the chart is optional.

Grain	Water	Salt	Cooking Time	Yield
Barley	3 cups	1 teaspoon	40 min.	3 ½ cups
Buckwheat	2 cups	1 teaspoon	12 min.	3 ½ cups
Bulgur	2 cups	¼ teaspoon	20 min.	3 cups
Grits	4 cups	1 teaspoon	5 min.	4 cups
Millet	2 cups	½ teaspoon	30 min.	4 cups
Oat Groats	2 cups	½ teaspoon	60 min.	2 ½ cups
Oats Rolled	2 ¼ cups	½ teaspoon	7 min.	1 ½ cups
Oats, Quick	2 cups	¼ teaspoon	2 min.	1 ¼ cups
Rice, White	2 cups	1 teaspoon	20 min.	3 cups
Rice, Brown	2 ½ cups	1 teaspoon	45 min.	3 cups
Wheat Berries	2 ½ cups	½ teaspoon	2 hours	3 cups

HOW TO CAN HOMEMADE CONDIMENTS

Since I admittedly do not like to spend a lot of time in the kitchen, you may be surprised to see directions here for a time consuming task like home canning. Once in a blue moon I am overcome by a brief spell of domesticity. When this happens, I usually end up canning something, or making a loaf or two of homemade whole-grain bread. Condiments such as chow-chow, chutney and chili sauce can add a special zip to bean dishes, so I like to keep a variety on hand. While there are many good commercial brands on the market, it can be fun to create some gourmet chutneys, relishes or sauces at home. I had never canned a thing in my life until about a year ago. My husband and I were on vacation in a rustic mountain resort when we stumbled upon a gourmet food shop that specialized in unique homemade condiments. They averaged $5.00 per half pint. I decided that if they could do it, so could I. I purchased a few canning supplies and periodically, when I am in the mood, I put up a few jars of homemade chutney, relish or whatever else strikes my fancy, for us to enjoy with our meals. I usually can them rather than store them in the refrigerator or freezer. I do this because it keeps my freezer and refrigerator space free, and because I like to give a few jars to friends.

You may want to give home canning a try, too. It gives you a great feeling to look in the cupboard and see these lovely jars of gourmet treats that you have prepared yourself. You may enjoy making some of my favorite chutney and relish recipes. I have included them in the condiment section of this book. These recipes do call for quite a bit of sugar. However most people only eat a spoonful or two as an accompaniment, so the actual amount of sugar in a normal serving is quite small.

When home canning, it is very important to follow proper canning procedures. Otherwise, spoilage may occur. Never eat a canned food if the lid is bulging or if the food looks or smells like it may be spoiled. Do not use the following method to can meat or vegetables. They must be processed in a pressure canner. The boiling water bath method described here is used to process chutneys, relishes, pickles, fruits, tomatoes, jams and jellies.

You will need a kettle or pot deep enough to permit water to cover the tops of the canning jars by at least an inch. You will also need a rack, or insert that will hold the jars at least ½ inch above the bottom of the pot. It is essential to have a jar lifter to remove the hot jars from the water. You will also need pint or half pint canning jars, lids and bands that have been sterilized. This is done by pouring boiling water over them. Allow them to remain in the water so that they will still be hot when you are ready to use them. Use new canning jar lids and jars that have no cracks or chips.

Use only blemish-free, firm fruits and vegetables when preparing recipes for canning. While the chutney, relish or sauce is being cooked, bring sufficient water to a boil in your canning kettle to cover the tops of the filled jars by one inch. Allow room at the top so that the water will not boil over the sides of the kettle when the filled jars are placed in it. Pour the hot, cooked food into the hot, sterilized canning jars. Place the lids and seals on the jars. Place the filled jars in the boiling water. Allow enough room around each jar for free circulation of the water. If the water does not come at least one inch above the tops of the jars, add additional boiling water. Begin counting the processing time when the water returns to a full rolling boil. Keep the water boiling all during the processing period. Add additional boiling water if at any time the water boils down below the required height.

When the processing time ends, remove the jars from the kettle. Place the hot jars on a rack or on several thicknesses of cloth to cool. Do not put the jars on a cold surface or in a cold place or they may crack. After several hours test the seal by pressing down on the middle of the lid. If it will not move, the jar should be sealed. If it is not sealed, replace the lid with a new one and reprocess in the boiling water bath.

Don't be put off by the lengthy directions for processing canned condiments. It is really kind of fun and a few hours work will give you a lot of good things to eat, as well as save you money.

BASIC VEGETABLE COOKING

When we begin a low-fat lifestyle, we have to rethink our old cooking habits. I personally used to never prepare basic, cooked vegetables without several heaping tablespoons of butter. I just didn't think I could like them any other way. It is really all a matter of habit. When you get used to foods cooked without the butter or oil, you really begin to prefer them that way.

To prepare basic vegetables or legumes, add 1 chicken bouillon cube per 1-2 cups of cooking water. If you cannot do without a bit of butter or margarine, add 1 teaspoon to the recipe before serving. One way to get more bang for the buck, so to speak, if you must add butter, is to make browned butter. You simply melt real butter in a saucepan and cook over medium heat until the solids turn a rich brown. Watch carefully, since it can burn quickly. Remove the butter from the heat. As it cools, stir so that the solids are distributed throughout. Keep in the refrigerator and use a teaspoon or less only on those occasions when you feel that you must. The browned butter adds a delicious richness. A level teaspoon full has approximately 4 fat grams. I personally prefer to avoid any butter or margarine except for the ultra-light brands.

Remember, fat-free butter-flavored granules, sauces, spices or even plain catsup can give you much more taste than butter or margarine. If you want more seasoning in your basic vegetables, give them a try. Remember, butter, margarine and oil all have 12-14 fat grams per tablespoon. Butter should also be avoided if you have high cholesterol.

Oven roasting is a delicious way to prepare many vegetables. Simply cut them into chunks and place in a baking dish that has been sprayed with butter-flavored cooking spray. After the vegetables have been placed in the pan, spray them with the butter-flavored spray. Bake at 400° until the vegetables are tender and lightly browned.

Steaming is probably the most nutritious way to cook basic vegetables. See the steaming chart in this book for steaming methods and cooking times. Light soy sauce, liquefied butter-flavored granules, or even a light spray with butter-flavored cooking spray are quick and simple ways to season steamed vegetables.

Of course, another easy way to prepare many vegetables is to sauté or stir-fry them. Place them in a skillet or wok that has been sprayed with no-stick cooking spray and cook until done to your preference. A bit of chicken broth or water may also be added. Vegetables are often more tasty and retain more color and nutrients if they are served tender-crisp.

A SHORT GUIDE TO STEAMING

Steaming is a very nutritious way to prepare vegetables, chicken or seafood. It is also quick and easy. A simple, inexpensive insert that can turn any pot into a steamer can be purchased at almost any grocery or discount store for just a few dollars. For those who are willing to spend a little more for convenience, there are electric steamers which will steam a whole meal and then cut themselves off. Steaming allows the true taste of the food to shine, a fact that you will especially like as you decrease your dependence on fat and increase your appreciation of naturally good tasting food.

Basic steaming is simply a matter of suspending the food above boiling water so that the steam rising from the water cooks the food. As in other methods of cooking, timing is everything. A few extra minutes of steaming can change a tender-crisp stalk of asparagus into a sodden lump. Following is a general guide to the steaming times for some commonly steamed foods.

Artichokes: Choose blemish-free, compact artichokes. Trim off about an inch from the top, as well as the sharp tip from each leaf. Steaming time ranges from 30-45 minutes, depending on size.

Asparagus: Choose blemish-free, deep green, thin stalks. Break off the tough, woody end of each stalk. If the stalks are left whole, they will be tender-crisp in 8 minutes. If cut into pieces, it will take about 6 minutes.

Beans, Green: Choose blemish-free, crisp beans that snap easily. Remove the ends. Break into pieces or steam whole. Whole green beans will be tender-crisp in about 12 minutes. Beans that have been broken into pieces will take 10 minutes.

Beets: Choose deep red, firm beets with healthy green tops. Before steaming, cut off the tops, leaving about 2" of stem. Scrub the beets well. They will cook in 30-40 minutes.

Broccoli: Choose blemish-free, deep green stalks with no sign of yellow in the florets. Trim off the tough portion of the stalk. Cut into small pieces or steam whole. Broccoli will be tender-crisp in about 10-15 minutes.

Brussels Sprouts: Choose blemish-free, compact sprouts with no wilted leaves. Trim the ends and cut a small x in the base. They will steam in about 15 minutes.

Cabbage: Choose blemish-free, compact heads. Remove any wilted leaves and cut into wedges or shred. Shredded cabbage will steam in about 10 minutes, wedges will take about 15 minutes.

Carrots: Choose well-shaped, bright orange carrots. Peel them, using a vegetable peeler, and slice, or steam whole. Sliced carrots steam in about 10 minutes. Whole carrots take about 15-20 minutes.

Cauliflower: Choose compact, blemish-free heads. Trim away the outer leaves and cut into florets or steam whole. Florets will steam in 10-15 minutes. Whole heads will take about 15-20 minutes.

Chicken: Select boneless, skinless chicken breast halves. Trim away any remaining fat or skin. The steaming time will be 12-15 minutes.

Corn: Choose ears of corn with green, fresh looking husks. The kernels should be full and plump. Remove the husks and silk. An ear of corn steams in 8-10 minutes.

Eggplant: Choose blemish-free, deep purple eggplant. It can be steamed peeled or unpeeled, whole or in slices or cubes. Eggplant steams in 10-20 minutes, depending on whether it is cooked whole or cut into slices or cubes.

Fish fillets: Select fresh-smelling fillets of uniform thickness. Allow 10 minutes of steaming for each inch of thickness. If the fish is frozen, allow at least 20 minutes per inch.

Onions: Select blemish-free, firm onions. They may be peeled or steamed with the skin on. Steaming time will be about 15 minutes for sliced or chopped onions and 20 minutes for whole onions.

Peas, Green: Select peas with crisp, healthy pods. Sugar snap peas or snow peas should be steamed whole. Other green peas should be shelled shortly before steaming. Peas should steam for about 10 minutes.

Potatoes, Sweet: Choose plump potatoes with deep orange flesh. They may be steamed peeled or unpeeled, whole or in pieces. Whole sweet potatoes steam in about 25-40 minutes depending on size. Cut up sweet potatoes steam in 10-15 minutes.

Potatoes, White: Choose blemish-free, firm potatoes. They may be steamed peeled or unpeeled, whole or cut into pieces. Whole potatoes steam in 25-40 minutes. Potatoes cut up into slices or cubes should steam in about 20-30 minutes.

Rice, White or Brown: Add approximately 1½ cups water or chicken broth per cup of rice. Steam for about 40 minutes.

Shrimp: Choose fresh-looking peeled or unpeeled shrimp. Steam for about 11 minutes per pound. When they turn pink, they are done.

Spinach: Choose healthy, fresh-looking leaves. Remove any large or thick stems. Steam for 5-10 minutes.

Squash, Acorn: Choose heavy, dark green squash. Cut them in half and remove the strings and seeds. Place cut side down in the steaming basket. Steam for 25-30 minutes.

Squash, Summer: Choose blemish-free yellow squash or zucchini. Steam whole or cut into slices, for about 15 minutes.

Steamed vegetables, chicken and seafood are delicious alone or with very simple dressings, such as a squirt of lemon, a dash of soy sauce or a sprinkle of butter-flavored granules. A light sauce is also a good accompaniment.

Quick and Healthy Cooking the Microwave Way

Like steaming, microwaving is a particularly good way to prepare vegetables. Since little water is used, the vegetables retain their fresh, bright color and taste. They also lose fewer nutrients in the cooking process than vegetables boiled in water. As an added bonus, microwaved foods can often be cooked and served in the same dish. In general, vegetables and other foods cooked in the microwave should be placed in covered, microwave-safe casserole dishes. Often the water that remains on them after washing is enough to cook them properly. Below is a short guide to microwaving vegetables and other commonly microwaved foods. (The cooking times given are for 600-700 watt microwave ovens. Rotate the dish halfway through the cooking process.)

Artichokes: Wrap in waxed paper. Microwave on high 6-7 minutes per pound.

Asparagus: Arrange in a glass dish with 1 tablespoon water. Cover and microwave 6-7 minutes per pound on high.

Beans, Green: Place 3 cups green beans in a glass casserole. Add about ¼ cup water and microwave, covered, on high, for 8 minutes.

Corn: Remove the husks and silk and place the washed ears of corn in a covered dish or wrap in waxed paper with some of the water still clinging to them. Microwave on high 2-3 minutes for 1 ear, 6-7 minutes for 4 ears or 10-12 minutes for 8 ears.

Eggplant: May be cooked peeled or unpeeled. Cut into cubes and microwave on high, covered, for 6-7 minutes per pound.

Fish: Place boneless fish fillets in a glass baking dish with the thicker portions to the outside of the dish. Cover and microwave on medium power for 10 minutes per pound.

Greens: Place about 4 cups of washed greens in a casserole dish with the water still clinging to the leaves. Cover and microwave on high for 6-8 minutes.

Mushrooms: Clean the mushrooms and microwave whole or sliced in a covered glass dish on high for 6-7 minutes per pound.

Onions: May be left whole, sliced, or chopped. Microwave, covered, on high for 6-7 minutes per pound.

Peas, Green: Place 2 cups green peas in a casserole dish with 3 tablespoons water. Microwave, covered, on high for 5-6 minutes per pound. Stir halfway through the cooking time.

Beets: Place 2-4 beets in a glass casserole. Cover them with water and microwave on high, covered, for 15-18 minutes.

Broccoli: Arrange the stalks of broccoli with the stems pointing outward. Add 3-4 tablespoons water to the dish and cook, covered, on high for 8-10 minutes, depending on the size and number of stalks.

Cabbage: Shred, chop or slice into wedges. Place the cabbage in a glass cooking dish with 3 tablespoons water. Microwave on high, covered, for 7-8 minutes per pound.

Carrots: Slice carrots and place in a covered casserole with ¼ cup water. Microwave on high for 7-8 minutes per pound. Stir halfway through the cooking time.

Cauliflower: Leave whole or cut into florets. Add 3 tablespoons water to the cooking dish. Microwave, covered, on high for 6-7 minutes per pound. If the cauliflower has been cut into florets, stir halfway through the cooking time.

Chicken: Place boneless breast halves in a glass baking dish with the thicker parts to the outside of the dish. Cover and microwave on high for 4-5 minutes. Rearrange and turn the breasts and cook an additional 4-5 minutes.

Peppers: Place the washed, cored peppers in a glass baking dish. They may be sliced, chopped or left whole. Microwave, covered, on high for 6-7 minutes per pound.

Potatoes, Baked: Potatoes need to be similar in size and shape. Pierce skins. Arrange the potatoes in a circle in a baking dish, plate, or on the bottom of the oven. Microwave on high, 3-4 minutes for 1 potato, 6-7 minutes for two potatoes, 10-11 minutes for four potatoes.

Potatoes, Boiled: Peel and chop potatoes. Add about ½ cup water and microwave on high, covered, 18-20 minutes for four potatoes.

Potatoes, Sweet: Choose potatoes similar in size and shape. Arrange in a circle in a baking dish, on a plate, or on the bottom of the oven. Microwave on high 3-4 minutes for 1 potato, 5-6 minutes for two potatoes, 7-8 minutes for four potatoes, or 8-9 minutes for six potatoes.

Squash, Acorn: Pierce the whole squash in several places. Microwave 6-9 minutes on high. Let stand about 5 minutes, then cut in half and remove seeds.

Squash, Summer: Slice squash; place in a glass baking dish with 2 tablespoons water. Microwave, covered, on high for 6-7 minutes.

The Low-fat Kitchen

Kitchen Equipment For A Low-fat Lifestyle

Let's Go Grocery Shopping

KITCHEN EQUIPMENT FOR A LOW FAT LIFESTYLE

Good kitchen equipment can add enjoyment to the time you spend in the kitchen! Invest in the best you can afford.

Kitchen Basics:
Good quality nonstick cookware with tight fitting lids
Good quality nonstick bakeware
Good quality, sharp kitchen knives in assorted sizes
Mixing spoons, metal and wooden
Measuring spoons and cups
Metal and plastic colanders
A vegetable peeler
Strainers in several sizes
Wire whisks in several sizes
A spatula
A shredder/grater
A can opener
A kitchen scale
A cutting board

Helpful But not Essential Kitchen Equipment:
A blender
A food processor
An electric mixer
A garlic press
An instant reading thermometer
A slow cooker
A microwave oven
A steamer insert or bamboo steamer
A defatting cup
Kitchen shears
A pressure cooker
A wok
A waffle iron
A crepe skillet
A mini chopper
Microwaveable dishes

Kitchen Luxuries:
A Belgian waffle maker
An electric tortilla maker
An electric crepe maker
A pizza stone
An electric pasta maker
An electric bread maker
A grain mill
A wide slot toaster
An indoor electric grill
A convection oven
An air popcorn popper
An electric juicer
An ice cream maker
A pepper mill
A milkshake maker

LET'S GO GROCERY SHOPPING

Grocery shopping can be a lot of fun when you see all of the new low-fat products that come out weekly! The following is a general guideline to low-fat grocery shopping. Don't faint! You don't have to buy all of it! My best shopping tip: READ ALL NUTRITION LABELS! Make sure the goods you are buying are low-fat.

The Canned Goods section:
Any canned vegetable
Any canned water or juice-packed fruit
Fat-free spaghetti sauce
Canned Chinese vegetables, including water chestnuts
Canned dried beans
Canned tomatoes, tomato sauce and tomato paste (low sodium)
Canned fish, such as tuna, packed in water
Canned white chicken chunks, packed in water
Canned vegetable and fruit juices
Canned Mexican foods, such as chilies and fat-free refried beans
Canned evaporated skim milk
Canned baked beans
Canned 99% fat-free soups

Pasta, Grains, Beans, and Related:
White and brown rice
Noodles in various sizes, egg-free if possible
Gourmet rice, such as basmati and arborio
Instant rice
Packaged rice mixes and sauce mixes, low-fat
Packaged noodle and sauce mixes, low-fat
Dried beans of all kinds
Dried bean soup mixes
Barley
Assorted grains, such as oat groats, millet and bulgur
Instant mashed potatoes
Packaged potato and sauce mixes, low-fat
Packaged stuffing mix, low-fat

Breads, Crackers and Cookies:
Fat-free crackers
Fat-free rice cakes
Whole-grain crisp breads
Whole-grain reduced-calorie breads, rolls and buns
English muffins, assorted flavors
Bagels, assorted flavors
Pita bread
Melba toast
Fat-free and low-fat cookies
Fat-free croutons

Beverages:
Coffee, regular and assorted gourmet flavors
Tea, regular, and assorted flavored tea, regular and herbal
Diet hot cocoa mix (25 calories per cup)
Diet hot cider mix
Sugar-free powdered drink mixes
Diet soda

Baking Supplies:
White and whole-wheat flour (plain and self-rising)
Cornmeal
Buttermilk cornmeal mix
Fat-free baking mix
Yeast (rapid rise and regular)
Cocoa
Baking powder and baking soda
Dried skim milk powder

Cereals:
Rolled oats
Quick cooking oatmeal
Bran cereal
Fat-free or low-fat, low-sugar breakfast cereals
Grits

Cooking oils:
No-stick butter-flavored spray
No-stick olive oil-flavored spray
No-stick spray, unflavored
Small bottle olive oil
Small bottle canola oil

Packaged Dessert Mixes:
Sugar-free gelatin
Sugar-free pudding mix
Light cake mixes
Light frosting

Spices, Condiments and Related:
Louisiana hot sauce
Assorted mustards
Catsup (low sodium if possible)
Fat-free barbecue sauce
Worcestershire sauce
Liquid smoke

Fat-free and reduced-fat mayonnaise
Fat- free mayonnaise-type salad dressing
Fat-free salad dressing, assorted flavors
Pickles and pickle relish
Assorted vinegars
Imitation bacon bits
Light soy sauce
Light teriyaki sauce
Light salt
Coarse ground black pepper and whole peppercorns
Assorted spices and herbs
Salt-free spice blends
Salt substitute
Fat-free butter-flavor granules, in both package and shaker

The Meat Department:
Chicken pieces or boneless breasts (remove all skin and fat)
Whole turkey breast (remove skin)
Ultra-lean ground beef or butcher ground top round
97% fat-free wieners
Eye of round beef roast (all fat removed)
Pork tenderloin (all fat removed)
99% fat-free precooked turkey
98% fat-free precooked ham
Deli sliced 99% fat-free turkey
Deli sliced 98% fat-free ham
Fresh shrimp and other shellfish
Fresh fish fillets

Soups:
99% fat-free canned soups
Dehydrated soup mixes, including onion and vegetable
Bouillon cubes, chicken, vegetable, and beef (low sodium)
Instant bouillon granules, chicken and beef (low sodium)

The Dairy Case:
Fat-free egg substitute
Ultra-low-fat or fat-free margarine
Fat-free cream cheese
Fat-free hard cheeses, such as Cheddar and mozzarella
Fat-free sour cream
Fat-free yogurt
Skim milk
Fresh pasta
Fresh pasta sauces (fat-free)
Low-fat canned biscuits
Fresh refrigerated corn and flour tortillas

Frozen Foods:
Plain frozen vegetables
Frozen fat-free and low-fat dinners and entrées
Frozen pancakes
Frozen waffles (regular and Belgian)
Frozen sugar-free fruits
Frozen bread and roll dough
Frozen yogurt
Ice milk
Sherbet
Frozen juice bars

Produce:
Any fresh fruit, except avocado
Any fresh vegetable

Snack Foods:
Fat-free potato chips and corn chips
Popcorn (regular and low-fat microwave)
Fat-free dips
Pretzels

Miscellaneous:
Jelly, jams, and preserves-low or no-sugar brands preferred
Light pancake syrup, maple flavor
Light pancake syrup, blueberry flavor
Light chocolate sauce

Section 6

The Low-fat Recipes That Helped Me Lose

Breakfast Foods

Appetizers and Snacks

Breads

Soups and Stews

Salads

Main Dishes

Vegetables

Grains and Pasta

The Fast Food Lover's Low-fat Path To Happiness

Desserts

Sauces and Condiments

Miscellaneous

JUST A FEW MORE WORDS ABOUT LOW-FAT RECIPES

On the following pages are the recipes that are a part of my low-fat lifestyle. Many are adaptations of recipes I used before I began counting fat grams. It is so simple to adapt recipes. Just replace the high-fat ingredients with low-fat alternatives. I have no trouble sticking with a low-fat lifestyle because I can enjoy most of my old favorites, with just a few modifications.

I am not a person who likes to spend a lot of time in the kitchen. As a matter of fact, the less time, the better. My recipes reflect that. They are short and uncomplicated. You may want to prepare more challenging recipes than I present here. If so, visit your local bookstore. There are a lot of cookbooks devoted to more sophisticated low-fat recipes. That is one thing I love about the low-fat lifestyle. Many conventional diets assume that people with weight problems love to cook and think about food all of the time. They believe that they must keep you busy cooking, weighing and measuring so that you won't notice that you are hungry. On a low-fat lifestyle you can have it either way. If you hate to cook, you fix it quick and get out of the kitchen. If you love to cook, you can find low-fat recipes that will make the most demanding gourmet happy.

Whether you love to cook or hate it, I imagine that you despise cleaning up afterwards. Everyone does. One great bonus of a low-fat lifestyle is that none of your dirty dishes will have the horrible greasy residue that is so hard to scrub off dishes in which fatty foods have been cooked or eaten. Is this a terrific lifestyle or what? Lots of great food to eat and dishes that are easier to clean, too!

You may notice that I list the number of fat grams, but not the calorie count per serving for each of my recipes. I do this because of my own experience. It is hard to forget about counting calories when you see them attached to every recipe.

When you prepare any of the recipes in this book, do not hesitate to modify them to your own taste. You may find that you prefer more or less herbs or spices. You might want to throw in a few extra low-fat ingredients. You may want to use some of your daily fat gram allowance to sauté or oven fry in a tablespoon of oil instead of using only the no-stick cooking spray that is suggested in a recipe. Please do not just take one taste of any low-fat dish or product and dismiss it just because it doesn't taste just like you think it should. Tinker with it if you must, but, above all, do not forget our words to live by: I WILL NOT LET MYSELF COMPARE THE TASTE OF MY LOW-FAT FOODS TO THEIR HIGH-FAT COUNTERPARTS. I WILL SIMPLY ENJOY THEM, WITHOUT MAKING ANY COMPARISON. You will come to love the taste of your low-fat dishes. After all, they can help you lose weight without dieting or deprivation.

BREAKFAST FOODS

I never skip breakfast! It gets my body cranked up in the morning! My personal favorites are oatmeal with sugar substitute, spices and/or fruit, pancakes with reduced-calorie syrup, or whole-grain toast with jam. I sometimes also throw in a bowl of cereal, an English muffin or a bagel if I am really hungry. If you are a bacon and eggs type person, you may decide to enjoy biscuits, several slices of low-fat precooked ham and scrambled eggs made with fat-free egg substitute or egg whites.

French Toast

½ cup fat-free egg substitute
½ cup skim milk
⅛ teaspoon nutmeg
1 teaspoon sugar or granular sugar substitute
fat-free, reduced-calorie bread slices
butter-flavored no-stick cooking spray

Combine the egg substitute, milk, nutmeg and sugar or sugar substitute. Cut the bread slices in half. Dip the bread into the egg mixture and sauté until golden on a griddle that has been sprayed with butter-flavor no-stick cooking spray. Good with light syrup, preserves or fruit sauce.

4 servings
0 fat grams per serving

Homemade Pancakes

I usually make pancakes with fat-free baking mix, or I buy the frozen ones at the grocery that are quite low in fat. However, when I have the time and inclination, I make them from scratch.

2 cups all-purpose flour
4 teaspoons baking powder
1 teaspoon light salt
1½ cups skim milk
¼ cup fat-free egg substitute
4 tablespoons fat-free cottage cheese
butter-flavored no-stick cooking spray

Combine the dry ingredients. In another bowl, combine the milk, egg substitute and the cottage cheese. Combine with the flour mixture. Cook the pancakes on a griddle that has been coated with butter-flavor no-stick cooking spray.

Variation: Add blueberries or sliced bananas to the batter.

4 servings
Less than 1 fat gram per serving

TERRIFIC OATMEAL

Frankly, oatmeal has probably done more to help me lose weight than anything else. Before I started following a low-fat lifestyle, I didn't eat oatmeal once a year. I didn't even particularly like it. Now I love it. I eat it often for breakfast. It also makes a great snack. It is healthy, wonderfully filling, and very versatile. Some people like it plain or with milk. I personally like to doctor it with lots or fruit, sugar substitute, and butter-flavored granules. Prepared this way, it becomes almost a dessert. With raisins and nutmeg, it is a little like rice pudding. With chopped peaches or apple it is tastes rather like fruit cobbler. I have even added a bit of cocoa powder! The results were not unlike a rich, fudgy dessert. Oatmeal has become one of my favorite comfort foods.

My Favorite Breakfast and Snack Oatmeal

Prepare as much quick cooking plain oatmeal as desired, according to the directions on the package. Add sugar substitute or sugar to taste. Blend in a sprinkle of nutmeg or cinnamon. Top with a sprinkling of butter-flavored granules and granular sugar substitute or sugar. Add raisins, cooked apple, or other fruit, if desired. A dash of vanilla, maple, or coconut flavoring instead of the spices is also terrific.

Approximately 2 fat grams
per cup of prepared oatmeal

APPETIZERS AND SNACKS

Appetizers and snacks can take the edge off hunger. However, they can also slow down your weight loss efforts if you overindulge. I could eat an entire family-size bag of fat-free tortilla chips and a whole recipe of dip by myself, so I try to save most traditional snack foods for an occasional treat. If I get hungry between meals, I most often have a piece of fruit, a bowl of oatmeal, or a cup of diet hot cocoa. Whole-grain reduced-calorie toast with jam also makes a filling snack.

Buffalo Chicken Breasts

This is a less fatty version of popular Buffalo Chicken Wings. For an authentic Buffalo Wings experience, serve with celery sticks and a small container of fat-free blue cheese dressing.

4 4-ounce chicken breast halves, boned and skinned
no-stick cooking spray
1 tablespoon melted margarine
1 tablespoon water
Louisiana hot sauce to taste

Cut the chicken breasts into strips, if serving as an appetizer, or leave whole to serve as an entrée. Sauté the chicken until brown in a skillet that has been coated with no-stick cooking spray. Combine the margarine, water and hot sauce. Add to the chicken in the skillet and simmer briefly.

4 servings
7 fat grams per serving

"Beanuts"

One day I happened to taste some raw chickpeas that had been soaked overnight in preparation for cooking. The flavor was very similar to that old southern favorite—boiled peanuts. I decided that the chickpeas might also taste good roasted. Since roasted peanuts are high in fat, these make a great substitute. Other dry beans may be substituted for the chickpeas.

2 cups dried chickpeas, soaked overnight/drained well

Arrange the chickpeas in a single layer on a baking sheet with low sides. Bake for about 40 minutes at 350°, stirring occasionally.

4 servings
2 fat grams per serving

Hummus

This is a popular dip that is delicious with toasted pita chips. Tahini (sesame seed paste), is quite high in fat, but the amount used in this recipe is not enough to blow your fat gram allowance.

1 16-ounce can chickpeas
1 tablespoon tahini (sesame seed paste)
2 tablespoons fresh lemon juice
2 cloves garlic, minced, or ¼ teaspoons garlic powder

Combine all of the ingredients in a food processor and puree.

8 servings
Less than 2 fat grams per serving

Lasagna Chips

1 8-ounce package lasagna noodles, cooked as directed
    on package
butter-flavored no-stick cooking spray
light salt
1 tablespoon grated Parmesan cheese

Cut the cooked noodles into 1" lengths. Place on a baking sheet that has been coated with butter-flavored no-stick cooking spray. Lightly coat the noodles with cooking spray. Sprinkle the noodles with salt and Parmesan cheese. Bake at 400° for about 15 minutes, or until brown. Heated spaghetti sauce makes a good dip with the chips.

6 fat grams in recipe

Lively Horseradish Dip

1 1-ounce envelope dehydrated onion soup mix
1 tablespoon imitation bacon bits
1 cup fat-free sour cream
horseradish to taste

Combine onion soup mix, imitation bacon bits, sour cream, and horseradish. Serve with fat-free chips, crackers, or crudities.

1 fat gram per serving

Mexican Bean Dip

2 cups cooked pinto beans or black beans, mashed
½ teaspoon garlic powder
1 can chopped chili peppers, drained
½ green pepper, chopped
½ medium onion, chopped
½ teaspoon cumin
hot sauce to taste

Combine the beans, garlic powder, chili peppers, green peppers, onion, cumin and hot sauce. Serve with baked tortilla chips

6 servings
0 fat grams per serving

Middle Eastern Eggplant Dip

1 medium eggplant
1 tablespoon tahini
2 cloves garlic, minced, or ¼ teaspoon garlic powder

Place the eggplant in a 375° oven and roast until the skin is charred. Let cool, cut in half, and remove the pulp. Mash the pulp and combine with the remaining ingredients. Serve with pita bread or toasted pita chips.

8 servings
1 fat gram per serving

Pineapple Cheese Spread

This recipe sounds just awful, but it is really good.

1 8-ounce container fat-free cream cheese, softened
1 8-ounce can crushed pineapple in its own juice,
    drained
2 tablespoons finely minced onion
2 tablespoons finely minced green pepper

Combine the softened cream cheese and the drained pineapple. Stir in the onion and the green pepper. Place the mixture in a small serving dish. Serve with fat-free snack crackers.

0 fat grams in the recipe

Sort of Guacamole

Since avocado is relatively high in fat, this recipe lets us have a guacamole-style dip without the avocado found in the traditional recipe. Serve with baked tortilla chips.

2 10-ounce packages frozen English peas, thawed
½ cup fat-free sour cream
1 small onion, finely minced
½ teaspoon dried cilantro
1 chopped tomato
½ teaspoon cumin

Puree the peas in a blender or food processor until smooth. Add the remaining ingredients. Serve chilled or at room temperature.

8 servings
0 fat grams per serving

BREADS

Breads are among the "Big Five" foods in my low-fat lifestyle. Along with beans, grains, fruits and vegetables, breads will fill you up and keep you satisfied. Whole-grain breads are the most nutritious and most filling, so choose them often.

Baked Hushpuppies

½ cup cornmeal
½ cup all-purpose flour
½ teaspoon sugar or granulated sugar substitute
½ teaspoon light salt
dash of ground red pepper
⅓ cup skim milk
¼ cup fat-free egg substitute
2 tablespoons fat-free sour cream
1 medium onion, finely minced

Combine the dry ingredients. Add the milk, egg substitute and sour cream. Mix in the onion. Bake in regular muffin tins, or mini tins, if you want them to be more like a traditional hushpuppy. Bake at 400° for 15-25 minutes, depending on the size of the muffin tins.

Less than 1 fat gram per muffin

Broccoli Cornbread

1 cup self-rising cornmeal mix
¼ cup fat-free egg substitute
½ cup water, or more if needed
½ cup fat-free cottage cheese
1 onion, chopped
1 10-ounce package frozen chopped broccoli,
   cooked and drained

Combine all of the ingredients. Pour into and 8" x 11.5" baking pan. Bake at 375° for 30-40 minutes.

8 servings
Less than 1 fat gram per serving

Cheese, Onion and Poppy Seed Dinner Bread

2 cups fat-free baking mix
1 medium onion, finely minced
¼ cup fat-free egg substitute
¾ cup water
4 ounces fat-free Cheddar cheese
1 tablespoon poppy seeds
1 tablespoon fat-free cottage cheese

Combine all of the ingredients. Pour into an 8" square baking pan. Top with a sprinkle of extra poppy seeds if desired. Bake at 400° for 20 minutes.

6 servings
Less than 1 fat gram per serving

Cinnamon Rolls

Since these contain sugar, they should be eaten only as a special treat. Too much sugar can hurt weight loss.

3 cups fat-free baking mix
¾ cup skim milk
¼ cup sugar
2 teaspoons cinnamon
butter-flavored no-stick cooking spray
¼ cup raisins
¼ cup powdered sugar mixed with 2 teaspoons skim milk

Combine the baking mix and the skim milk. Turn the dough out onto a flat surface that has been sprinkled with flour or baking mix. Roll the dough out into a 12" x 14" rectangle. Combine the sugar and cinnamon. Spray the dough with the cooking spray. Sprinkle the sugar-cinnamon mixture, then the raisins over the dough. Roll the dough up, beginning with the 14" side. Press the seam to help seal. Cut the roll into 12 1" pieces. Place in a 9" x 13" baking dish that has been sprayed with butter-flavored no-stick cooking spray. Bake for 25 minutes at 350°. Drizzle the powdered sugar mixture over the cinnamon rolls.

12 servings
0 fat grams per serving

Country Biscuits

A friend gave me this recipe long before I started watching fat grams. Luckily, they are low in fat so I didn't have to give them up. They are great served with fat-free margarine and reduced-sugar jam. You can even make a reasonable facsimile of the fast food chain favorite, breakfast in a biscuit, by adding a slice of 98% fat-free cooked ham and a scrambled egg made with fat-free egg substitute.

1 cup self-rising flour
1 tablespoon solid vegetable shortening
½ cup buttermilk
butter-flavored no-stick cooking spray

Cut the shortening into the flour, using a pastry blender or two knives. When completely blended, add the buttermilk. Roll out and use a biscuit cutter to cut into 8-10 biscuits. Place on a baking sheet that has been coated with butter-flavored no-stick cooking spray. After the biscuits have all been placed in the pan, spray the tops lightly with the butter-flavor spray. Bake at 425 for 10 minutes or until lightly browned.

8-10 servings
Less than 2 fat grams per serving

Our Daily Corn Bread

Okay, so it's not our daily corn bread, but I couldn't resist the pun. However, we do have it at least 3-4 times a week. My husband and I usually eat half the recipe each! I bake it in an 8" iron skillet that has been coated with no-stick cooking spray. We like it left in the oven for a long time, so that the outside becomes very crusty. This is especially good with dry beans. The onions and peppers are entirely optional. The corn bread is just as good without them. However, I like to add them because it doubles the size of the corn bread, while adding a lot of taste and no additional fat grams.

1 cup self-rising cornmeal mix
¼ cup fat-free egg substitute
½ cup water, or more for a thinner batter
¼ cup unsweetened applesauce
1 onion, chopped
1 green pepper chopped
no-stick cooking spray

Preheat the oven to 450°. Combine the cornmeal mix, egg substitute, water and applesauce. Add the onion and green pepper. Pour into an 8" skillet that has been coated with no-stick cooking spray. Bake for 30-45 minutes, depending upon how crisp you like the crust.

4 servings
1 fat gram per serving

Stuffed Bread

I do not make a habit of keeping this around the house because it is entirely too tempting to me. It is nice for a special treat, however.

butter-flavored no-stick spray
1 pound loaf frozen bread dough, thawed

Roll dough into a 9"x 12" rectangle, spray with butter-flavored no-stick cooking spray, and sprinkle with one of the following fillings. Then roll up and place in a loaf pan. Let rise and bake according to the directions on the bread dough label.

Double onion filling:
1 1-ounce package dehydrated onion soup mix,
½ medium onion, finely chopped, ⅛ teaspoon poppy
seeds

Apple-cinnamon filling:
¼ cup brown sugar substitute, 2 apples, peeled and grated, 1 teaspoon cinnamon

16 servings
1 fat gram per slice

Tasty Dinner Bread

Sometimes a meal just cries out for some special, delicious bread as an accompaniment. Who can eat pasta without a few slices of warm garlic bread? If you think you can't prepare it without lots of butter, think again. I personally like to reserve my daily fat gram allowance for things other than 12 grams per tablespoon butter or margarine, so I prefer one of the following methods of making the bread without the fat:

Method 1: Use fat-free, reduced-calorie Italian or sourdough bread. Spray each slice lightly with butter-flavored no-stick cooking spray. Sprinkle with garlic powder and dried oregano. Bake at 350° until just warm, or until brown and crisp, depending on your personal preference.

Method 2: Use fat-free, reduced-calorie Italian or sourdough bread. Spread with a teaspoon of ultra-low-fat (2 grams per tablespoon or less) margarine. Sprinkle with garlic powder and dried oregano. Bake at 350° until warm or crisp depending on your preference.

Variation: Poppy seeds and dehydrated onion are also tasty additions.

Less than 1 fat gram per slice

SOUPS AND STEWS

Make a lot of these for a warm, satisfied feeling. I make several pots of Twelve Bean or Northern Bean soup every week, often in the slow cooker. A hearty soup or stew, served with corn bread or whole-grain bread and a salad, makes a wonderful meal. I often eat three large bowls of soup at a time.

Baked Bean Soup

3 16-ounce cans fat-free vegetarian baked beans,
    undrained
1 16-ounce can chopped tomatoes, undrained
3 97% fat-free wieners, sliced
1 medium onion, finely chopped
1 green pepper, finely chopped
1 tablespoon granulated brown sugar substitute
1 teaspoon prepared mustard

Combine all ingredients. Simmer until the onion and green
pepper are tender.

6 servings
Less than 1 fat gram per serving

Chili

You may think if it doesn't have meat, then it's not chili, but it's still really good. You don't really miss the meat.

1 pound dry kidney beans
8 cups water
2 large onions, chopped
2 green peppers, chopped
2 15-ounce cans chunky Mexican-style tomato sauce
1 tablespoon chili powder
1 tablespoon cumin

Soak the beans overnight. Pour off the soaking water and replace with 8 cups fresh water. Cook the beans, onion and peppers for 1½ hours, or until tender. Add the tomato sauce, chili powder and cumin.

Variation: Add 6 ounces cooked ultra-lean ground beef or ½ cup dehydrated ground beef-style textured vegetable protein.

We like this chili with chopped onion and fat-free shredded Cheddar cheese on top.

6 servings
Less than 1 fat gram without meat

Cozy Corn Chowder

While a big steaming bowl of this tasty and filling chowder would be good any time of year, somehow it evokes thoughts of crisp fall days, red and gold leaves and football games. It would be just the thing to warm you up after a brisk day outdoors.

1 medium onion, minced
½ cup celery, minced
no-stick cooking spray
1 tablespoon all-purpose flour
2½ cups skim milk
1 ½-ounce package butter-flavored granules
1 17-ounce can creamed corn
2 medium potatoes, peeled and diced
8 ounces cooked 98% fat-free ham
light salt and pepper to taste

Sauté the onion and celery in a saucepan that has been coated with no-stick cooking spray. When they are wilted, add the flour and cook 1 minute. Gradually add the milk and stir until thickened. Add the butter-flavored granules, corn, potatoes, ham, salt and pepper. Simmer 20 minutes.

4 servings
2 fat grams per serving

Cream of Broccoli Soup

Since broccoli is supposed to be so good for us, we are sup-posed to eat lots of it, as often as possible. This is a good way to serve it.

2 cups water
1½ pounds fresh broccoli, chopped
½ cup onion
½ cup celery
2 tablespoons all-purpose flour blended with 2 table-
    spoons water
2½ cups water
½ cup evaporated skim milk
1 tablespoon chicken-flavor instant bouillon granules
salt and pepper to taste

Heat 2 cups of water until boiling. Add the vegetables and cook until tender. Purée half of the vegetables in the blender, along with the cooking liquid. Return the puréed vegetables to the cooking pot. Add the flour mixed with 2 tablespoons water. Stir until blended. Add the remaining 2½ cups of water, the evaporated skim milk and the bouillon granules. Bring to a boil and then simmer until slightly thickened. Add the remaining vegetables and continue cooking for 10 minutes.

9 cups
0 fat grams per serving

Northern Bean Soup

This is another regular on our menu. I love it because it, like most dishes made with dry beans, can cook all day in the slow cooker and be ready to serve when you get home from work.

1 pound dried northern beans, soaked overnight
8 cups water
3 medium potatoes, peeled and diced
2 carrots, peeled and sliced
1 cup celery, diced
8 ounces 98% fat-free precooked ham, cut into cubes
3 chicken bouillon cubes

After soaking the beans overnight, discard the soaking liquid. Add 8 cups fresh water and the rest of the ingredients. Cook up to 12 hours on low in a slow cooker or cook on medium heat for about 2 hours or until the vegetables are tender.

6 servings
2 fat grams per serving

Quick and Hearty Potato Soup

½ cup chopped onion
½ cup chopped celery
½ cup chopped carrots
no-stick cooking spray
6 cups skim milk
4 teaspoons chicken-flavor instant bouillon granules
2 medium potatoes, diced
1¾ cup instant mashed potato flakes

Sauté the onion, celery and carrots in a large saucepan that has been coated with no-stick cooking spray. When they are wilted, stir in the milk and the bouillon granules. Add the potatoes. Cook 8 minutes, stirring frequently. Add the potato flakes and cook 6 more minutes.

6 servings
Less than 1 fat gram per serving

Twelve Bean Soup Mix

Mix equal amounts of the following dry beans:

black beans	large lima beans	northern beans
pinto beans	split peas	field peas
kidney beans	baby limas	black-eyed peas
chickpeas	lentils	navy beans

It is a good idea to buy a pound of each of the beans and after mixing, store in a large container and remove as needed. It's much cheaper than buying the commercial multi-bean soup mixes.

To make 4-6 servings, soak 1½ cups of the mixed beans overnight. Discard the soaking water and replace with 8 cups of fresh water. Add 3 chicken bouillon cubes. Cook up to 12 hours on low in a slow cooker or simmer for 2½ hours on the stovetop. When the beans are done, mix them with the following:

1 15-ounce can mixed tomatoes and chilies
1 chopped onion
1 clove garlic, minced
salt and pepper to taste

Continue cooking for 30-40 additional minutes.

Less than 1 fat gram per serving

SALADS

A tasty salad can add interest to a meal and take the edge off your appetite! I keep a lot of assorted salad ingredients. They make great in-between-meal snacks, in addition to their usual role as a mealtime accompaniment or main dish. While I have prepared my own dressings on occasion, I usually buy a variety of the excellent fat-free dressings available at the market. Thousand Island, Ranch, Italian, French and Honey Mustard fat-free dressings can not only perk up a salad, or plain sliced fresh vegetables, they can also double as marinades and sandwich spreads. Fat-free mayonnaise can also benefit from the addition of a little fat-free salad dressing for a special taste.

Blueberry Salad

This could also double as a dessert.

1 6-ounce package sugar-free black cherry gelatin
2 cups hot water
1 15-ounce can crushed pineapple, juice-pack, drained
1 15-ounce can blueberries, drained

Dissolve the gelatin in hot water. Add pineapple and blueberries. Place in the refrigerator until jelled. Spread with the topping.

Topping:

4 ounces fat-free sour cream
4 ounces fat-free cream cheese
1 teaspoon vanilla
3 tablespoons sugar or granulated sugar substitute

Combine the topping ingredients. Spread on the gelatin layer.

8 servings
0 fat grams per serving

Carrot and Raisin Salad

5 cups shredded carrots

1 8-ounce can crushed pineapple (in its own juice), drained

¼ cup raisins

4 tablespoons reduced-fat mayonnaise (3 grams per tablespoon brand)

Combine all of the ingredients. Chill before serving.

5 servings
Less than 2 fat grams per serving

Chef's Salad

1 head iceberg lettuce, shredded

1 onion, thinly sliced

1 tomato, chopped

8 radishes, thinly sliced

1 cucumber, thinly sliced

8 ounces 98% fat-free precooked ham, cut into matchstick size pieces

4 hard boiled eggs, whites only, chopped

4 ounces fat-free Cheddar cheese, shredded

fat-free salad dressing

Place a layer of the shredded lettuce on a dinner plate, followed by layers of each of the other vegetables. Top with a portion of the ham, egg whites and the cheese. Add your favorite fat-free dressing. Serve with fat-free crackers.

4 servings
2 fat grams per serving

"Couldn't Be Better For You" Salad

1 small cauliflower, chopped
1 bunch broccoli, chopped
1 bunch green onions, chopped
4 ounces fat-free Cheddar cheese, shredded
1 bottle fat-free Ranch salad dressing

Combine all ingredients and chill.

8 servings
0 fat grams per serving

Crisp Corn Salad

3 cans whole kernel corn, drained
1 cucumber, chopped
1 green pepper, chopped
1 small onion, chopped
3 fresh tomatoes, chopped
1 cup fat-free Italian salad dressing

Combine all ingredients. Serve cold.

6 servings
0 fat grams

Crispy Slaw

Slaw:

1 head cabbage, shredded
1 carrot, shredded
1 onion, finely chopped
1 green pepper, finely chopped

Dressing:

2 packets sugar substitute
4 tablespoons vinegar
4 tablespoons evaporated skim milk
½ teaspoon dry mustard
3 tablespoons fat-free mayonnaise
light salt and pepper to taste

Combine the slaw ingredients. In a separate container, mix the dressing ingredients. Combine the slaw and dressing.

8 servings
0 fat grams per serving

Deluxe Fruit Salad Bowl

4 navel oranges, peeled and sectioned
1 cup strawberries, halved
2 bananas, sliced
1 cup seedless grapes
½ cup fat-free sour cream
1 tablespoon honey
1 tablespoon orange juice

Combine the fruits. Combine the sour cream, honey and orange juice. Pour over the mixed fruits. Toss to coat. Chill.

4 servings
0 fat grams per serving

English Pea Salad

2 boxes frozen English peas, thawed
1 medium onion, chopped
2 stalks celery, thinly sliced
4 ounces fat-free Cheddar cheese
1 tablespoon sweet pickle relish
commercial fat-free Ranch salad dressing

Combine all ingredients. Serve chilled.

6 servings
0 fat grams per serving

Fancy Fruit Salad

1 16-ounce can fruit cocktail, juice-packed, undrained
1 16-ounce can mandarin oranges, rinsed and drained
1 16-ounce can crushed pineapple, juice-packed,
    undrained
2 ripe bananas
1 .9-ounce box sugar-free vanilla instant pudding

Combine all ingredients. Chill.

0 fat grams per serving

Freezer Cole Slaw

1 medium cabbage, shredded
1 medium onion, chopped
1 green pepper, chopped
2 carrots, shredded
1 tablespoon salt
½ cup sugar
2 teaspoons dry mustard
2 cups cider vinegar

Combine the vegetables and the salt. Let stand 2 hours. Taste the vegetables. If they are too salty, rinse and drain. Combine the sugar, dry mustard and vinegar. Heat the dressing briefly and pour over the vegetables while still hot. Divide the slaw among pint freezer containers. Freeze. Thaw several hours before serving.

0 fat grams per serving

Fruit Salad with Poppy Seed Dressing

1 cup apple, chopped
1 cup seedless grapes
1 cup strawberries
1 cup melon balls, in season
2 bananas, sliced

Combine all of the fruits. Mix with poppy seed dressing. Serve chilled.

Dressing:
1 cup water
3 tablespoons cider vinegar
1 tablespoon cornstarch
3 tablespoons sugar
½ teaspoon dry mustard
2 teaspoons poppy seeds

Combine all of the ingredients and cook over medium heat until thickened. Let cool before mixing with the fruit.

6 servings
0 fat grams per serving

GELATIN SALADS

While these are usually considered salads, I actually use them as desserts, when I want something sweet. I usually keep a gelatin salad in my refrigerator at all times. Since the gelatin is a fat-free and sugar-free and other ingredients are fat-free, this is a guilt-free treat! I usually eat some several times a day. Just between you and me, I have been known to eat an entire recipe in one day. You can use your favorite sugar-free gelatin and favorite fruits to create your own gelatin treats.

Double Strawberry Delight

Prepare a large (.6-ounce) package of sugar-free strawberry gelatin, using the quick set method. When the gelatin is partially jelled, add 2 cups sliced strawberries (unsweetened) and ½ cup fat-free sour cream.

Chill in the refrigerator until jelled.

0 fat grams per serving

Lime Cooler

Prepare one large (.6-ounce) package of lime sugar-free gelatin according to the quick set method. When partially jelled, add 1 small can crushed pineapple (juice-pack), drained, and ½ cup fat-free cottage cheese. Chill until jelled.

0 fat grams per serving

German Potato Salad

6 medium potatoes, peeled and sliced
½ cup water
2 tablespoons all-purpose flour
4 tablespoons cider vinegar
¼ teaspoon celery seeds
2 tablespoons sugar or granulated sugar substitute
1 medium onion, thinly sliced
1 tablespoon imitation bacon bits

Boil the potatoes until tender. Meanwhile, combine the water and flour in a saucepan. Stir until the flour is dissolved. Add the vinegar and cook over medium heat until thickened. Add the celery seeds and sugar, or sugar substitute. Combine the potatoes and onion with the dressing. Serve warm, topped with the bacon bits.

6 servings
Less than 1 fat gram per serving

Guilt Free Potato Salad

6 baking potatoes, peeled, diced and cooked
2 stalks celery, chopped
1 medium onion, chopped
½ cup fat-free Ranch or Thousand Island dressing

Combine all ingredients. Serve chilled.

6 servings
0 fat grams per serving

Italian Vegetable and Pasta Salad

1 package frozen mixed broccoli, carrots and water
   chestnuts
8 ounces dry rotini, egg-free if possible, cooked
1 cup sliced mushrooms
1 medium onion, chopped
¾ cup bottled fat-free Italian dressing

Thaw the frozen vegetables under cold tap water. Drain completely. Add the remaining ingredients. Serve chilled.

4 servings
1 fat gram per serving

Marinated Cucumber and Onion Salad

1 large cucumber, very thinly sliced
1 large onion, very thinly sliced
⅓ cup cider vinegar
3 tablespoons sugar or granulated sugar substitute

Mix all ingredients. Chill, stirring occasionally.

4 servings
0 fat grams

Meal In One Dish Salad

8 cups shredded cabbage
½ pound cooked 98% fat-free ham, cut into thin strips
12 ounces fat-free shredded Cheddar cheese
1 medium onion, chopped
1 11-ounce can mandarin oranges, drained
fat-free Blue Cheese salad dressing

Toss all of the ingredients together in a large salad bowl.

4 servings
2 fat grams per serving

Middle Eastern Tabouli

1½ cups cooked bulgur
¼ cup lemon juice
¼ teaspoon garlic powder
2 tomatoes, diced
1 medium onion, chopped
1 tablespoon olive oil

Combine all of the ingredients except the tomatoes and the onions. Chill for several hours. Just before serving, add the vegetables.

4 servings
5 fat grams per serving

My Favorite Salad

I make this salad year round at mealtime and also as a snack. In the winter, when fresh tomatoes are not very good, I use cherry tomatoes or Italian plum tomatoes. Instead of croutons, I will sometimes crumble a few fat-free saltines over the top.

3 fresh tomatoes, chopped
1 medium onion, thinly sliced
1 large cucumber, thinly sliced
1 clove garlic, minced
4 ounces fat-free Cheddar cheese, shredded
commercial fat-free Italian dressing

Combine the vegetables and cheese. Top with the salad dressing.

4 servings
0 fat grams per serving

Spinach Salad

2 bags fresh spinach, torn into bite sized pieces
1 medium onion, thinly sliced
3 hard boiled egg whites, chopped
1 cup fat-free Cheddar cheese, shredded
1 tablespoon imitation bacon bits
commercial fat-free Ranch salad dressing

Combine all of the ingredients except the salad dressing. Add it immediately before serving.

6 servings
Less than 1 fat gram per serving

Springtime Salad

1 head iceberg lettuce, torn into bite-size pieces
1 cup fresh strawberries, sliced
1 mild onion, thinly sliced
1 cup fresh peaches or nectarines, peeled and sliced
commercial fat-free red French dressing

Combine the vegetables and fruits. Chill. Just before serving, add the salad dressing.

6 servings
0 fat grams per serving

Three Bean Salad

1 16-ounce can chickpeas, drained
1 16-ounce red kidney beans, drained
1 16-ounce can black beans, rinsed and drained
1 medium onion, chopped
1 green pepper, chopped
1 carrot, shredded
1 cup fat-free Italian salad dressing

Combine all of the above ingredients. Serve chilled.

4 servings
Less than 1 fat gram per serving

Turkey Salad

2 cups 99% fat-free, precooked turkey, chopped
1 cup celery, chopped
1 tablespoon mild onion, chopped
2 hard boiled egg whites, chopped
4 tablespoons fat-free Thousand Island or Ranch dress-
     ing

Combine all ingredients. Serve chilled as a salad with toma-to slices and fat-free crackers, or as a sandwich filling.

4 servings
2 fat grams per serving

Easy Blue Cheese Salad Dressing

There are a lot of excellent fat-free salad dressings on the market, but sometimes it's fun to make them at home. This can also be used as a dip with vegetables.

1 cup fat-free cottage cheese
½ cup skim milk
1 tablespoon crumbled blue cheese

Mix all ingredients. Chill

4 servings
1 fat gram per serving

MAIN DISHES

Make meatless main dishes and main dishes with just a bit of meat often. Pasta, grains, and vegetables should be the stars of a meal. Meat, if served, should only be a supporting player.

BEEF MAIN DISHES:

Baked Chow Mein

6 ounces browned ground round, drained and patted
    dry
3 cups cooked rice
1 onion chopped
2 stalks celery, finely chopped
1 cup mushrooms, sliced
1 16-ounce can mixed Chinese vegetables
1 10¾-ounce can 99% fat-free cream of mushroom soup

Combine all ingredients. Bake in a casserole dish for 30 minutes at 350°.

4 servings
5 fat grams per serving

Cheesy Ground Beef Casserole

This is one of those recipes that has been around for years. It has probably appeared at every pot luck supper ever held. It is very rich, full of ground beef, sour cream and cream cheese. It doesn't have to be that way. In a casserole, a little ground beef goes a long way, and our trusty fat-free sour cream, Cheddar cheese and cream cheese help lighten it up even more.

6 ounces browned ground round, rinsed and patted dry
¼ teaspoon garlic powder
1 16-ounce can tomato sauce
1 8-ounce package dry noodles, egg free if possible
1 medium onion chopped
8 ounces fat-free cream cheese, softened
8 ounces fat-free sour cream
4 ounces fat-free Cheddar cheese, shredded
no-stick cooking spray

Combine the ground round with the garlic and the tomato sauce. Prepare the noodles according to package directions. Combine the onion with the cream cheese, sour cream and Cheddar. Place a layer of the noodles in a baking dish that has been coated with no-stick cooking spray. Top with a layer of the meat sauce and then a layer of the cheese mixture. Repeat the layers. Bake at 350° for 30 minutes.

4 servings
5 fat grams per serving

Chili Mac

8 ounces ground top round or ultra-lean ground beef,
    browned and rinsed
1 medium onion, chopped
1 green pepper, chopped
½ teaspoon garlic powder
4 cups elbow macaroni, cooked
½ cup water
1 tablespoon chili powder
2 teaspoons ground cumin
1 16-ounce can Mexican style chunky tomato sauce
1 15 ounce can kidney beans, drained
1 6-ounce can tomato paste

Combine the cooked ground beef, onion and green pepper in a skillet. Cook until the vegetables are tender. Add the remaining ingredients and simmer 20 minutes, stirring occasionally.

4 servings
5 fat grams per serving

Corn Bread Pie

Filling:

1 onion, chopped
1 green pepper, chopped
no-stick cooking spray
6 ounces browned ground round, rinsed and patted dry
1 11-ounce can whole kernel corn, drained
1 tablespoon chili powder
1 16-ounce can chunky tomato sauce

Corn Bread Crust:

1 cup self-rising cornmeal mix
½ cup water
¼ cup fat-free egg substitute
2 tablespoons fat-free sour cream

Sauté the onion and green pepper in a skillet that has been coated with no-stick cooking spray. Add the remaining filling ingredients and place in a casserole dish. Prepare topping ingredients and pour over the filling. Bake at 350° for about 30 minutes, or until the topping is brown.

4 serving
6 fat grams per serving

English Cottage Pie

1 large onion, chopped
2 carrots, thinly sliced
1 cup frozen English peas
3 cups potatoes, peeled and diced
6 ounces browned ground round, rinsed and patted dry
1 can low-fat prepared brown gravy
1 tablespoon Worcestershire sauce
2 cups fat-free prepared mashed potatoes
butter-flavored cooking spray

Cook the onion, carrots, peas and diced potatoes in boiling water until tender. Combine with the beef, brown gravy and Worcestershire sauce. Pour into a casserole dish and spread the mashed potatoes over the top. Spray the potatoes with a bit of butter-flavored cooking spray. Bake at 375° for 30 minutes.

4 servings
5 fat grams per serving

Hamburger and Macaroni Casserole

6 ounces browned ground round, rinsed and patted dry
2 cups cooked macaroni
1 8-ounce can tomato sauce
1 16-ounce can tomatoes, chopped and drained
1 onion, diced
¼ teaspoon garlic powder
4 ounces fat-free sour cream

Combine the ground round, macaroni, tomato sauce, tomatoes, onion, garlic powder and sour cream. Pour into a casserole dish. Bake at 350° for 30 minutes.

4 servings
5 fat grams per serving

Hamburger Steak with Mushroom Gravy

1 pound ultra-lean ground beef or ground top round
1 10¾-ounce can 99% fat-free cream of mushroom soup
2 slices fat-free, reduced-calorie bread, made into
    crumbs
¼ cup fat-free egg substitute
½ medium onion, finely minced
¼ teaspoon garlic powder
⅛ teaspoon light salt
⅛ teaspoon black pepper
no-stick cooking spray
½ soup can water

Combine the ground beef, 2 tablespoons cream of mushroom soup, the bread crumbs, egg substitute, onion, garlic powder, salt and pepper. Thoroughly blend the ingredients. Shape into four small loaves. Place the loaves on a rack in a baking pan that has been coated with no-stick cooking spray. Bake at 350° for 20 minutes. Remove from the oven and place in a small baking dish that has been coated with no-stick cooking spray. Combine the remaining mushroom soup with ½ soup can of water. Pour over the meat. Return to the oven and bake 15 additional minutes.

4 servings
8 fat grams per serving

Inside Out Cabbage Rolls

Do you like cabbage rolls but don't have the time or inclination to go to all that trouble? You might try this recipe.

½ medium cabbage, chopped
1 medium onion, finely chopped
no-stick cooking spray
1 16-ounce can chunky tomato sauce
light salt and pepper to taste
6 ounces browned ground round, rinsed and patted dry
2 cups cooked rice

Sauté the cabbage and onion in a skillet that has been coated with no-stick cooking spray. When tender, combine with the remaining ingredients and pour into a casserole dish that has been sprayed with no-stick cooking spray. Bake at 350° for 20 minutes.

4 servings
4 fat grams per serving

Pepper Steak

12 ounces eye of round, all fat removed
no-stick cooking spray
1-ounce envelope dehydrated onion soup mix
2 cups water
2 medium green peppers, seeded and cut into strips
1 onion, cut into wedges
1½ tablespoons cornstarch
½ cup cold water

Slice the beef into thin strips. Stir-fry over medium heat until browned in a skillet or wok that has been coated with no-stick cooking spray. Add the dry soup mix and the water. Simmer, covered, for 15 minutes. Add the green pepper and onion. Simmer an additional 10 minutes. Mix the cornstarch with ½ cup cold water. Add to the skillet and stir. Continue to cook the mixture briefly, until thickened. Serve over cooked, hot rice.

4 servings
6 fat grams per serving

Pizzagetti

8 ounces angel hair pasta
1 16-ounce can fat-free pizza sauce or spaghetti sauce
no-stick cooking spray
6 ounces browned ground round, rinsed and patted dry
1 medium onion, thinly sliced
1 cup mushrooms, thinly sliced
1 green pepper, thinly sliced
4 ounces fat-free mozzarella cheese, shredded

Prepare the angel hair pasta according to package directions. When done, drain and mix with the pizza sauce. Place the pasta in a 9"x 13" baking dish that has been coated with no-stick cooking spray. Top the pasta with the beef, then with the vegetables. Bake uncovered at 350° for 20 minutes. While still very warm, just before serving, top with the cheese.

6 servings
3 fat grams per serving

Reduced Fat Meat Loaf

1 pound ultra-lean ground beef or ground top round
2 slices fat-free, reduced-calorie wheat bread, made into
    crumbs
½ medium onion, finely minced
½ green pepper, finely minced
1 carrot, shredded
¼ cup fat-free egg substitute
¼ teaspoon garlic powder
⅛ teaspoon light salt
⅛ teaspoon black pepper
4 tablespoons catsup, divided
no-stick cooking spray

Combine the beef, bread crumbs, vegetables, egg substitute, garlic powder, salt, pepper and 2 tablespoons catsup. Blend the ingredients thoroughly. Shape into four small individual loaves. Place the loaves on a rack in a baking pan that has been sprayed with no-stick cooking spray. Spread a bit of the remaining catsup atop each loaf. Bake at 350° for 20 minutes, or until done to your taste.

4 servings
7 fat grams per serving

Smothered Steak With Country Gravy

1 pound eye of round roast, trimmed of all fat and sliced
    into 4-ounce steaks
4 tablespoons all-purpose flour
½ teaspoon light salt
¼ teaspoon pepper
1 tablespoon vegetable oil
no-stick cooking spray
1½ cups water
8 ounces skim milk
4 teaspoons all-purpose flour

Place the steak slices between two pieces of plastic wrap and gently flatten with the flat side of a meat mallet. Combine the 4 tablespoons flour, ½ teaspoon salt and ¼ teaspoon pepper. Dredge the steak in the flour mixture. Coat the skillet with no-stick cooking spray. Brown the steaks over medium heat in the oil. Add the water and simmer, covered, for one hour. Check occasionally to see if more water is needed. Remove the meat from the pan and set aside. Combine the milk with the 4 teaspoons all-purpose flour. Add to the skillet. You may need to add additional water if much of it has cooked away. Stir the mixture until thickened. Return the meat to the gravy and simmer 5 minutes.

4 servings
11 fat grams per serving

Very Simple "Stroganoff"

6 ounces browned ground round, rinsed and patted dry
4 cups cooked rice
1 10¾-ounce can 99% fat-free cream of mushroom soup
1 cup fat-free sour cream
1 1-ounce package dehydrated onion soup mix
light salt and pepper to taste
no-stick cooking spray

Combine the ground round, rice, mushroom soup, sour cream, onion soup mix, salt and pepper. Pour into a casserole dish that has been coated with no-stick cooking spray. Bake for 30 minutes at 350°.

4 servings
5 fat grams per serving

CHICKEN MAIN DISHES

Barbecued Chicken

4 4-ounce chicken breast halves, skinned and boned
no-stick cooking spray
¾ cup water
¾ cup catsup
3 tablespoons cider vinegar
2 tablespoons granulated sugar substitute
1 teaspoon hickory smoke flavoring

Place the chicken breasts in a baking dish that has been sprayed with no-stick cooking spray. Combine the sauce ingredients and pour over the chicken. Bake, covered, for 30 minutes at 350°.

Shortcut: Use bottled barbecue sauce thinned with water. Read the label carefully. Some bottled sauces are rather high in fat, while some are fat-free.

4 servings
4 fat grams per serving

Chicken a la King

4 tablespoons all-purpose flour
1 ½-ounce package butter-flavored granules
2 cups skim milk
2 cups diced cooked chicken breast
3 hard boiled eggs, whites only, chopped
1 cup mushrooms, sliced and sautéed
1 tablespoon pimento, chopped

Prepare a white sauce using the flour, butter-flavored granules and milk. When thickened, add the remaining ingredients. Serve over cooked rice.

4 servings
4 fat grams per serving

Chicken Cacciatore

no-stick cooking spray
4 4-ounce chicken breast halves, boned and skinned
1 medium onion, sliced
1 pound fresh mushrooms, sliced
1 bell pepper, sliced
1 15-ounce can tomato sauce
1 15-ounce can tomatoes, chopped and drained
1-2 teaspoons dried oregano, to taste
¼ teaspoon garlic powder

Coat a skillet with no-stick cooking spray. Sauté the chicken over medium heat until cooked throughout and lightly browned on both sides. Remove the chicken from the skillet. Sauté the onion, mushrooms and peppers until tender-crisp. Add the tomato sauce, the tomatoes, the oregano and the garlic to the vegetables in the skillet. Return the chicken to the skillet. Simmer a few minutes to blend the flavors. Good with pasta or rice.

4 servings
4 fat grams per serving

Chicken-Mushroom Casserole

4 4-ounce boneless, skinless chicken breast halves, cooked and
    chopped or 3 5-ounce cans chunk white chicken packed in
    water.
1 10¾-ounce can 99% fat-free cream of mushroom soup
8 ounces fat-free sour cream
1 package long grain and wild rice mix, prepared
    according to package directions, omitting margarine
    or butter
1 8-ounce can sliced water chestnuts, drained
1 4-ounce can sliced mushrooms, drained
1 medium onion, chopped
2 stalks celery, chopped
no-stick cook spray

Mix the cooked chicken cubes with the mushroom soup and
the sour cream. Add the cooked rice, water chestnuts, mushrooms, onion and celery. Turn into a 2-quart casserole dish that
has been sprayed with no-stick cooking spray. Bake at 350°, covered, for 30 minutes.

4 servings
6 fat grams per serving

Chicken Casserole

1 8-ounce package angel hair pasta
2 cups cooked chicken breast meat, cubed
1 10 ¾-ounce can 99% fat-free cream of chicken soup
1 cup fat-free sour cream
1 cup sliced mushrooms
light salt and pepper to taste
no-stick cooking spray

Cook the pasta according to package directions. Drain well. Add the chicken, soup, sour cream, mushrooms, salt and pepper. Pour into a casserole dish that has been coated with no-stick cooking spray. Bake at 375° for 20 minutes.

4 servings
5 fat grams per serving

Crispy Broiled Chicken

6 4-ounce chicken breast halves, skinned and boned
no-stick cooking spray
2 tablespoons cornmeal
2 cloves garlic, minced, or ¼ teaspoon garlic powder
½ teaspoon black pepper
3 tablespoons lemon juice
2 teaspoons vegetable oil

Place the chicken breasts in a 9" x 13" baking dish that has been coated with cooking spray. Combine cornmeal, garlic, pepper, lemon juice and oil. Spread the cornmeal mixture on top of each breast. Refrigerate for one hour. Broil 8" from heat until chicken is done and topping is crispy.

6 servings
7 fat grams per serving

The Easiest Chicken and Dumplings Ever

4 4-ounce chicken breasts halves, skinned and boned
6 cups water
1 13.5-ounce package fat-free flour tortillas
1 10¾-ounce can 99% fat-free cream of chicken soup
½ cup water

Cover the chicken with water and boil until tender. Remove the chicken from the broth and cut into bite-size pieces. Set aside. Cut the tortillas into approximately 2" square pieces. Bring the chicken broth to a boil and drop in the tortilla pieces, one at a time, stirring frequently to keep the tortillas from sticking together. They will be done in a short time. Combine the cream of chicken soup with ½ cup water. Add to the dumplings. Return the chicken pieces to the pot. Good with English peas and sliced tomatoes.

6 servings
4 fat grams per serving.

Easy Italian Chicken

6 4-ounce chicken breast halves, skinned and boned
1 cup fat-free Italian salad dressing
olive oil-flavored no-stick cooking spray

Marinate the chicken breasts in the salad dressing for at least 20 minutes. Remove the chicken from the marinade. Place in a baking dish that has been sprayed with olive oil-flavored no-stick cooking spray. Also spray the chicken with the cooking spray. Bake at 375° for 25 minutes.

6 servings
4 fat grams per serving

Greek Chicken

A personal favorite. Very easy to fix and very good served with cooked rice.

4 4-ounce skinned and boned chicken breast halves
¼ cup lemon juice
1 clove garlic, minced or ⅛ teaspoon garlic powder
1 teaspoon dried oregano
½ teaspoon coarsely ground black pepper
butter-flavored no-stick cooking spray

Sprinkle the chicken breasts with the lemon juice, then the garlic, oregano and pepper. Let marinate 10 minutes. Place the breasts in a baking dish that has been coated with the butter-flavored cooking spray. Lightly coat the breasts with the cooking spray. Bake at 350°, 15-20 minutes until well done and lightly browned. Do not overcook.

4 servings
4 fat grams per serving

Lemon Chicken

4 4-ounce chicken breast halves, skinned and boned
¼ cup lemon juice
1 teaspoon dried tarragon
¼ teaspoon garlic powder

Place each chicken breast on a 12" square of aluminum foil. Sprinkle 1 tablespoon lemon juice on each breast, then sprinkle with the tarragon and garlic powder. Carefully fold the foil so that the lemon juice can't run out. Bake at 350° for 20-25 minutes.

4 servings
4 fat grams per serving

Moist and Tender Oven Fried Chicken

4 4-ounce chicken breast halves, boned and skinned
1 cup cold buttermilk
¾ cup fine, dry bread crumbs
1 teaspoon garlic powder
1 teaspoon dried oregano
1 tablespoon grated Parmesan cheese
⅛ teaspoon light salt
no-stick cooking spray

Place the chicken in the buttermilk, making sure that the buttermilk coats each chicken piece. Place in the refrigerator for 4 hours. Meanwhile, combine the crumbs, garlic powder, oregano, Parmesan cheese and salt. Remove the chicken from the buttermilk and roll each piece in the crumb mixture. Place the chicken into a baking pan that has been sprayed with no-stick cooking spray. Bake at 425° for 25 minutes, turning halfway through the cooking time.

4 servings
4 fat grams per serving

Mongolian Chicken

Mongolian beef is a very popular Chinese restaurant entrée that my family loves for me to make at home. While it can be prepared with a fairly low-fat cut of beef, such as eye of round, it is equally good with chicken breast or, for even less fat, turkey breast.

4 4-ounce chicken breast halves, boned and skinned
2 tablespoons fat-free chicken broth
2 bunches green onions, including tops, cut into 2"
    pieces
1 tablespoon brown sugar
½ teaspoon sesame oil
3 tablespoons reduced-sodium soy sauce
1 tablespoon dark soy sauce
1 dried red pepper or dried red pepper flakes to taste

Cut the chicken breasts into bite size pieces. Bring the chicken broth to a boil over high heat in a wok or skillet. Sauté the chicken in the broth. Set aside. Sauté the green onions in the same manner. Mix the remaining ingredients together and add to the wok or skillet, along with the chicken. Serve with hot, cooked rice.

4 servings
5 fat grams per serving

No Watch Chicken Dinner

4 4-ounce breast halves, skinned and boned
1 tablespoon Dijon mustard
¼ teaspoon garlic powder
1 teaspoon tarragon
1 teaspoon paprika
4 yellow squash, sliced
1 large onion, sliced
3 baking potatoes, sliced

Place each chicken breast on a 12" square piece of foil. Top with a bit of Dijon mustard and a sprinkle of the garlic powder and tarragon and paprika. Add sliced squash, onion and potatoes. Tightly close the foil packets and place in a shallow baking dish. Bake at 400° for 30 minutes.

4 servings
4 fat grams per serving

Oniony Oven Fried Chicken

½ cup fine, dry bread crumbs
1 1-ounce package dehydrated onion soup mix
4 4-ounce chicken breast halves, skinned and boned
no-stick cooking spray

Combine the dry ingredients. Spray the chicken very lightly with the cooking spray. Coat each piece of chicken with the dry mixture. Spray the coated pieces again. Bake at 350° for 20-25 minutes.

4 servings
5 fat grams per serving

Oven Fried Sesame Chicken

While sesame seeds are quite high in fat, they add so much to a dish that a few shouldn't hurt from time to time. A tablespoon contains 4.5 fat grams, but they are so small that just a few go a long way.

2 tablespoons sesame seeds
4 tablespoons fine, dry bread crumbs
¼ teaspoon pepper
4 4-ounce chicken breast halves, boned and skinned
2 tablespoons soy sauce
no-stick cooking spray

Combine sesame seeds, bread crumbs and pepper. Dip chicken breasts in the soy sauce and roll in the sesame seed mixture. Place the chicken on a baking sheet that has been coated with no-stick cooking spray. Also spray each breast after placing them on the baking sheet. Bake for 25 minutes at 450° or until browned. Turn halfway through cooking time. Do not overcook.

4 servings
7 fat grams per serving

Pan Fried Chicken Breasts

4 4-ounce chicken breast halves, boneless and skinless
1 cup fine, dry bread crumbs
½ teaspoon garlic powder
⅛ teaspoon light salt
no-stick cooking spray
1 tablespoon canola oil

Lightly flatten the chicken breasts. Combine the crumbs, garlic powder and salt. Dredge the chicken in the crumb mixture. Set aside for a few minutes to help the coating adhere to the chicken when cooked. Spray a skillet with no-stick cooking spray. Place the pan over medium heat. When it is hot, add one half of the oil, swirling the pan to evenly coat the bottom. Add the chicken. Pan fry the chicken till brown on one side. Add the remaining oil and turn the chicken to cook the other side until brown.

4 servings
9 fat grams per serving

Stir-Fried Chicken and Vegetables

4 4-ounce chicken breast halves, skinned and boned, cut
   into strips
no-stick cooking spray
1 large onion, sliced
1 green pepper, sliced
2 tablespoons cornstarch
3 tablespoons soy sauce
1 cup fat-free chicken broth
2 large tomatoes, cut into wedges

Stir-fry the chicken in a skillet or wok that has been coated
with no-stick cooking spray. Remove from the skillet or wok and
stir-fry the onion and pepper in the same manner. Combine the
sauce ingredients. Add to the skillet, along with the chicken.
When sauce is thickened, add the tomatoes. Continue cooking
until tomatoes are heated through. Serve with rice.

4 servings
4 fat grams per serving

Sweet and Sour Chicken

4 4-ounce chicken breast halves, skinned and boned, cut into
strips
no-stick cooking spray
1 8-ounce can pineapple tidbits, juice-packed, juice
reserved
1 8-ounce can water chestnuts, sliced
1 carrot, thinly sliced
1 green pepper, cut into cubes

Sauce:
½ cup tomato paste
½ cup water
½ cup reserved pineapple juice
3 tablespoons brown sugar or granulated brown sugar
substitute
3 tablespoons vinegar

Stir-fry the chicken in a skillet or wok that has been coated
with no-stick cooking spray. Remove. Stir-fry the pineapple and
vegetables in the same way. Combine the sauce ingredients and
add to the vegetables, along with the chicken. Stir until thickened. Serve with rice.

4 servings
4 fat grams per serving

Teriyaki Kabobs

1 8-ounce can pineapple chunks, juice reserved
½ cup light soy sauce
¼ cup sherry
1 tablespoon sugar
½ teaspoon ground ginger
¼ teaspoon garlic powder
4 4-ounce chicken breasts, boned and skinned, each cut
   into 4 pieces
1 teaspoon cornstarch
16 cherry tomatoes
16 mushrooms

Combine the reserved pineapple juice, soy sauce, sherry, sugar, ground ginger and garlic powder. Add the chicken and marinate 20 minutes. Remove the chicken from the marinade and set aside. Add the cornstarch to the marinade and boil until slightly thickened.

Thread 4 pieces of chicken breast, 4 pineapple chunks, 4 cherry tomatoes and 4 mushrooms onto each of 4 skewers. Grill over hot coals until done, brushing with the marinade frequently.

4 servings
4 fat grams per serving

FISH MAIN DISHES

Always Moist Fish in Foil
For each serving:
4-ounce fish fillet
no-stick cooking spray
dash of dill or tarragon to taste

Place the fish fillet on a square of aluminum foil that has been sprayed with no-stick cooking spray. Coat the fillet with a bit of the cooking spray. Sprinkle with herbs as desired. Tightly close the foil. Close carefully so that juices cannot leak out during cooking. Place the foil packets in a baking dish. Bake at 400° for 15 minutes per inch of thickness.

1 serving
Less than 2 fat grams per serving

Baked Flounder
1 pound flounder fillets
1 10¾ ounce can 99% fat-free cream of mushroom
    soup
1 4-ounce can sliced mushrooms
chopped fresh parsley
no-stick cooking spray

Place the fish in a baking dish that has been coated with no-stick cooking spray. Cover with the undiluted soup. Top with the mushrooms. Sprinkle with chopped parsley. Bake at 400° for 30 minutes

4 servings
3 fat grams per serving

Baked Tuna Croquettes

1 7-ounce can water packed tuna
2 slices fat-free, reduced-calorie bread, made into
    crumbs
2 tablespoons onion, chopped
¼ cup fat-free sour cream
1 teaspoon lemon juice
2 tablespoons evaporated skim milk
¼ cup wheat germ
no-stick cooking spray

Combine the tuna, bread crumbs, onion, sour cream, lemon juice and evaporated skim milk. Shape the combined mixture into croquettes. Roll in the wheat germ. Place on a baking sheet that has been coated with no-stick cooking spray. Also spray the croquettes lightly with the cooking spray. Bake at 375° for 20 minutes.

4 servings
3 fat grams per serving

Dilled Baked Fish

2 pounds fish fillets
butter-flavored no-stick cooking spray
2 teaspoons chopped parsley
1 teaspoon dill weed

Spray a baking dish with butter-flavored no-stick cooking spray. Arrange fish fillets in the dish, then spray the fillets with the butter-flavored spray. Sprinkle with the parsley and the dill weed. Cover tightly with foil. Bake at 400° for 30 minutes.

8 servings
2 fat grams per serving

Gulf Coast Broiled Fish
1 pound fish fillets
no-stick cooking spray
4 teaspoons reduced-fat mayonnaise
lemon pepper, to taste
garlic powder, to taste

Place the fish in a baking dish that has been coated with no-stick cooking spray. Spread 1 teaspoon reduced-fat mayonnaise on each piece. Sprinkle with lemon pepper and garlic powder. Broil 4" from the heat source until done.

4 servings
3 fat grams per serving

Oven Fried Fish
This recipe can also be used with skinless, boneless chicken breasts.

⅓ cup fine, dry bread crumbs
⅛ teaspoon light salt
⅛ teaspoon pepper
1 tablespoon vegetable oil
4 4-ounce fish fillets
no-stick cooking spray

Combine the crumbs, salt, pepper and oil in a small bowl. Blend the mixture thoroughly. Sprinkle the tops of the fish fillets with the crumb mixture. Place the fillets in a baking dish that has been coated with no-stick cooking spray. Bake at 450° until the fish is opaque and flakes easily.

4 servings
5 fat grams per serving

Shrimp Creole

1 pound medium shrimp, peeled and deveined
no-stick cooking spray
1 clove garlic, minced or ⅛ teaspoon garlic powder
1 medium onion, chopped
1 green pepper, chopped
3 tablespoons all-purpose flour
1 cup water
1 8-ounce can tomato sauce
½ teaspoon red pepper
light salt and pepper to taste

Sauté the shrimp in a saucepan that has been coated with no-stick cooking spray. Remove. Sauté the vegetables in the same manner. Add the flour to the water. Add to the vegetable mixture. Add the tomato sauce and the seasoning, as well as the shrimp. Simmer for about 20 minutes. Serve with rice.

4 servings
2 fat grams per serving

Shrimp Scampi

1 tablespoon vegetable oil
2 tablespoons fresh lemon juice
¼ teaspoon garlic powder
dash of hot sauce, or to taste
butter-flavored no-stick cooking spray
1 pound medium fresh shrimp, peeled and deveined

Combine the oil, lemon juice, garlic powder and hot sauce in a skillet that has been coated with butter-flavored no-stick cooking spray. Sauté the shrimp in the oil mixture until they turn pink. Serve with rice.

4 servings
6 fat grams per serving

Tuna Casserole-Again?

The title of this recipe refers to the fact that every cook in America has probably heard those words. This dish is a reliable old standby that we have all probably served too much, but it is good, quick and easy.

1 10¾-ounce can 99% fat-free cream of mushroom
    soup
½ cup fat-free sour cream
¾ cup skim milk
7-ounce can white tuna, packed in water
2 cups cooked medium noodles
1 cup sliced mushrooms
light salt and pepper to taste
no-stick cooking spray

Combine the soup, sour cream and milk. Add tuna, noodles, mushrooms, salt and pepper. Pour the tuna mixture into a casserole dish that has been coated with the cooking spray. Bake at 350° for 30 minutes.

4 servings
2 fat grams per serving

Tuna Puff

1 7-ounce can white tuna, packed in water
½ cup chopped onion
2½ cups fat-free prepared mashed potatoes
¼ cup fat-free egg substitute
4 ounces fat-free Cheddar cheese, shredded
light salt and pepper to taste
no-stick cooking spray

Combine the tuna, onion, mashed potatoes, egg substitute, cheese, salt and pepper. Pour into a baking dish that has been coated with no-stick cooking spray. Bake at 350° for 30 minutes.

4 servings
1 fat gram per serving

HAM MAIN DISHES

Barbecued Ham and Corn Casserole
8 ounces 98% fat-free precooked ham
1 medium onion, chopped
1 medium green pepper, chopped
1 16-ounce can whole kernel corn, drained
1 cup catsup
1 teaspoon chili powder
¼ teaspoon garlic powder
dash of hot sauce

Sauté the vegetables and ham in a skillet that has been coated with no-stick cooking spray. Add the other ingredients. Pour into a casserole dish and bake 20 minutes at 350°.

4 servings
2 fat grams per serving

Calico Beans

½ pound 98% fat-free cooked ham, diced
1 chopped onion
½ cup catsup
2 teaspoons mustard
1 tablespoon vinegar
2 tablespoons brown sugar or 2 tablespoons granulated
    brown sugar substitute
1 16-ounce can fat-free baked beans
1 16-ounce can kidney beans, drained
1 19-ounce can chickpeas, drained
no-stick cooking spray

Combine all of the ingredients and pour into a casserole dish that has been coated with no-stick cooking spray. Bake at 350°, uncovered, for 40 minutes.

6 servings
2 fat grams per serving

Chunky Ham Casserole

6 ounces 98% fat-free precooked ham, chopped
1 8-ounce package noodles, cooked according to pack-
    age directions
1 10¾-ounce can 99% fat-free cream of mushroom soup
½ cup fat-free sour cream
1 teaspoon poppy seeds
1 tablespoon dehydrated onion flakes

Combine all of the ingredients and pour into a casserole dish. Bake at 350° for 20 minutes

4 servings
4 fat grams per serving

Creamy Ham and Macaroni Casserole

1 green pepper, chopped
1 medium onion, chopped
no-stick cooking spray
3 tablespoons all-purpose flour
1½ cups skim milk
light salt and pepper to taste
1 8-ounce package macaroni, egg free if possible,
   cooked
8 ounces 98% fat-free cooked ham, cut into cubes
1 cup fat-free cottage cheese

Sauté the vegetables in a skillet that has been sprayed with no-stick cooking spray. Stir in the flour, then the milk, salt and pepper. Bring to a boil, stirring constantly. Add the macaroni, ham and cottage cheese. Pour into a casserole dish and bake at 350° for 30 minutes.

4 servings
3 fat grams per serving

Ham and Cheese Crepes

Versatile crepes can be lifesavers when unexpected company comes for dinner. Keep a supply of unfilled crepes in the freezer. Then just prepare a quick filling and you're ready to eat.

8 crepes (see recipe index)
1 cup fat-free cottage cheese
6 ounces 98% fat-free precooked ham, cut into matchstick sized pieces
4 ounces fat-free Cheddar cheese, shredded
1 10¾-ounce can 99% fat-free cream of mushroom soup
½ soup can water or skim milk
1 4-ounce can sliced mushrooms, drained

Combine the cottage cheese, ham and Cheddar cheese. Place several tablespoons of filling down the center of each crepe, then fold the sides over the filling. Place the filled crepes in a 9" x 13" baking dish. Combine the mushroom soup, water or milk and sliced mushrooms. Pour over the crepes. Bake for 20 minutes at 350°.

4 servings
8 fat grams per serving

Ham With Raisin Sauce

Ham with raisin sauce is a popular Sunday dinner entrée that you can serve while staying well within your fat gram goal. Many of the boneless, precooked hams in the grocery store today are 98%-99% fat-free and have only 100 calories and 3 fat grams per 3-ounce serving.

1 99% fat-free precooked ham
¼ cup seedless raisins
½ cup water
½ cup brown sugar or substitute to equal ½ cup sugar
2 teaspoons cornstarch
¼ teaspoon light salt
1 teaspoon vinegar

Wrap the ham in foil and bake at 350° for approximately 1 hour. Meanwhile, simmer the raisins in the water for 10 minutes. Mix the remaining ingredients and add to the raisin-water mixture. Simmer 3 minutes or until thickened.

3 fat grams per 3 ounce serving of ham
0 fat grams for the sauce

Microwave Ham Loaves

½ cup fat-free egg substitute
2 slices fat-free, reduced-calorie bread, made into
    crumbs
¼ cup finely chopped onion
2 teaspoons Dijon mustard
2 5-ounce cans chunk ham or 10 ounces ground 98%
    fat-free cooked ham
3 tablespoons reduced-sugar orange marmalade

Combine the egg substitute, bread crumbs, onion, mustard
and ham. Shape into 4 individual loaves. Place in a microwave
safe dish with a cover. Microwave on high for 6 minutes, rotating after 3 minutes. Spread each loaf with marmalade and
microwave uncovered for 1 minute.

4 servings
7 fat grams each serving

Skillet Cabbage and Ham

½ pound 98% fat-free cooked ham, chopped
no-stick cooking spray
½ head cabbage, coarsely chopped
1 onion, chopped
¼ cup water

Briefly sauté the cooked ham in a skillet that has been
sprayed with no-stick cooking spray. Add the cabbage, onion and
water. Cook, covered, over medium heat, for 15 minutes or until
the cabbage is done to your preference.

4 servings
2 fat grams per serving

TURKEY MAIN DISHES

Almost Instant Turkey and Dressing

You can prepare this when you have the taste but not the time for the holiday favorite.

1 onion chopped
½ cups celery chopped
no-stick cooking spray
1 box corn bread stuffing mix
1 16-ounce can fat-free chicken broth
¼ cup fat-free egg substitute
8 1-ounce slices 99% fat-free precooked turkey
1 10¼ -ounce can low-fat prepared turkey or chicken
    gravy

Sauté the onion and celery in a skillet that has been sprayed with no-stick cooking spray. Prepare the boxed stuffing mix according to package directions, omitting the margarine. Use the chicken broth instead of the water specified in the directions. Add the sautéed vegetables and the egg substitute to the dressing. Pour into a casserole dish and bake at 350° for 30 minutes or until brown. Serve with the heated, sliced turkey and gravy.

4 servings
4 fat grams per serving

Chinese Lo-Mein

Another staple around our house. Adding lots of vegetables and a little meat to the pasta makes this a one dish meal.

8 ounces angel hair pasta, egg free if possible
8 ounces precooked 99% fat-free turkey breast, cut into
    matchstick size pieces
1 cup cabbage, shredded
1 cup fresh mushrooms, sliced
1 onion, cut into wedges
no-stick cooking spray
light soy sauce to taste

Cook the pasta according to package directions. Drain well. Sauté the turkey, cabbage, mushrooms and onion in a skillet that has been coated with no-stick cooking spray. When the vegetables are tender-crisp, add the mixture to the cooked pasta. Toss with the light soy sauce before serving.

4 servings
3 fat grams per serving

Turkey Cutlets, Scallopini
4 4-ounce fresh turkey breast cutlets
butter-flavored no-stick cooking spray
1 cup mushrooms, sliced
⅛ teaspoon garlic powder
1 teaspoon dried rosemary
fresh lemon juice

Sauté the turkey cutlets in a skillet that has been sprayed with butter-flavored no-stick cooking spray. Remove the cooked turkey. Sauté the mushrooms in the same manner. Return the turkey to the skillet and sprinkle with the garlic and rosemary, as well as a bit of fresh lemon juice. Serve with rice or noodles.

4 servings
4 fat grams per serving

WEINER MAIN DISHES

Hot Dog Casserole

This casserole is a lot like hot dogs without the bun. Great with mashed potatoes.

1 cup catsup
¼ cup prepared mustard
sugar substitute to equal ¼ cup sugar
2 tablespoons Worcestershire sauce
2 16-ounce cans baked beans, drained
1 medium onion, chopped
1 green pepper, chopped
no-stick cooking spray
1 pound 97% fat-free wieners
1 16-ounce can sauerkraut

Mix the catsup, mustard, sugar substitute and Worcestershire together. Set aside. Pour the baked beans into a baking dish that has been coated with no-stick cooking spray. Sauté the onion and pepper in a skillet that has been coated with cooking spray. Spread the onion and pepper over the beans. Spread half of the sauce over the onion and pepper. Place the wieners on top of the sauce. Top with the sauerkraut and then the remaining sauce. Bake at 350° for 25-30 minutes.

5 servings
2 fat grams per serving

Weiners and Baked Beans

This is an old standby for grocery shopping night. After working all day, then buying groceries and putting them up, I really am in a hurry to get out of the kitchen. This is super quick and popular with the family too.

2 16-ounce cans fat-free baked beans
no-stick cooking spray
1 chopped onion
5 97% fat-free weiners, cut into thirds

Pour the baked beans into a 2 quart casserole that has been sprayed with no-stick cooking spray. Add the chopped onion and mix well. Top with the weiners. Bake uncovered at 350° until the weiners are lightly browned and the beans are bubbly. Good with Mom's Mashed Potatoes or in a real pinch, instant mashed potatoes.

4 servings
Less than 2 fat grams per serving

MEATLESS MAIN DISHES

Cheese Enchiladas
12 corn tortillas (1 8-ounce package)
2 cups fat-free cottage cheese
4 ounces fat-free Cheddar cheese
1 medium onion, finely minced
1 15-ounce can Mexican style tomato sauce

Briefly warm the tortillas to make them pliable. If you have a microwave oven, you can just make a few slits in the package and heat them on high for about 30 seconds. Combine the cheeses and the onion. Place a spoonful of the cheese filling on each tortilla and roll up. Place the enchiladas in a 9" x 13" casserole after lightly coating the bottom of the dish with tomato sauce. Pour the remaining sauce over the enchiladas. Cover tightly with foil and bake at 350° for 30 minutes.

4 servings
3 fat grams per serving

Lasagna

1 26¾-ounce can fat-free spaghetti sauce
9 lasagna noodles, cooked
2 cups fat-free cottage cheese
¼ cup fine, dry bread crumbs
1 cup fat-free shredded mozzarella cheese
1 tablespoon grated Parmesan cheese
1 teaspoon oregano
¼ teaspoon garlic powder, or 2 cloves garlic, minced

Place a thin layer of spaghetti sauce in a 8" x 11½" baking dish. Place three cooked lasagna noodles on top of the sauce. Combine the cottage cheese, bread crumbs mozzarella cheese, Parmesan cheese, oregano and garlic. Place one half of the cheese mixture on the noodles. Top the cheese layer with one third of the remaining spaghetti sauce. Repeat the layers until all ingredients are used. Bake at 350° for 30 minutes. Let stand for 15 minutes before serving.

8 servings
1 fat gram per serving

Manicotti Florentine

2 cups fat-free cottage cheese
½ cup fat-free mozzarella cheese, shredded
1 tablespoon grated Parmesan cheese
¼ cup fine, dry bread crumbs
1 10-ounce package frozen chopped spinach, thawed and
    squeezed dry
¼ teaspoon garlic powder
1 teaspoon dried oregano
12 manicotti shells, cooked
1 26¾-ounce can fat-free spaghetti sauce

Combine the cottage cheese, mozzarella, Parmesan, dry bread crumbs, spinach, garlic and oregano. Stuff each shell with some of the cheese mixture. Spread a thin layer of spaghetti sauce in the bottom of a 9" x 13" baking dish. Place the filled shells in the dish. Cover with the remaining spaghetti sauce. Cover tightly with aluminum foil and bake at 350° for 30 minutes. Uncover and let stand 15 minutes before serving.

4 servings
2 fat grams per serving

Mexican Lasagna

no-stick cooking spray
1 8-ounce bottle taco sauce
1 8-ounce package corn tortillas
2 16-ounce cans fat-free refried beans
2 cups fat-free cottage cheese
1 green pepper minced
1 onion, minced
4 ounces fat-free Cheddar cheese, shredded

Spray a 9" x 13" baking dish with no-stick cooking spray. Spread a thin layer of taco sauce in the pan. Place a single layer of tortillas on the sauce. Spread the contents of one can of refried beans on the tortillas, followed by 1 cup of cottage cheese. Add ½ of the pepper and onion, then ½ of the Cheddar cheese. Dollop spoonfuls of taco sauce evenly on top. Repeat all the layers. Cover with foil and bake at 350° for 30 minutes.

6 large servings
3 fat grams per serving

No Bake Lasagna Style Casserole

I make this dish once a week. It is one of my favorites because it is so much fun to see a huge plateful and to know that I can eat it all without guilt! I usually serve it with sliced tomatoes, onions and cucumbers marinated in Italian dressing and garlic bread.

12-ounce package rotini or pasta shells, egg free if possible
1 cup fresh mushrooms, sliced
1 medium onion, chopped
1 medium green pepper, chopped
1 cup fat-free cottage cheese
¼ teaspoon garlic powder
1 teaspoon oregano
½ of a 26¾-ounce can fat-free spaghetti sauce, heated

Cook the pasta according to package directions. When done, drain thoroughly. Add the vegetables to the hot pasta in the cooking vessel. Allow the pasta and vegetables to stand, covered, for about 5 minutes to allow the heat of the pasta to lightly steam the vegetables. Add the cottage cheese, garlic powder and oregano to the pasta just before serving. Place each serving on a dinner plate and top with heated sauce.

4 servings
Less than 2 fat grams per serving

Spaghetti Dinner

I used to spend half a day making spaghetti sauce. Now I open a can. My husband likes it even better than my homemade sauce. I usually purchase the basic sauce and dress it up by adding some additional vegetables.

1 26¾-ounce can fat-free spaghetti sauce
1 cup sliced mushrooms
1 medium onion, chopped

Combine all ingredients and simmer until the vegetables are tender. Serve over cooked spaghetti. Good with salad and garlic bread.

4-6 servings
0 fat grams per serving

Vegetable Lasagna

1 medium eggplant, peeled and sliced
3 cups zucchini, sliced
no-stick cooking spray
2 cups fat-free cottage cheese
¼ cup fine, dry breadcrumbs
½ cup fat-free mozzarella, shredded
1 tablespoon Parmesan cheese, grated
1 26¾-ounce can fat-free spaghetti sauce

Sauté the eggplant slices, then the zucchini slices, in a skillet that has been sprayed with no-stick cooking spray. Place half of the cooked vegetables in a single layer in an 8" x 11½" casserole dish. Mix the cottage cheese with the breadcrumbs, the mozzarella and 2 teaspoons of the Parmesan cheese. Top the vegetables with ½ of the cheese mixture, then half of the spaghetti sauce. Repeat the layers. Bake at 350° for 20-25 minutes, uncovered. Let stand 10 minutes before serving. Just before serving, sprinkle with the remaining Parmesan cheese.

6 servings
Less than 1 fat gram per serving

VEGETABLES

Vegetables should be the heart and soul of low-fat meals. Buy and enjoy a wide variety of vegetables and prepare them in an interesting manner. Herbs, spices, butter-flavored granules, lemon juice, garlic, and homemade or commercially prepared gravies or sauces can add punch to plain vegetables. Even plain ketchup is not bad in a pinch. You can also add a can of 99% fat-free cream soup, a little fat-free sour cream, and fat-free shredded or sliced Cheddar cheese to vegetables to create an easy, cheesy casserole. It's a good idea to keep a lot of aromatic vegetables, such as onion, sweet peppers and celery on hand. They can be chopped and included in any number of dishes to add bulk and flavor. You can even keep a supply of chopped aromatic vegetables in the freezer. Just add a handful to any dish if it strikes your fancy.

Busy Day Pinto Beans

2 cans pinto beans, rinsed and drained
½ cup chopped green pepper
½ cup chopped onion
½ cup catsup
1 tablespoon Worcestershire sauce

Combine all of the ingredients in a saucepan. Cook over medium heat until the onions and peppers are tender.

4 servings
Less than 1 fat gram per serving

Country Style Black-Eyed Peas

1 cup dried black-eyed peas
6 cups hot water
3 chicken bouillon cubes
1 onion, chopped
1 whole hot pepper

After washing the peas, combine them in a saucepan with the rest of the ingredients. Simmer over low heat for 2-2½ hours or until tender. Discard the pepper before serving.

4 servings
Less than 1 fat gram per serving

Deluxe Refried Beans

Serve these as an accompaniment to any Mexican style meal, or as a dip with baked tortilla chips.

2 16-ounce cans fat-free refried beans
1 medium onion, finely chopped
4 ounces fat-free Cheddar cheese
1 4-ounce can chopped chili peppers
no-stick cooking spray
fat-free sour cream

Mix the beans, onion, cheese and chili peppers. Pour into a casserole dish that has been coated with no-stick cooking spray. Bake at 350° until bubbly. When serving, add a dollop of sour cream to individual portions.

4 large servings
Less than 2 fat grams per serving

English Pea Casserole

This old standby is still popular with my family. Many food critics disdain the use of mushroom soup in recipes. I make no apologies for using it frequently. It adds a creamy richness to dishes, and thankfully is available in an almost fat-free version.

2 16-ounce cans small English peas, drained
1 10¾-ounce can 99% fat-free cream of mushroom soup
3 tablespoons fat-free sour cream
2 tablespoons dehydrated minced onion
1 8-ounce can sliced water chestnuts, drained
4 ¾-ounce slices fat-free Swiss or Cheddar cheese
1 slice fat-free, reduced-calorie bread, made into crumbs

Combine the peas, mushroom soup, sour cream, onion and water chestnuts. Pour half of the mixture into a 1½ quart casserole dish. Top with the cheese slices. Pour the remaining mixture over the cheese slices. Top the casserole with the bread crumbs. Bake at 350° for 20 minutes, or until the crumbs are brown.

Variation: Use 2 16-ounce cans of asparagus or mixed vegetables.

6 servings
Less than 2 fat grams per serving

Green Beans and Potatoes
2 16-ounce cans green beans, rinsed and drained
8 new potatoes, quartered
1 cup water
1 chicken bouillon cube

Combine all of the ingredients in a saucepan. Simmer, covered, over medium heat until the potatoes are tender.

4 servings
0 fat grams per serving

Hopping John
Hopping John is a traditional southern dish. It is often served on New Year's Day to bring good luck in the coming year. Because it contains both blackeyed peas and rice, it is especially filling. Since part of the good luck is supposed to come from cooking the peas, it is usually prepared from scratch, but in case you don't have the time, here is a speedier version.

2 16-ounce cans blackeyed peas, rinsed and drained
1 cup cooked rice
1 tablespoon dehydrated onion flakes
⅛ teaspoon liquid smoke
1 tablespoon imitation bacon bits
hot sauce to taste

Combine all of the ingredients and simmer over medium heat until warmed through.

4 servings
Less than 1 fat gram per serving

Luau Baked Beans

This is a classic example of how vegetables can be used to add bulk to a dish. While you don't have to count calories on a low-fat lifestyle, it is good to add low-fat, low-calorie extenders to dishes whenever possible.

2 green peppers, cut into squares
1 large onion chopped
no-stick cooking spray
1 clove garlic or ⅛ teaspoon garlic powder
2 cans fat-free baked beans
½ cup juice-packed pineapple tidbits, drained
1 8-ounce can sliced water chestnuts, drained

Sauté the green peppers and onions in a skillet that has been coated with no-stick cooking spray. Add the other ingredients. Pour into a casserole dish and bake at 350° for 20 minutes. This is good with ham or grilled chicken.

4 servings
0 fat grams

Red Beans and Rice

This New Orleans favorite has become a favorite around our house too. Traditionally, New Orleans cooks prepared it on wash day, so that the cook could just start the beans and forget them while doing the washing. Then at the end of the long tiring day, dinner was ready without much preparation. My sentiments exactly. I love to come in from work to a slow cooker full of delicious red beans. I know that I can have a nutritious dinner on the table and be out of the kitchen in no time.

1 pound dry kidney beans
6 cups water
2 medium onions, chopped
3 chicken bouillon cubes
¼ teaspoon garlic powder
2 tablespoons chili powder, or to taste
hot sauce to taste

Soak the beans overnight. Pour off the soaking liquid and replace with about 6 cups of fresh water. Place in a slow cooker with the remaining ingredients. Cook for 8-12 hours on low. Serve with rice.

Variation: Can be cooked with 8 ounces 98% fat-free cubed ham.

8 servings
Less than 1 fat gram per serving
if prepared without ham

Versatile Cuban Black Beans

Another bean dish that I serve often. I usually prepare a recipe of the basic beans in the slow cooker. The first day we eat the basic beans on a bed of hot, cooked rice, topped with chopped onions and hot sauce. Later in the week I add a large can of Mexican style tomato sauce and serve it as black bean soup. Anything to cut down on time in the kitchen!

1 pound black beans, picked over and soaked overnight
6 cups water
3 chicken bouillon cubes
1 large onion, chopped
1 green pepper, chopped
1 teaspoon liquid smoke
1 tablespoon cumin, or to taste
1 tablespoon chili powder, or to taste

Carefully pick over the black beans before soaking. After soaking overnight, discard the water and replace with 8 cups fresh water. Add the remaining ingredients. Cook 8-12 hours on low in a slow cooker.

8 servings
Less than 1 fat gram per serving

Broccoli and Potato Casserole
6 medium baking potatoes, peeled and cut into chunks
1 ½-ounce package butter-flavored granules
¼ cup skim milk
1 10-ounce package frozen chopped broccoli, cooked
    and drained
1 teaspoon dehydrated minced onion
4 ounces fat-free Cheddar cheese, shredded
no-stick cooking spray

Boil the potatoes over medium heat until tender. Mash the potatoes. Add the butter-flavored granules, milk, cooked broccoli, dehydrated onion and cheese. Pour into a casserole dish that has been sprayed with no-stick cooking spray. bake at 350° for 15 minutes.

6 servings
0 fat grams per serving

Sesame Broccoli
1 bunch broccoli, trimmed
1 tablespoon soy sauce
1 teaspoon sesame seeds
1 teaspoon sesame oil

Steam the broccoli until tender-crisp. Mix the dressing ingredients together and pour over the broccoli. Serve warm.

4 servings
Less than 1 fat gram per serving

Baked Cabbage

4 cups shredded cabbage
no-stick cooking spray
½ cup skim milk
¼ cup fat-free egg substitute
1 ½-ounce package butter-flavored granules
½ teaspoon poppy seed
salt and pepper to taste

Place the shredded cabbage in a 1 quart casserole that has been sprayed with no-stick cooking spray. Mix the remaining ingredients together and pour over the cabbage. Bake at 350° for 40-45 minutes until the custard is set.

4 servings
0 fat grams per serving

Cabbage and New Potatoes

no-stick cooking spray
2 medium onions, chopped
6 new potatoes, cut into wedges
1½ cups fat-free chicken broth
½ small head of cabbage, chopped

Spray a medium skillet with no-stick cooking spray. Sauté the onion until soft. Add the potatoes and the broth. Cook about 10 minutes over medium heat, covered. Add the cabbage and cook about 10 more minutes.

4 servings
Less than 1 fat gram per serving

Holiday Corn Pudding

A dish from my holiday meal menu from which I have removed the fat. My guests don't seem to miss it.

½ cup fat-free egg substitute
1 cup soft bread crumbs
2 cups skim milk
3 cups cream-style corn
1 ½-ounce package butter-flavored granules
1½ tablespoons sugar or granulated sugar substitute
no-stick cooking spray

Combine the egg substitute, bread crumbs, milk, corn, butter-flavored granules and sugar or sugar substitute. Pour into a casserole dish that has been coated with no-stick cooking spray. Bake for 40 minutes at 350°.

6 servings
0 fat grams per serving

Cheesy Eggplant Casserole

Eggplant has a wonderful meaty quality that makes it a great addition to an all vegetable dinner.

1 medium eggplant, peeled, boiled and mashed
¼ cup fat-free egg substitute
½ of a 10¾ ounce can 99% fat-free cream of mushroom
    soup
½ cup fat-free Cheddar cheese, shredded
½ medium onion, chopped
2 tablespoons catsup
no-stick cooking spray

Combine the eggplant, egg substitute, soup, cheese, onion and catsup. Pour into a casserole dish that has been coated with no-stick cooking spray. Bake at 350° for 35 minutes.

4 servings
1 fat gram per serving

Southern Greens

1 bunch turnip greens, collards or mustard greens
2 chicken bouillon cubes
1 cup water
1 teaspoon light salt

Strip the leaves from the stems and wash thoroughly. Combine all ingredients. Cook in a covered saucepan for 45 minutes or until tender.

4 servings
0 fat grams per serving

Oven Fried Okra

We southerners love our fried okra. This almost fat-free version is not bad. Another alternative is the pre-breaded frozen okra sold in the grocery store. Just read the ingredients label to make sure that oil is not included in the breading.

1¼ cup cornmeal
¼ teaspoon light salt
1½ pound fresh okra, tip and stems removed
no-stick cooking spray

Combine the meal and salt. Slice the okra and coat with the cornmeal mixture. It must be slightly damp for the cornmeal to adhere. Place in a single layer in a shallow pan or iron skillet that has been coated with no-stick cooking spray. Also coat the okra lightly with the spray. Bake at 450° for 30-40 minutes.

4 servings
Less than 1 fat gram per serving

Pepper and Onion Sauté

1 large onion, sliced
2 green peppers, chopped
1 clove garlic, minced or ⅛ teaspoon garlic powder
butter-flavored or olive oil-flavored no-stick cooking
    spray

Sauté the onion, peppers and garlic in a skillet that has been coated with no-stick cooking spray until tender-crisp.

4 servings
0 fat grams per serving

Hash Brown Potato Casserole

It's good to know that many of the frozen hash brown potatoes sold in the grocery store are fat-free. I somehow assumed that they probably had oil as one of the ingredients, since some come ready to cook. The frozen hash brown patties do well sprayed with butter-flavored cooking spray and oven fried, or sautéed in no-stick spray or a teaspoon of oil on the stovetop. This recipe calls for the tiny cubed potatoes that are also sold for use in making hash browns. It's a fat-free version of the old recipe that has been a standby for years.

2 pound bag hash brown potatoes, thawed
1 10¾-ounce can 99% fat-free cream of mushroom soup
1 cup fat-free sour cream
1 cup fat-free Cheddar cheese
1 medium onion, finely minced
light salt and pepper to taste
no-stick cooking spray

Combine all of the ingredients in a casserole dish that has been coated with no-stick cooking spray. Bake at 350° for 45 minutes.

8 servings
Less than 1 fat gram per serving

Irish Potato and Cabbage Casserole

In Ireland this dish is called colcannon. The combination of mashed potatoes and cabbage makes it very filling.

6 medium potatoes, peeled and boiled until tender
¼ cup water
¼ cup skim milk
1 ½-ounce package butter-flavored granules
½ head cabbage, chopped
1 medium onion, chopped
no-stick cooking spray

Mash the potatoes, adding the water, milk and butter-flavored granules. Sauté the cabbage and onion in a skillet that has been coated with no-stick cooking spray. Add the cabbage and onions to the potatoes. Pour the mixture into a casserole that has been sprayed with no-stick cooking spray. Bake at 350° for 15 minutes

6 servings
0 fat grams

Low-fat Potato Patties

2 large potatoes, peeled and grated
1 medium onion, grated
light salt and pepper to taste
1 tablespoon vegetable oil

Combine the potatoes, onion, salt and pepper. Shape into 10 small flat patties. Sauté in the vegetable oil until browned on both sides.

4 servings
4 fat grams per serving

Mashed Potato Casserole

6 medium potatoes, peeled and boiled
3 tablespoons non-fat dry milk powder
½-ounce package butter-flavored granules
½ cup fat-free sour cream
1 medium onion, chopped
4 ounces fat-free Cheddar cheese
light salt and pepper to taste

Mash the potatoes, using as much of the cooking liquid as necessary to achieve the proper consistency. Add the remaining ingredients. Pour into a casserole dish. Bake at 350° for 30 minutes.

4 servings
0 fat grams

Microwave Scalloped Potatoes

4 medium potatoes, peeled and thinly sliced
1 medium onion, thinly sliced
1 tablespoon all-purpose flour
1½ cups skim milk
light salt and pepper to taste

Arrange the potatoes and onion in a 2 quart baking dish. Combine the remaining ingredients and pour over the vegetables. Microwave on high, covered, for 15 minutes. Let stand at least 5 minutes before serving.

4 servings
0 fat grams per serving

Mom's Mashed Potatoes

Some trendy restaurants now serve their mashed potatoes with bits of skin mashed in with the potatoes. You might want to try it for a change of pace. It saves peeling time too! Top each serving with a little fat-free gravy or ultra-low-fat margarine, if desired.

6 medium baking potatoes, peeled or unpeeled, as
    desired, cut into large chunks
1 ½-ounce packet butter-flavored granules
3 tablespoons non-fat dry milk powder
3 tablespoons non-fat sour cream
light salt and pepper to taste

Boil the potatoes until they are tender, then drain. Reserve the cooking liquid. Mash the potatoes until they are free from lumps. Add the butter-flavored granules, the milk powder, sour cream, salt, pepper and enough cooking liquid to achieve the desired consistency. Stir until the ingredients are well blended.

6 servings
0 fat grams per serving

Old Fashioned Creamed Potatoes

2 cups skim milk
3 tablespoons all-purpose flour
1 ½-ounce package butter-flavored granules
4 cups cooked potatoes, peeled and in chunks
light salt and pepper to taste

Add the flour and butter-flavored granules to the milk and cook over medium heat, stirring frequently, until thickened. Add salt and pepper to taste. Add the cooked potatoes and serve.

4 servings
0 fat grams per serving

Oven Fried Potatoes and Onions

4 medium potatoes, peeled and cut into large cubes
1 medium onion, coarsely chopped
1 tablespoon vegetable oil
no-stick cooking spray

Boil the potatoes until half done. This should take about 10 minutes. Drain them well. When cool, place them in a zipper top bag, along with the onion and oil. Shake lightly to distribute the oil. Place the onion and potatoes on a large baking pan with low sides that has been coated with no-stick cooking spray. Bake at 425° for about 25 minutes or until the potatoes are browned. Stir occasionally.

4 servings
4 fat grams per serving

Oven Roasted Potatoes

1 1-ounce envelope dehydrated onion soup mix
5 medium potatoes, unpeeled, cut into chunks
1 onion, chopped
butter-flavor no-stick cooking spray

Preheat the oven to 450°. Combine the soup mix, the potatoes and the onion in a large bowl. Stir gently, so that the vegetables are well coated with the soup mix. Place the vegetables in a shallow baking dish that has been well coated with butter-flavor no-stick cooking spray. Spray the vegetables lightly with the spray. Bake for 40-45 minutes, stirring occasionally until the vegetables are tender and browned.

4 servings
1 fat gram per serving

Potato Pancakes

1 pound baking potatoes, peeled and grated
3 tablespoons all-purpose flour
1 tablespoon dehydrated onion flakes
light salt and pepper to taste
butter-flavor no-stick cooking spray

Combine the potatoes, flour, onion flakes, salt and pepper. Form into cakes and sauté in a skillet that has been coated with butter-flavored no-stick cooking spray.

6 servings
Less than 1 fat gram per serving

Potatoes and Onions in Foil

4 medium baking potatoes
2 tablespoons ultra-low-fat (2 grams per tablespoon)
    margarine
2 medium onions, sliced

Cut each potato crosswise into 4 slices. Spread a bit of the margarine on each slice of potato. Reassemble each potato, placing a slice of onion between each of the potato slices. Wrap each potato in foil. Bake at 375° for 1 hour.

4 servings
Less than 1 fat gram per serving

Skillet Hash Browns

3 medium potatoes, peeled and cut into quarters
1 tablespoon vegetable oil
1 medium onion, minced
½ teaspoon light salt
¼ teaspoon black pepper

Cover the potatoes with water and boil until they are tender. This should take about 10 minutes after the water begins to boil. Drain the potatoes and allow them to cool. (They may be refrigerated at this point for later use.) Cut the potatoes into small cubes and set aside. Heat a large nonstick skillet over medium heat. When the skillet is hot, add 1 tablespoon vegetable oil. Add the onions and sauté until tender. Add the potatoes and continue cooking until the potatoes are browned. Season with the salt and pepper.

4 servings
4 fat grams per serving

Old Fashioned Corn Bread Dressing

I have served this dressing, along with turkey and all the trimmings, for several Thanksgiving and Christmas dinners since I began watching fat grams, and no one has apparently noticed that I took out the entire stick of margarine that I used to add

4 cups corn bread (made from my low-fat recipe),
    crumbled
2 cups bread crumbs made with reduced-calorie, fat-free
    bread
3½ cups fat-free chicken broth
1 cup skim milk
½ cup fat-free egg substitute
light salt and pepper to taste
1 tablespoon sage or poultry seasoning
1 large onion, finely chopped
4 stalks celery, finely chopped
no-stick cooking spray

Mix the corn bread and the bread crumbs with the chicken broth. Combine the milk, egg substitute, salt and pepper. Add to the bread mixture. Add the sage or poultry seasoning and the vegetables. Pour into a casserole dish that has been coated with no-stick cooking spray. Bake at 425° for 30 minutes.

6 servings
2 fat grams per serving

Ratatouille

1 medium eggplant, diced
1 medium onion, chopped
2 zucchini, sliced
1 green pepper, chopped
no-stick cooking spray
1 16-ounce can tomatoes, chopped and drained
¼ teaspoon garlic powder
½ teaspoon dried basil
½ teaspoon dried oregano

Sauté the eggplant, onion, zucchini and green pepper in a skillet that has been coated with olive oil no-stick cooking spray. When tender, add the tomatoes and seasonings. Cook for 5 additional minutes.

6 servings
0 fat grams per serving

Spinach and Sour Cream Casserole

3 10-ounce packages frozen chopped spinach, thawed
   and drained
1 10¾-ounce can 99% fat-free cream of mushroom soup
4 ounces fat-free sour cream
½ 1-ounce packet dehydrated onion soup mix.

Combine all ingredients. Pour into a casserole dish and bake at 350° for 20 minutes.

6 servings
Less than 1 fat gram per serving

Holiday Sweet Potatoes

These are the potatoes that I serve, along with my turkey and dressing, at Thanksgiving and Christmas dinner. No one seems to notice that it is any different from my old sweet potato casserole, yet this one has no fat.

6 large sweet potatoes, baked and mashed
sugar substitute to equal 1 cup sugar
½-ounce package butter-flavor granules
½ cup fat-free egg substitute
1 teaspoon vanilla
1 tablespoon grated orange rind
1 tablespoon orange juice
cinnamon and nutmeg to taste
2 cups miniature marshmallows

Combine all of the ingredients, except the marshmallows. Pour into a large baking dish and bake at 350° for 30 minutes. Remove from the oven and top with a single layer of the marshmallows. Briefly run under the broiler until the marshmallows are lightly browned.

6 servings
0 fat grams per serving

Broiled Tomatoes

4 firm ripe tomatoes
butter-flavored no-stick cooking spray
2 tablespoons fat-free Italian salad dressing
2 slices fat-free, reduced-calorie wheat bread, made into
   crumbs
⅛ teaspoon light salt
⅛ teaspoon garlic powder
⅛ teaspoon black pepper

Core the tomatoes and cut in half. Squeeze gently to remove the seeds. Place the tomatoes in a baking dish that has been coated with no-stick cooking spray. Brush the tomatoes with the fat-free Italian dressing. Combine the crumbs and seasoning. Place some of the crumb mixture on each tomato half. Spray each tomato half with the no-stick cooking spray. Bake at 400° for approximately 20 minutes.

8 servings
0 fat grams per serving

Country Style Scalloped Tomatoes

1 medium onion, chopped
½ cup celery, chopped
½ green pepper, chopped
no-stick cooking spray
1 tablespoon all-purpose flour
16-ounce can tomatoes, chopped and undrained
1 tablespoon sugar or granulated sugar substitute
1 teaspoon mustard
3 slices toasted reduced-calorie, fat-free bread, cubed

Sauté the onions, celery and green pepper in a skillet that has been coated with no-stick cooking spray. When the vegetables are wilted, add the flour, undrained tomatoes, sugar or sugar substitute and mustard. Place ½ of the bread cubes in a casserole dish. Top with ½ of the tomato mixture. Repeat the layers. Bake at 350° for 30 minutes.

4 servings
0 fat grams per serving

Oven Fried Green Tomatoes or Yellow Squash

½ cup cornmeal
⅛ teaspoon light salt
¼ cup fat-free egg substitute
1 tablespoon water
3 medium firm green tomatoes or 3 yellow squash,
    sliced into ¼ inch rounds.
no-stick cooking spray

Combine the meal and salt. In a separate bowl, combine the egg substitute and the water. Dip the tomato or squash slices into the egg mixture and then into the cornmeal. Coat a large baking pan with no-stick cooking spray. Place the tomato or squash slices in the pan in a single layer. Coat the slices lightly with the cooking spray. Bake at 450° for 30-40 minutes. Turn the slices halfway through the cooking time.

4 servings
Less than 1 fat gram per serving

Marinated Vegetables

This is the type of dish that is ideal to keep on hand at all times. Not only is it a great side dish with a meal, but it makes a great snack anytime you just have to have something to eat.

1 16-ounce package frozen mixed broccoli, cauliflower
    and carrots
1 medium onion, thinly sliced
½ cup cherry tomatoes, halved
½ cup fat-free Italian dressing

Thaw the frozen vegetables under running water. Drain thoroughly. Combine the drained vegetables with the onion, tomatoes and the Italian dressing. Marinate for several hours.

4 servings
0 fat grams per serving

Microwave Fancy Glazed Vegetables

2 tablespoons brown sugar
2 tablespoons water
½ of ½-ounce package butter-flavored granules
3 carrots, sliced
1 medium onion, cut into wedges
1 cup fresh mushrooms, sliced
2 teaspoons Dijon mustard

Combine the brown sugar, water and the butter-flavored granules in a microwave proof casserole dish. Add all of the vegetables, except the mushrooms. Microwave on high for 2 minutes, covered. Add the mushrooms and cook 8 more minutes. Add the mustard and cook 1 minute longer.

4 servings
0 fat grams

Oven Roasted Vegetable Medley

Many vegetables are good when oven roasted. It is a simple and easy way to cook them.

2 onions, cut into wedges
2 carrots, cut into 1" lengths
2 potatoes, unpeeled, cut into 1" dice
1 eggplant, unpeeled, cut into 1" dice
butter-flavored no-stick cooking spray

Place the vegetables in a single layer in a baking dish that has been coated with no-stick butter-flavored cooking spray. Also spray the vegetables with the spray. Bake at 400° until the vegetables are tender and slightly brown.

6 servings
0 fat grams per serving

Super Simple Casserole

You can use this recipe, to doctor up just about any vegetable or combination of vegetables. Try it with potatoes, eggplant or zucchini.

3 cups cooked vegetable(s)
1 cup fat-free spaghetti sauce
1 tablespoon Parmesan cheese, grated
1 tablespoon dehydrated onion flakes

Combine the vegetable(s), spaghetti sauce and onion flakes. Bake at 350° for 20 minutes. Before serving, sprinkle with the Parmesan.

4 servings
Less than 1 fat gram per serving

GRAINS AND PASTA

These were strictly limited on conventional diets. I love to eat a lot of them because they are so delicious, and especially because they are so filling.

Delicious Barley

Many of us have only eaten barley when we serve canned vegetable or beef soup, which frequently contains this delicious grain. It is important to eat as many whole grains as possible. This is one good way to do it.

1 cup uncooked barley
3 cups water
2 tablespoons instant chicken bouillon granules
1 cup mushrooms, sliced
1 medium onion, chopped
¼ teaspoon garlic powder

Place all of the ingredients in a saucepan and simmer, covered, until done. It will take approximately 40 minutes. Check occasionally to see if additional water is needed.

4 servings
1 fat gram per serving

Basic Bulgur

Bulgur is a wheat product that is very popular in Middle Eastern cooking. It is very versatile and really easy to prepare. It can be purchased in health food stores and larger grocery stores.

1 cup bulgur
3 cups boiling water
1 chicken bouillon cube

Add the bulgur to the boiling water. Simmer for 10 minutes. Remove from the heat and let stand 15 minutes. Drain well.

8 servings
2 fat grams per serving

Bean Burgers and Sausage

With the ultra-low-fat ground beef in the grocery stores and the lower-fat burgers available in restaurants, we can have a hamburger without sabotaging our fat allowance. Granted, some lower-fat burgers can still contain around 10-12 fat grams, but it's worth it sometimes! If you really want the burger without the extra fat, you might try one of the vegetarian burger mixes available in health food stores (some are very good) or you might want to give the following recipe a shot. If you really miss sausage, you might want to try that recipe also.

Bean Burgers

2 cups cooked pinto beans
3 slices fat-free reduced-calorie bread, made into
    crumbs
½ cup egg substitute
½ cup skim milk
2 tablespoons onion, finely minced
¼ teaspoon garlic powder
light salt and pepper to taste
1 tablespoon vegetable oil

Use your hands to "squeeze" everything together, excluding the oil. Shape into patties and sauté in the oil.

Bean Sausage

Follow the directions for bean burgers, omitting the onion and garlic. Add 1 teaspoon sage. Shape into patties and sauté.

17 fat grams per recipe. Divide by # of patties

Delicious Brown Rice

1 cup uncooked brown rice
2½ cups water
1 1-ounce package dehydrated onion soup mix
3 chicken bouillon cubes
1 4-ounce can mushrooms

Combine all ingredients and bring to a boil on the stovetop. Pour into a casserole dish and bake, covered, at 350° for 1 hour or until done.

4 servings
1 fat gram per serving

Deluxe Macaroni and Cheese With Ease

Check out some of the boxed rice and pasta side dish mixes on your grocery store shelves. You may be surprised that many of them have very few fat grams per serving before the milk and butter is added. The brand of macaroni and cheese that I use has 1 fat gram per serving for the dry mix but 13 grams per serving when prepared with milk and butter. The trick is to forget the milk and butter and substitute fat-free goodies.

1 box macaroni and cheese mix (read the label for fat content)
½ cup fat-free cottage cheese
½ cup fat-free sour cream

Cook the macaroni according to package directions. When tender, drain all but 1-2 tablespoon water. Add the dry cheese sauce mix and stir. Add the remaining ingredients. Continue cooking on low until the mixture is heated through.

4 servings
1 fat gram per serving

Green Rice

½ cup chopped celery
1 medium onion, chopped
no-stick cooking spray
1 10-ounce package frozen chopped broccoli, cooked
    and drained
1 10¾-ounce can 99% fat-free cream of mushroom soup
½ cup water or fat-free chicken broth
3 cups cooked rice
½ cup fat-free sour cream

Sauté the onion and celery in a saucepan that has been coated with no-stick cooking spray. Add remaining ingredients. Pour into a casserole dish and bake at 350° for 30 minutes.

6 servings
Less than 2 fat grams per serving

Marvelous Millet

Millet is another whole grain that we should eat more often. It is really delicious, and as a whole grain food, is very good for us. You can buy it at health food stores or large grocery stores. It is great served in place of rice or potatoes. A few tablespoons of uncooked millet can also be used as a crunchy topping for casseroles or as a great addition to homemade bread. I seldom make my own bread, but when I do, I always throw in millet to add texture.

1 cup millet
1 teaspoon vegetable oil
2 cups boiling water
2 tablespoons chicken bouillon granules

Sauté the millet in the oil until it is lightly toasted. Add the boiling water and the bouillon granules. Simmer, covered, for 30 minutes.

6 servings
Less than 2 fat grams per serving

Creamy Noodles

1 8-ounce package dry wide noodles, egg free if possible
1 cup fat-free sour cream
1 tablespoon grated Parmesan cheese
1 tablespoon onion, finely minced
1 clove garlic, minced or ⅛ teaspoon garlic powder
1 ½-ounce package butter-flavored granules

Cook noodles according to package directions. Add the remaining ingredients. Serve warm.

4 servings
Less than 2 fat grams per serving

Spanish Rice

2 medium onions, chopped
2 green peppers, chopped
no-stick cooking spray
1 16-ounce can tomatoes, chopped and undrained
1 8-ounce can tomato sauce
1 teaspoon hot sauce, or to taste
1 tablespoon imitation bacon bits, optional
2 cups cooked rice

Sauté the onions and peppers in a skillet that has been coated with no-stick cooking spray. Add the tomatoes, tomato sauce, hot sauce, bacon bits and rice. Pour into a casserole dish and bake at 350° for 30 minutes.

Variation: Add 6 ounces browned ground round, rinsed and patted dry.

4 servings
1 fat gram per serving, if bacon bits are used
3 grams per serving, if ground round is used

THE FAST FOOD LOVER'S
LOW-FAT PATH TO HAPPINESS

HOMEMADE LOW-FAT VERSIONS OF FAST FOOD FAVORITES

Most of us have eaten at fast food restaurants all of our lives. We have come to view our fast food favorites as real comfort foods that we just cannot give up. While we can on occasion work fast food treats into our low-fat lifestyles, we may not always want to blow a major portion of our daily fat gram allowance on a high fat fast food favorite. The solution is clear. Make it at home the low-fat way!

The Almost Fat-free Grilled Cheese Sandwich

The good old grilled cheese sandwich can be made in a way that is almost fat-free. It is tasty, and tons better for you than the old greasy version.

Method One

Heat a griddle on the stovetop. For each sandwich, use 2 slices of 25 calorie per slice, fat-free Cheddar cheese and 2 slices of reduced-calorie, fat-free bread. You may also wish to add 1 ounce of thinly sliced ham or turkey. Spray both sides of the sandwich with butter-flavored no-stick cooking spray. Grill on both sides until golden brown. Add lettuce and tomato.

Method Two

Follow the same directions given for method one, except spread the outside of the bread with approximately 1 teaspoon ultra-low-fat margarine (2 fat grams per tablespoon or less brand).

Less than 1 fat gram per serving, without meat

Amazingly Easy Fat-free Homemade Potato Chips

The key to this recipe is slicing the potatoes super thin. I use an inexpensive plastic slicer that has inserts for thin and thick slicing, as well as chopping. The chips can be served plain or jazzed up with one of the seasoning mixes that you will find in the recipe index.

3 medium size baking potatoes
no-stick cooking spray
light salt or seasoning mix (optional)

Slice the potatoes as thin as possible. Soak the potato slices briefly in cold water. Pat dry. Sprinkle with salt or seasoning, if desired.

Microwave directions: Coat a large, flat plate with no-stick cooking spray. Place a single layer of potato slices on the plate. Microwave on high for 4-6 minutes, or until the chips are crisp and light brown. Rotate the dish halfway through the cooking time. You may also place the potato slices around the inside of a microwave safe plastic colander that has been coated with cooking spray. This allows you to make a few more chips at a time.

Oven Method: Layer the potato slices on a baking sheet that has been coated with cooking spray. Bake at 400° until the chips are light brown.

0 fat grams in the recipe

Baked Corn Dogs

1½ cups self-rising cornmeal mix
½ cup fat-free egg substitute
¾ cup water or more if needed
3 tablespoons applesauce
5 97% fat-free wieners

Combine the cornmeal mix, egg substitute, water and apple-sauce. Space the wieners evenly in a 8" square baking pan. Pour the cornmeal mixture over the wieners. Bake at 425° for 30-40 minutes. Cut apart so that there is a whole wiener in each serving.

5 servings
2 fat grams in each serving

Baked Tortilla Chips

12 corn tortillas
no-stick cooking spray
salt

Lightly spray each tortilla with the no-stick cooking spray. Sprinkle with salt. They may also be sprinkled with chili powder if desired. Cut each tortilla into 6-8 wedges. Place in a single layer on a nonstick baking sheet. Bake in 350° oven for about 10 minutes, or until brown and crisp.

Less than 2 fat grams in 8 chips

Barbecue Sandwiches

Twice a day, every weekday, I must pass one of the best barbecue restaurants in our area. The aroma of the cooking meat
that always permeates the air around the restaurant is enough
to make you want to forget your best low-fat intentions. One
thought alone has saved me. I don't have to be deprived of barbecue. I can just make my own at home the low-fat way with
pork tenderloin. At only 4 fat grams per 3- ounce serving, it is a
great substitute for other higher fat cuts of pork.

1 pork tenderloin, carefully trimmed of all fat
black pepper, garlic powder and chili powder to taste
1 bottle commercial fat-free barbecue sauce or home-
    made sauce
low-fat or fat-free reduced-calorie hamburger buns

Prepare an outdoor grill for cooking by throwing a handful
of water soaked hickory chips on the heat source (charcoal, gas
or electric). Rub the tenderloin with a bit of black pepper, garlic
powder and chili powder. Cook on the grill, covered if possible,
until done. The cooking time will depend on the size and thickness of the tenderloin. It shouldn't take long. Thinly slice the
meat, allowing 3 ounces per sandwich. Add a bit of the sauce to
a heated bun and pile on the meat. For a restaurant-style touch,
you can lightly spray the outside of the bun with no-stick cooking spray and briefly warm the completed sandwich in a skillet
or on a griddle until it is slightly toasted.

With fat-free sauce and bun 4 fat grams each.

Broccoli Stuffed Baked Potatoes

Stuffed baked potatoes are becoming a fixture on fast food restaurant menus. The amount of fat in these potatoes is generally quite high. Our homemade version is fat-free.

1 10-ounce package frozen chopped broccoli, cooked and drained
1 ½-ounce package butter-flavored granules
4 large baked potatoes
1 recipe fat-free cheese sauce (recipe follows)
4 tablespoons fat-free sour cream

Add the butter-flavored granules to the cooked broccoli. Split the baked potatoes open. Top with ¼ of the broccoli. Add cheese sauce, followed by 1 tablespoon sour cream.

Fat-free cheese sauce:
6 ¾-ounce slices fat-free Cheddar cheese
3 tablespoons skim milk
¼ teaspoon prepared mustard

Tear the cheese slices into strips. Place in a microwave safe measuring cup. Add the milk. Microwave on medium power for less than 1 minute, or until the cheese is melted, stirring frequently. Add the mustard.

4 servings
0 fat grams per serving

Burritos

For each burrito:
2 tablespoons canned fat-free refried beans
1 fat-free flour tortilla, heated to soften
1 tablespoon fat-free sour cream
shredded lettuce
chopped tomato
chopped onion
shredded fat-free Cheddar cheese
bottled taco sauce

Place the refried beans down the center of the tortilla. Add the other ingredients, as desired. Roll the two sides of the tortilla toward the center.

1 serving
0 fat grams per serving

Instant Pizza

Do you ever need a snack or a lunch in a hurry? Try these simple, quick pizzas.

For each pizza:
¼ cup fat-free spaghetti sauce
1 ounce fat-free mozzarella cheese, shredded
1 tablespoon onion, chopped (optional
1 tablespoon green pepper, chopped (optional)
garlic powder and oregano to taste
1 English muffin half, toasted

Layer the topping ingredients on the toasted muffin half. Bake at 350° until the cheese just melts, about 5 minutes.

1 serving
1 fat gram per serving

Chicken Nuggets

For each serving:
1 4-ounce chicken breast half, skinned and boned
no-stick cooking spray
¼ cup fine, dry bread crumbs
light salt to taste
pepper
1 teaspoon vegetable oil

Cut the chicken breast into 6 bite size pieces. Coat lightly with no-stick cooking spray. Combine the bread crumbs, salt and pepper. Roll the chicken breast pieces in the crumb mixture. Sauté the chicken pieces in the oil. Serve with Sweet and Tangy Sauce or fat-free barbecue sauce.

Sweet and Tangy Sauce:
2 tablespoons reduced-sugar peach preserves
1 teaspoon prepared mustard
horseradish to taste

Combine all sauce ingredients and blend well.

1 serving
10 fat grams per serving

Deep Dish Pizza

I made up this recipe after seeing endless commercials for a restaurant that served Chicago style pizzas. They would cut into one, exposing layer after layer of cheeses, meats and vegetables. To keep myself from jumping in the car and rushing out to get one, I knew I better come up with a substitute version.

Crust:
1½ cups all-purpose flour
⅓ cup plus 2 tablespoons warm water
1 package dry yeast
½ teaspoon light salt

Combine all ingredients and knead briefly. Cover and set aside in a warm place until doubled. Spread dough on the bottom and up the sides of a 12" deep-dish pizza pan or casserole dish that has been coated with olive oil no-stick cooking spray. Dust with a bit of cornmeal to keep crust from getting soggy, Layer the following ingredients on the crust:

1 cup fat-free cottage cheese mixed with ¼ cup fat-free egg substitute
1 cup mushrooms, sliced
4 ounces fat-free mozzarella cheese
1 cup onion, chopped
1 cup tomatoes, chopped and squeezed dry
oregano, garlic and basil to taste

Bake at 450° for 20-25 minutes.

4 servings
1 fat gram per serving

The Deli Style Sandwich

For each serving:

2 tablespoons fat-free Italian salad dressing
1 hoagie sandwich roll, sliced lengthwise
2 very thin slices precooked ham
2 very thin slices precooked turkey breast
2 ¾-ounce slices fat-free 25-calorie per slice mozzarella
     or Swiss cheese
shredded lettuce
thinly sliced onion rings
thinly sliced green pepper rings
thinly sliced tomato
dill pickle slices
pickled jalapeno pepper rings or mild pickled pepper rings

Sprinkle the salad dressing onto the two cut sides of the bread. Layer the ham, turkey and cheese on the roll. Top with the vegetables to taste.

1 serving
4 fat grams per serving

The Fast Food Burger

For each hamburger:

4 ounces uncooked ultra-lean ground beef or ground top
    round
1½ low-fat or fat-free reduced-calorie sesame seed ham-
    burger buns
no-stick cooking spray
1 tablespoon fat-free Thousand Island dressing
shredded iceberg lettuce
1 teaspoon finely minced mild onion
1 ¾-ounce slice fat-free Cheddar cheese
dill pickle slices

Shape the beef into two very thin patties. Cook until well done on a ridged griddle that allows any fat in the meat to drip away. When the meat is almost done, toast the cut side of the hamburger bun and both sides of the extra half bun on a griddle that has been coated with no-stick cooking spray.

Assemble the hamburger as follows: Place 1½ teaspoons Thousand Island dressing on the bottom half of the bun. Add shredded lettuce, cheese, a hamburger patty and a sprinkle of chopped onion. Top with the extra bun half. Add the rest of the dressing, shredded lettuce, a hamburger patty, the remaining onion, several dill pickle slices and the top bun section.

1 serving
7 fat grams per serving if fat-free bun is used

The Fast Food Style Chicken Filet Sandwich
1 low-fat or fat-free reduced-calorie hamburger bun
no-stick cooking spray
1 tablespoon reduced-fat mayonnaise
1 4-ounce pan fried boneless, skinless chicken breast
    half (see recipe index)
lettuce and tomato slices

Lightly toast the cut sides of the bun on a griddle that has been coated with no-stick cooking spray. Spread the bun with the mayonnaise. Layer the chicken breast, lettuce and tomato on the bun.

1 serving
12 fat grams per serving
(Use fat-free mayo and oven fry the chicken breast
without oil to reduce the fat grams to 6 per serving)

The Fast Food Style Grilled Chicken Sandwich
For each sandwich:
1 4-ounce chicken breast half, skinned and boned
½ teaspoon chili powder
½ teaspoon garlic powder
1 tablespoon fat-free Ranch salad dressing
1 low-fat or fat-free soft sandwich roll
lettuce and tomato slices

Sprinkle the chicken with the chili powder and garlic powder. Grill or sauté until completely cooked. Spread the Ranch dressing on each half of the sandwich roll. Layer the chicken, lettuce and tomato on the roll.

1 serving
4 fat grams per serving if fat-free roll is used

Fast Food Style Mini-Burgers

These are sold all over the country as the specialty of several fast food chains. The name of the chain and the burger may differ from area to area, but the wonderful aroma of the cooking beef and onions makes many of us remember these steamy little burgers fondly.

For each hamburger:
1 tablespoon finely minced onion
no-stick cooking spray
1 ounce uncooked ultra-lean ground beef or ground top
    round
1 commercially prepared 2" square ready to serve soft
    roll
mustard
dill pickle slice

Sauté the onion in a skillet that has been coated with no-stick cooking spray. When tender, remove from the skillet. Shape the meat into a very thin 2" square patty. Sauté until well done. Blot the cooked meat with a paper towel to remove any fat on the surface. Return the onion to the skillet. Cut the roll in half crosswise. Place the cut sides on the meat and onion in the skillet and allow the bun to steam briefly. Place the meat and onion on the bun, adding a dollop of mustard and a dill pickle slice. Most people eat 3-4 each. Prepare plenty!

1 serving
4 fat grams per serving

Fast Food Style Roast Beef Sandwich
1 pound cooked eye of round roast, all fat removed
¼ cup beef broth
4 low-fat or fat-free reduced-calorie hamburger buns
no-stick cooking spray
fat-free barbecue sauce
fat-free horseradish sauce (recipe follows)

Thinly slice the roast beef. Pour the beef broth over the beef to keep it moist. Toast the cut sides of the buns on a griddle that has been coated with no-stick cooking spray. Divide the roast beef among the 4 buns. Serve with barbecue sauce or horseradish sauce.

Horseradish sauce:
½ cup fat-free mayonnaise
horseradish to taste

4 sandwiches
8 fat grams per sandwich if a fat-free bun is used

Good Old Sloppy Joes

These are good served as sandwiches or served open faced with mashed potatoes and another vegetable for a full meal.

1 pound ultra-lean ground beef or ground top round,
    browned and rinsed
1 medium onion, minced
1 green pepper, minced
½ cup catsup
½ cup tomato sauce
¼ teaspoon garlic powder
1 tablespoon Worcestershire sauce
toasted fat-free or low-fat hamburger buns

Combine the browned, rinsed ground beef and vegetables in a skillet. Sauté together until the vegetables are tender. Add the catsup, tomato sauce, garlic powder and Worcestershire sauce. Simmer over low heat for 10 minutes. Serve on the toasted hamburger buns.

4 servings
7 fat grams per serving if fat-free buns are used

Heavenly Hot Dogs

In the area where I live, hot dogs are an art form. There are dozens of small hot dog stands around town, each proudly boasting a special secret sauce that takes hours of preparation. I know one man who spends his lunch hour each day eating at a different hot dog stand. When he works his way through all of them, he starts over. People who have moved away have been known to have their favorite hot dog stand ship them a few by air when they can't stand the deprivation any longer. Thanks to the wonderful ultra-low-fat hot dogs now on the market, we can enjoy a good hot dog anytime. I serve them once or twice a week!

Fast and Tasty Hot Dog Sauce:
1 8-ounce can tomato sauce
2 teaspoons chili powder or more, to taste
1 teaspoon cumin
1 teaspoon sugar or granulated sugar substitute
red pepper flakes to taste

Combine the ingredients and simmer over low heat for 5 minutes. Serve on hot dogs, using 97% fat-free wieners and fat-free or low-fat buns. Pile on the onions, kraut and whatever else you like.

1 gram fat per hot dog if fat-free buns are used

Guiltless French Fries

French fries are one of those foods that we would hate to have to give up. While I can't indulge in the real thing, golden, crisp and loaded with fat, I can enjoy a reasonable facsimile to my heart's (and body's) content. They are also much less messy to make! Spice them up with some of the seasoning mixes in the recipe index, if desired.

4 large potatoes, unpeeled or peeled, as desired
butter-flavored no-stick cooking spray
light salt to taste

Preheat the oven to 450°. Slice the potatoes into standard size fries, steak fries or wedges. Coat a 10" x 13" baking pan with the no-stick cooking spray. Place the potatoes in the baking pan in a single layer. Spray the potatoes with the cooking spray. Bake 30 minutes, or until brown, stirring occasionally.

4 serving
Less than 1 fat gram per serving

Lunch in a Pita

2 cups shredded lettuce
½ medium onion, thinly sliced
1 medium tomato, chopped
4 ounces 99% fat-free precooked turkey breast, sliced
    into matchstick size strips
½ cup fat-free Italian salad dressing
2 whole pitas, cut in half to form pockets

Combine the vegetables and the turkey. Add the salad dressing. Fill each pita half with ¼ of the mixture.

4 servings
2 fat grams per serving

Zippy Mustard Fries

1 tablespoon vegetable oil
1 tablespoon Dijon mustard or prepared mustard
4 medium baking potatoes, cut into strips
no-stick cooking spray

Combine the oil and mustard. Add the potatoes and toss to coat. Place the potatoes in a single layer in 10" x 15" baking pan that has been sprayed with no-stick cooking spray. Bake at 450° for about 30 minutes, stirring every 10 minutes, until brown and crisp.

4 servings
5 fat grams per serving

Nachos

6 ¾-ounce slices fat-free Cheddar cheese
3 tablespoons skim milk
½ teaspoon mustard
baked tortilla chips (See recipe index.)
pickled jalapeno slices

Tear the cheese slices into strips. Combine the cheese strips and milk in a microwave proof measuring cup. Microwave on medium power for less than 1 minute, stirring twice. Add the mustard. Pour the cheese sauce over the tortilla chips. Sprinkle the jalapeno pepper slices over the chips and cheese. Serve immediately.

0 fat grams in cheese sauce
Less than 2 fat grams in 8 chips

The Old Fashioned Hamburger

For each hamburger:

dash Worcestershire sauce (optional)
dash garlic powder (optional)
4 ounces uncooked ultra-lean ground beef or ground
     top round
1 low-fat or fat-free reduced-calorie hamburger bun
mustard to taste
catsup to taste
thinly sliced onion rings
thinly sliced tomato
lettuce
dill pickle slices

Add the garlic powder and Worcestershire sauce to the meat, if desired. Shape the beef into a patty, handling as gently as possible. Either grill outdoors or cook on a ridged stovetop griddle that allows any fat that cooks out of the meat to drip away. Warm the bun, add the cooked hamburger patty, and top with condiments as desired. If you prefer cheeseburgers, add a ¾-ounce slice of fat-free Cheddar cheese.

1 serving
7 fat grams per serving if fat-free buns are used

Oven Fried Onion Rings

French fried onion rings are my weakness. This recipe has kept me from straying when the temptation to indulge in the original version has almost gotten to me.

¾ cup fine, dry bread crumbs
⅛ teaspoon light salt
¼ cup fat-free egg substitute
¼ cup water
2 large onions, sliced into rings
no-stick cooking spray

Combine the bread crumbs and salt. In another bowl, combine the egg substitute and water. Dip the onion rings into this mixture, then in the crumbs. Place on a baking sheet that has been coated with no-stick cooking spray. After the onion rings have been placed on the baking sheet, also coat them with the spray. Bake at 425° for about 15 minutes, or until brown and crisp.

4 servings
Less than 2 fat grams per serving

Philly-Style Cheese Steak Sandwich

For each sandwich:
3 ounces cooked eye of round roast, all fat removed
½ medium onion, thinly sliced
no-stick cooking spray
2 ¾-ounce slices fat-free Cheddar cheese
1 tablespoon skim milk
1 soft low-fat or fat-free sandwich roll

Thinly slice the roast beef and heat until warm. Sauté the onion until limp in a skillet that has been coated with no-stick cooking spray. Meanwhile, tear the cheese slices into small bits. Place them in a measuring cup with 1 tablespoon skim milk. Microwave on medium for 45 seconds, stirring twice. Layer the roast beef on the roll, followed by the onion and the cheese sauce. Wrap in foil and warm in a 350° oven for several minutes.

1 serving
7 fat grams per serving if fat-free buns are used.

The Reuben-Style Sandwich

For each sandwich:
2 slices low-fat or fat-free rye bread
1 tablespoon fat-free Thousand Island salad dressing
4 deli thin slices 99% fat-free corned beef
1 1-ounce slice fat-free Swiss cheese
¼ cup sauerkraut, drained
no-stick cooking spray

Spread Thousand Island dressing on each slice of bread. Layer the corned beef, cheese and sauerkraut on one slice. Top with the remaining slice. Grill the sandwich on both sides on a griddle that has been coated with no-stick cooking spray.

1 serving
3 fat grams per serving if fat-free buns are used

Snow Cones

Many people remember these treats from trips to fairs or carnivals. They are equally tasty when prepared at home. Most good blenders or food processors will crush ice to a snowy consistency. Just read the directions to make sure your machine is made to crush ice. Use your favorite fruit juice flavors.

For each serving:
1 cup finely crushed ice
1½ tablespoons frozen fruit juice concentrate, thawed

Place the crushed ice in a small paper cup. Drizzle the fruit juice concentrate over the ice. Serve immediately.

1 serving
0 fat grams per serving

Taco Time

I love tacos, but not the fat that you get in take-out tacos or homemade versions that contain regular ground beef. Even store bought taco shells have two grams of fat each. Tacos are kind of like hamburgers. When you dress them up with all the fixings, you can't really tell if there's any meat in them or not.

12 corn tortillas (1 8-ounce package)
1 can fat-free refried beans
shredded lettuce
chopped onions
shredded fat-free cheese
commercial taco sauce

You may use commercially prepared taco shells or save about a fat gram per shell by making your own. Drape corn tortillas over the wires of your oven rack so that they form the traditional taco shape. Heat at 350° until they are crisp. Fill each shell with a heaping spoonful of the heated refried beans, then dress with the toppings you prefer.

Variation: Add 6 ounces browned, well drained ultra-lean ground beef to the refried beans

4 servings
1-2 fat grams per taco without beef

Thin Crust Pizza

Thin crust pizza dough:
1 package dry active yeast
1 cup very warm water (110°-120°)
3½ cups all-purpose flour
1 teaspoon salt
1 tablespoon oil
no-stick cooking spray

Combine the yeast and warm water. In a separate bowl, combine the flour and salt. Add the yeast mixture and the oil to the dry ingredients. Knead the dough until it is smooth and elastic. Let the dough rest, covered, in a warm place for about 1½ hours, or until doubled in bulk. Punch the dough down. Press ½ of the dough into a 12" pizza pan that has been coated with no-stick cooking spray. If the dough resists spreading, let it rest in the pan for ten minutes. Repeat with remaining dough.

Topping:
2 cups fat-free spaghetti sauce or pizza sauce
chopped onion
chopped green pepper
sliced mushrooms
12 ounces fat-free mozzarella cheese, shredded

Divide the sauce and vegetables between the two pizzas. Bake at 425° for 20 minutes. After removing the pizzas from the oven, add half of the shredded cheese to each pizza. Return the pizzas to the oven for 1 minute to melt the cheese.

This recipe makes 2 pizzas.
Each pizza has 9 fat grams.

The Zesty Pizza Burger

For each pizza burger:

4 ounces uncooked ultra-lean ground beef or ground
  top round
1 low-fat or fat-free hamburger bun
2 tablespoons fat-free spaghetti sauce or pizza sauce
1 ¾-ounce slice fat-free mozzarella cheese

Shape the ground beef into a patty, handling as little as possible. Cook on a ridged griddle that allows any fat in the meat to drip away. Place ½ of the sauce on the bottom bun half. Add the cooked hamburger patty. Top with the cheese slice and the remaining sauce. Wrap the burger in foil and place in a 350° oven for 4-5 minutes to melt the cheese and warm the bun.

1 serving
7 fat grams per serving if fat-free buns are used

DESSERTS

I have been known to use a large part of my daily fat gram allowance to indulge in an especially beloved dessert. However, I make desserts an occasional special treat. They are not very filling and often just create a desire for more. When I crave something sweet, a piece of fruit or a cup of diet hot chocolate often is enough to satisfy my sweet tooth.

Almost Fat-free Banana Pudding

2 cups skim milk
2 tablespoons cornstarch
¼ cup sugar
2 teaspoons vanilla flavoring
2 bananas, sliced
12 vanilla wafers

Heat 1½ cups of the milk, stirring constantly. Mix the rest of the milk with the cornstarch and stir until the cornstarch dissolves. Add this mixture to the heated milk. Add the sugar and the vanilla. Cook until thick. When cool, add the sliced bananas. Place 6 of the vanilla wafers in a serving dish. Top with half of the pudding. Repeat the layers. Serve with a dollop of light nondairy whipped topping.

6 servings
2 fat grams per serving

Apple Cobbler

1 20-ounce can light apple pie filling
¼ teaspoon ground cinnamon
1½ cups fat-free baking mix
⅓ cup sugar
¼ cup skim milk

Combine the apple pie filling and the cinnamon. Pour into an 8"x 8" baking dish. Combine the baking mix and sugar. Stir in the skim milk. Drop by spoonfuls on top of the apples. Bake at 350° for 30 minutes.

Variation: Use other light pie fillings, such as peach or blueberry instead of the apple filling.

9 servings
0 fat grams per serving

Frozen Fruit Snacks

Frozen pieces of fruit make a really great and healthy snack. I try to keep some on hand at all times. They are filling and very refreshing, especially when you are hot and tired.

Frozen Bananas

Peel ripe bananas and slice into ¼ inch pieces. Place slices in a single layer on a plate and freeze until firm. Remove the slices from the plate and place in a freezer proof plastic bag, making sure the air is pressed out before sealing. The bananas can also be frozen whole after peeling. This is a good way to use excess bananas before they become too ripe to eat.

Frozen Strawberries

Wash and remove caps from fresh strawberries. Follow the same freezing process used for bananas.

Frozen Seedless Grapes

Select blemish free firm red or green seedless grapes. Follow the same process used for bananas.

Frozen Peach Slices

Peel and slice fresh peaches. Follow the same process used for bananas.

0 fat grams

Belgian Waffle Shortcake
For each serving:
1 Belgian waffle, toasted (Purchase those with 1 fat
    gram per waffle.)
½ cup fat-free vanilla frozen yogurt
1 cup fresh or sugar free frozen strawberries, mashed
    and sweetened with sugar substitute to taste

Place the frozen yogurt on the waffle and top with the straw-berries.

Variation: Use fat-free fudge topping instead of strawberries.
1 fat gram per serving

Bread Pudding
6 slices fat-free, reduced-calorie bread, made into
    crumbs
3 cups skim milk
½ cup fat-free egg substitute
½ cup sugar or granulated sugar substitute
¼ teaspoon light salt
¼ teaspoon nutmeg
1 teaspoon vanilla
1 ½-ounce package butter-flavored granules
butter-flavored no-stick cooking spray

Soak the bread in the milk for several minutes. Add the remaining ingredients. Pour into a baking dish that has been coated with no-stick cooking spray. Bake at 350° for 30 minutes, or until a knife inserted in the center comes out clean.
4 servings
0 fat grams per serving

Cinnamon Apples

1 cup water
⅓ cup sugar
½ cup orange juice
1 teaspoon cinnamon
4-5 firm apples, peeled and sliced
1 tablespoon cornstarch dissolved in ¼ cup cold water

Bring the water, sugar, juice and cinnamon to a boil. Simmer 5 minutes. Add the apples. Cover the pot and simmer 20 minutes. Remove the apples. Add the cornstarch mixture to the cooking liquid. Bring to a boil and simmer until thickened. Return the apples to the thickened liquid.

These are good as a dinner side dish, served with ham, or as a pancake topping. You can also serve them warm, topped with ice milk or low-fat frozen yogurt for dessert. For a mock apple cobbler, crumble a cinnamon-sugar graham cracker over a dish of the apples.

4 servings
0 fat grams

Easy Fruit Sorbet

You cannot come up with a less complicated dessert than this one. It is really appealing on a hot summer day. You can make it with any canned fruit that you like. Some possibilities are pineapple, peaches, pears or mixed fruit.

1 16-ounce can of fruit, packed in its own juice,
    undrained

Puree the fruit and juice in the blender or food processor. Pour into an 8" square pan and freeze until almost firm. Remove from the freezer and break up. Blend again briefly, then return to freezer to finish freezing.

4 servings
0 fat grams

English Trifle

This is a very pretty and light dessert. I usually only serve it when I am having guests. I don't like to keep any leftover trifle around. It is too tempting.

1 large (1.4-ounce) package vanilla sugar-free pudding mix
4 cups skim milk
1 light yellow cake mix
½ cup fat-free egg substitute
1 20-ounce can light cherry pie filling
1 cup light nondairy whipped topping

Prepare the pudding, using the skim milk. Prepare the cake, using the egg substitute. Bake in a 9" x 13" pan. Layer 1" thick slices of the cake in a serving dish. A clear glass dish is preferred. Over the slices of cake place a layer of pudding, followed by a layer of the pie filling. Repeat the layers until all of the cake, pudding, and pie filling have been used. Top with the whipped topping.

Variation: Sliced, fresh strawberries or blueberries can be used instead of the pie filling.

12 servings
5 fat grams per serving

Fat-free Microwave Chocolate Pudding

This can save you when the craving for chocolate gets to you. Knowing that you can fix yourself a big dish of warm chocolate pudding when you get home can get you through watching a fellow diner wade through one of those super fattening chocolate creations that restaurants love to trot out on the dessert cart.

3 tablespoons cornstarch
2¼ cups skim milk
¼ cup sugar
6 packets sugar substitute
¼ cup cocoa powder
2 teaspoons vanilla
⅛ teaspoon salt

Combine the cornstarch and milk. Stir until the cornstarch is dissolved. Add the sugar, the sugar substitute, the cocoa, the vanilla and the salt. Microwave at 100% power for 6 minutes, stirring every 2 minutes

5 servings
Less than 1 fat gram per serving

Fresh Fruit with "Cream" Topping

Topping:
2 cups fat-free cottage cheese
¼ cup skim milk
6 tablespoons sugar or granulated sugar substitute
1 tablespoon vanilla
6 cups fresh fruit

Combine the cottage cheese, milk, sugar or sugar substitute and vanilla in a blender or food processor. Puree until no lumps remain. Serve the topping over the fresh fruit or as a substitute for whipped cream atop any dessert.

6 servings
0 fat grams per serving

Lemon Ice

1 .3-ounce envelope sugar-free lemon gelatin
1 cup boiling water
1½ cups cold water
2 teaspoons liquid sugar substitute
½ cup lemon juice

Sprinkle the gelatin over the boiling water and stir until the gelatin is dissolved. Add the remaining ingredients. Pour in a shallow pan and place in the freezer until the mixture is almost firm. Remove from the freezer and place in a chilled bowl or in the food processor. Beat or process until smooth. Return to the freezer until firm.

4 servings
0 fat grams

Really Lazy Rice Pudding

1 1.4-ounce package sugar-free vanilla pudding
4 cups skim milk
¼ teaspoon nutmeg
2 tablespoons raisins
½ cup cooked rice

Prepare the pudding according to package directions, using skim milk instead of the low-fat milk specified. Add the nutmeg and the raisins, then the rice. Serve chilled.

4 servings
Less than 1 fat gram per serving

Sparkling Fruit Cup

This is a really refreshing variation on the classic fruit in champagne. It is non-alcoholic, and much cheaper to boot.

2 cups apple, peeled and chopped
1 15-ounce can pineapple tidbits (juice packed), drained
2 bananas, sliced
1 cup peaches, peeled and sliced
1 cup seedless grapes
½ cup carbonated lemon-lime beverage

Combine the fruits and chill. At serving time spoon into stemmed dessert glasses. Pour a tablespoon of the carbonated lemon-lime beverage over each portion. Serve immediately.

6 servings
0 fat grams per serving

Sunday Best Baked Apples

¼ cup raisins
3 tablespoons brown sugar
1 teaspoon cinnamon
½ of ½-ounce package butter-flavored granules
4 firm apples, cored
½ cup water

Combine the raisins, sugar, cinnamon and butter-flavored granules. Stuff the apples with the mixture. Pour the water around the apples. Bake at 350° for 45 minutes.

4 servings
0 fat grams per serving

SAUCES AND CONDIMENTS

Sauces and condiments add interest and sparkle to many dishes. Keep a lot of them on hand. I have a large cabinet full of both commercially prepared and homemade condiments of all kinds. I also keep an array of commercially prepared sauces, flavored vinegars and mustards. Many commercial sauces and condiments, with the exception of mayonnaise and mayonnaise-type salad dressing, are either low-fat or fat-free. Just remember to check the label.

Basic White Sauce
¼ cup chicken broth
¼ cup all-purpose flour
¼ cup nonfat dry milk powder
2 cups skim milk
1 ½-ounce package butter-flavored granules

Combine all ingredients. Cook in a saucepan over medium heat, stirring frequently, until thickened.

Uses: Add to vegetables to make creamed vegetables or use to make casserole dishes that call for white sauce.

8 servings
0 fat grams per serving

Easy Cheesy Sauce
This is a quick sauce that is good poured over cooked vegetables, or added to casseroles.

1 10¾-ounce can 99% fat-free cream of mushroom soup
½ soup can water
3 tablespoons fat-free sour cream
4 ¾-ounce slices fat-free Swiss or Cheddar cheese, torn into strips

Combine the soup and water in a saucepan. Stir to blend. Place over medium heat. When the soup is hot, add the sour cream and cheese strips. Stir until the cheese is melted.

4 servings
Less than 2 fat grams per serving

Easy Microwave Lemon Sauce

Did you know that gingerbread prepared from a packaged mix is a relatively low-fat treat? This lemon sauce is especially good on gingerbread. It can also serve as a tasty topping for fresh fruit or angel food cake.

½ cup sugar or granulated sugar substitute
1½ tablespoons cornstarch
⅛ teaspoon light salt
1 cup water
2-3 tablespoons lemon juice, to taste

Combine the sugar, cornstarch and salt. Stir in the water. Microwave on high 4-6 minutes, stirring every 2 minutes. Add the lemon juice. Microwave 1 additional minute.

4 servings
0 fat grams

Fat-free Barbecue Sauce

12-ounce can tomato paste
2 cups water
2 tablespoons cider vinegar
2 teaspoons lemon juice
½ medium onion, minced
1 tablespoon Worcestershire sauce
2 tablespoons sugar or granulated sugar substitute
2 teaspoons liquid smoke
1 teaspoon garlic powder
1 tablespoon dry mustard
hot sauce to taste

Combine all ingredients in a saucepan and bring to a boil. Simmer 20 minutes.

0 fat grams in the recipe

Guilt-free Pesto Sauce

A lot of us like pesto, that flavorful pasta sauce that is full of oil and Parmesan cheese. This version is a little more kind to our fat gram allowance.

3 cups fresh spinach
¼ teaspoon garlic powder
1 tablespoon olive oil
¼ cup fat-free sour cream
1 tablespoon Parmesan cheese, grated
1 tablespoon lemon juice

Combine all of the ingredients in a blender or food processor and puree. Serve with pasta.

4 servings
4 fat grams per serving

Fruit Topping

This is a very versatile topping. It can be used on muffins, pancakes or as an ice cream sauce. Try it with peaches or blueberries.

½ teaspoon cornstarch
¼ cup unsweetened apple juice
1 cup berries or sliced fruit
dash of nutmeg
dash of cinnamon

Combine the cornstarch and apple juice. Bring the mixture to a boil, reduce the heat, and simmer until slightly thickened. Add the fruit and spices. Continue to cook until the fruit is heated through.

2 servings
0 fat grams

Great Onion Gravy

This is terrific over mashed potatoes, rice, chicken or vegetables of any kind. On the "rare" occasions that you might treat yourself to a slice or two of eye of round roast, it is especially good with beef.

1 1-ounce package dehydrated onion soup mix
2 cups cold water
2 tablespoons all-purpose flour

Combine the ingredients in a saucepan and bring to a boil, stirring frequently. Continue cooking until thickened.

8 servings
0 fat grams

Salsa Magnifico!

What makes this salsa so magnifico is the fact that it is not only fat free, but almost calorie free also. I keep a jar in the refrigerator all the time. It is not only great served as an accompaniment to Mexican style dishes or with tortilla chips, but also as a quick topping for plain fat-free saltine crackers when you want a simple snack in a hurry.

1 28-ounce can whole tomatoes, undrained
6 ounce can tomato paste
1 medium onion, finely minced
1 green pepper, finely minced
1 4-ounce can diced green chili peppers, undrained
¾ cup cold water
¼ teaspoon garlic powder
¼ teaspoon dried coriander
hot sauce to taste
crushed red pepper flakes to taste

Dice the tomatoes. Mix all ingredients. Keeps indefinitely in the refrigerator.

0 fat grams in the recipe

Tartar Sauce

This classic sauce for seafood is easily prepared using fat-free ingredients. It is also good used as a sandwich spread.

1 cup fat-free mayonnaise
2 tablespoons sweet pickle relish
1 teaspoon dried dill weed
1 tablespoon white wine vinegar

Combine all of the ingredients. Store in the refrigerator and use as needed. Keeps indefinitely.

0 fat grams in the recipe

Apple Relish

4 cups tart, firm green apples, peeled and chopped
1 cup apple cider vinegar
1⅓ cups brown sugar
1 medium onion, chopped
¼ cup raisins
½ teaspoon ground cinnamon
½ teaspoon cloves
1 tablespoon mustard seed

Combine all of the ingredients in a large saucepan. Bring to a boil, then reduce the heat and simmer for 30 minutes, or until the relish is thick. Store in the refrigerator or freeze in pint freezer containers. If preferred, the relish may be canned for future use. Pour the hot relish into hot, sterilized, pint canning jars and process in a boiling water bath for 10 minutes. Makes 2 pints.

0 fat grams in the recipe

Blueberry Chutney

2 12-ounce packages frozen blueberries, unthawed
1 medium onion, chopped
½ cup sugar
1 cup apple cider vinegar
½ cup raisins
1 tablespoon mustard seeds
½ teaspoon ground ginger
½ teaspoon ground cinnamon
¼ teaspoon dried red pepper flakes
light salt to taste

Combine all of the ingredients in a large saucepan. Bring to a boil, then lower the heat and allow to simmer for 45 minutes or until thick. Store in the refrigerator or freeze in pint freezer containers. If preferred, the chutney may be canned for future use. Pour the hot chutney into hot, sterilized, pint canning jars and process in a boiling water bath for 10 minutes. Makes 3 pints.

0 fat grams in the recipe

Chili Sauce From Your Kitchen

4 quarts peeled, chopped fresh tomatoes
2 cups chopped onion
2 cups chopped green peppers
1 cup sugar
3 tablespoons light salt
3 tablespoons mixed pickling spice
1 tablespoon mustard seed
2½ cups cider vinegar

Combine the vegetables, sugar and salt. Tie the spices up in a cheesecloth bag and add them to the mixture. Simmer for about 45 minutes until thick. Add the vinegar and continue cooking briefly. Pour into pint jars, leaving ½-inch headspace. Fasten the lids and process in a boiling water bath for 15 minutes.

Makes approximately 6 pints
0 fat grams

Chunky Mexican Relish

1 16-ounce can chunky Mexican style tomato sauce
½ green pepper, chopped
½ medium onion, finely chopped
1 teaspoon garlic, minced
1 teaspoon cumin
1 teaspoon chili powder

Combine all ingredients. Keeps well in the refrigerator. This is a thick relish and becomes even thicker over time. May be thinned with a bit of water if desired.

0 fat grams

Dried Apricot Chutney

2 6-ounce packages dried apricot halves
2 cloves garlic, minced
1 cup water
1 cup cider vinegar
1 cup sugar
1 teaspoon ground ginger, or to taste

Combine all of the ingredients in a large saucepan. Bring to a boil, then lower the heat and simmer for 20 minutes, or until thick. Store in the refrigerator or freeze in a pint freezer container. If preferred, the chutney may be canned for future use. Pour the hot chutney into a hot, sterilized, pint canning jar and process in a boiling water bath for 10 minutes.

0 fat grams in the recipe

Fresh Cranberry-Orange Relish

This is a delicious relish that is often served at holiday dinners. However, it is a tasty addition to any meal. I like to buy plenty of cranberries and keep them in the freezer, since they freeze beautifully and are sometimes hard to find in stores.

1 pound fresh cranberries, rinsed and drained
1 unpeeled navel orange, quartered
6 tablespoons sugar or granulated sugar substitute

Place the cranberries and orange in a blender or food processor and finely chop. Add the sugar or sugar substitute. Serve chilled.

8 servings
0 fat grams per serving

Green Tomato Chutney

2 pounds firm green tomatoes, chopped
4 tart green apples, peeled and chopped
2 medium onions, chopped
½ cup raisins
1 cup sugar
½ teaspoon ground ginger
3 cloves garlic, minced
1¼ cups cider vinegar

Combine all of the ingredients in a large saucepan. Bring to a boil. Reduce the heat and allow to simmer for 30 minutes, or until thick. Store in the refrigerator or freeze in pint freezer containers. If preferred, the chutney may be canned for future use. Pour the chutney into hot sterilized jars and process in a boiling water bath for 10 minutes.

Makes 3 pints
0 fat grams in the recipe.

Microwave Peach Jam

4 cups unsweetened peaches
1 ¾-ounce package powdered pectin
2 tablespoons sugar
½ teaspoon ascorbic acid
1 tablespoon lemon juice

Mash the peaches. Combine with the remaining ingredients in a microwave safe bowl. Microwave, covered, on high for 2 minutes. Stir. Microwave 3-4 more minutes or until the mixture boils for 1 minute. Remove from microwave and let stand 1 minute. Stir again. Will keep in the freezer for up to 1 year or in the refrigerator for several weeks.

0 fat grams per serving

Mixed Fruit Chutney

2 cups peaches, peeled and chopped
2 cups plums, chopped
1 medium onion, chopped
¼ cup brown sugar
2 tablespoons raisins
⅛ teaspoon dry mustard powder
1 tablespoon mustard seed
½ teaspoon ground ginger
½ teaspoon allspice
¼ cup cider vinegar
½ cup orange juice

Combine all ingredients. Simmer about 30 minutes or until thick. Taste and adjust seasoning if needed. Store in the refrigerator or freeze in a pint freezer container. If preferred the chutney may be canned for future use. Pour the chutney into hot sterilized jars and process in a boiling water bath for 10 minutes.

8 servings
0 fat grams per serving

Mom's Chili Sauce
This makes a great relish with bean dishes.

1 15-ounce can diced tomatoes, undrained
chili powder to taste
1 teaspoon vinegar
½ small onion minced
1 teaspoon mustard seed
1 packet sugar substitute

Combine all of the ingredients except the sugar substitute. Simmer until thickened. When cool, add the sugar substitute.

6 servings
0 fat grams

Olden Days Apple Relish
2 dozen ripe tomatoes, peeled and chopped
12 firm cooking apples, peeled and chopped
6 hot peppers
1 dozen medium onions, chopped
4 teaspoons light salt
1½ teaspoons black pepper
2 cups sugar
2 cups vinegar

Combine the ingredients in a large kettle. Boil slowly until thick. Place in pint jars that have been prepared for canning and process in a boiling water bath for 15 minutes.

0 fat grams per serving

Picalilli

1 head green cabbage, chopped
5 firm green tomatoes, chopped
2 medium onions, chopped
2 green peppers, chopped
2 teaspoons pickling salt
1 tablespoon each mustard seed and celery seed
2 cups cider vinegar
1¼ cups sugar

Combine all of the ingredients in a large saucepan. Bring to a boil, then reduce the heat and simmer for 30 minutes, or until the vegetables are tender. Store in the refrigerator or freeze in pint freezer containers. If preferred, the picalilli may be canned for future use. Pour the hot picalilli into hot, sterilized, pint canning jars and process in a boiling water bath for 10 minutes.

Makes 3 pints.
0 fat grams in recipe

Pickled Beets

2 15-ounce cans sliced beets, undrained
2 medium onions, thinly sliced
1 cup apple cider vinegar
1 teaspoon light salt

Combine all of the ingredients. Store in the refrigerator. The beets are ready to eat when the onions turn pink.

4 servings
0 fat grams per serving

Pickled Onion Rings

These are good as an accompaniment to beans. They may also be used on hot dogs or hamburgers, especially in winter when mild onions are often not available.

2 large onions, thinly sliced or chopped if preferred
¼ cup water
½ cup cider vinegar
2 teaspoons light salt
½ cup sugar

Put the onion in a bowl. Combine the water, vinegar, salt and sugar in a saucepan. Heat to boiling. Pour over the onions. Chill 1 hour or longer. The liquid can be reused to make additional onions when needed.

4 servings
0 fat grams per serving

Pickled Pepper Relish

2 cups chopped green pepper
2 cups chopped onion
½ cup sugar or granulated sugar substitute
1 pint cider vinegar
2 teaspoons light salt

Place the peppers and onion in a saucepan. Combine the sugar, or substitute, vinegar and salt. Add them to the pepper and onions in the saucepan. Cook over medium heat until the vegetables are soft and the liquid is slightly thickened. This keeps well in the refrigerator for several months.

8 servings
0 fat grams

MISCELLANEOUS

Crepes

I keep a supply of crepes in my freezer all of the time. They can be used for main courses when filled with meat, side dishes when filled with vegetables, or as dessert when filled with fruit or frozen yogurt.

½ cup all-purpose flour
½ cup fat-free egg substitute
1 cup skim milk
1 tablespoon vegetable oil
no-stick cooking spray

Combine the flour, egg substitute, milk and oil. Let the batter rest in the refrigerator for at least 1 hour before preparing crepes. Spray a crepe pan or a small skillet with no-stick cooking spray. For each crepe, pour ¼ cup batter into the pan. Rotate the pan so that the batter spreads evenly. Bake on one side until the surface is slightly dry and the underside is lightly browned. Turn and cook the other side briefly.

Makes approximately 8 crepes
2 fat grams per crepe

Crisp Salad Croutons

2 plain or onion-flavored bagels, unsliced
butter-flavored no-stick cooking spray
¼ teaspoon garlic powder
¼ teaspoon dried oregano

Cut each bagel into thin coin sized slices. Place each slice on a baking sheet that has been sprayed with no-stick cooking spray. Coat the slices with the spray and sprinkle with the seasonings. Bake at 350° for 15 minutes, or until crisp and toasted, stirring occasionally. Use as a topping for salads.

4 fat grams in the recipe

Delicious "Butter" Spreads

Just because you choose not to blow your fat gram allowance on butter does not mean that you can't enjoy zesty spreads on bread, or added to hot vegetables or grilled chicken.

Easy Garlic Spread

4 garlic cloves, minced, or ½ teaspoon garlic powder
1 tub ultra-light or fat-free margarine

Combine all of the ingredients. Store in the refrigerator and use as needed.

Herb Spread

1 tub ultra-light or fat-free margarine
1 tablespoon chopped chives
1 tablespoon chopped parsley

Combine all ingredients and store in the refrigerator. Use as needed.

Savory Spread

1 tub ultra-light or fat-free margarine
1 tablespoon Worcestershire sauce
2 cloves garlic, minced, or ¼ teaspoon garlic powder

Combine all ingredients. Store in the refrigerator and use as needed.

0 fat grams if fat-free margarine is used
2 fat grams per tablespoon
if ultra-light margarine is used

Fat-free Sour Cream

Before fat-free sour cream became available in grocery stores, it was necessary to make your own. Thank goodness, those days are over! Here's how to make it, in case you want to compare it to the store bought kind.

1 cup fat-free cottage cheese
4 tablespoons skim milk
1 tablespoon lemon juice

Combine all ingredients in a blender. Blend until smooth.

Variations:
Add 1 tablespoon dried or fresh chives to use on baked potatoes.
Add 1 package dehydrated onion soup mix to use as a dip.
Add 2 tablespoons sugar or granulated sugar substitute and 1 teaspoon vanilla to use as a topping for fresh fruit.

4 servings
0 fat grams

Seasoning Mixes For Chips and Fries

Use these mixes to zip up anything. They are great on chips and French fries, but can add extra flavor to a lot of other dishes, from grilled chicken to cooked vegetables. The fat-free sour cream granules and Cheddar cheese-flavored granules can be found in grocery stores in the same section as butter-flavored granules.

Sour cream and onion seasoning mix: Combine 3 tablespoons fat-free sour cream-flavored granules with 3 tablespoons onion powder and ¼ teaspoon light salt.

Spicy seasoning mix: Combine 2 tablespoons chili powder with ½ teaspoon dried cumin powder and ¼ teaspoon light salt.
Ground red pepper may be added, if desired.

Cheese and garlic seasoning mix: Combine 2 tablespoons fat-free Cheddar-flavored granules with 2 tablespoons garlic powder and ¼ teaspoon light salt.

0 fat grams in each recipe.

Sweetened Condensed Milk

Commercially prepared sweetened condensed milk is high in fat and calories. This home made version reduces the calories quite a bit and reduces the fat grams to zero. Use in any recipe that calls for sweetened condensed milk, such as lemon ice box pie.

1 cup non-fat dry milk powder
¾ cup granulated sugar
½ cup warm water

Combine all of the ingredients in the top of a double boiler, adding the water a little at the time. If the mixture begins to seem too thin, do not add any more water. Simmer until the milk powder is completely dissolved. Place in the refrigerator. The mixture will continue to thicken as it cools.

0 fat grams in the recipe

Zesty Topping For Casseroles

This recipe is nice to keep on hand to top casseroles. It can also be used as a breading for chicken or fish. Keep a large batch in the freezer in a zipper top freezer bag and use as needed.

12 slices fat-free, reduced-calorie bread
2 teaspoons garlic powder
1 tablespoon grated Parmesan cheese
2 teaspoons dried oregano

Combine all of the ingredients, in a blender or food processor. Blend until the bread is reduced to fine crumbs.

Less than 2 fat grams in the recipe

Exceed The Feed Limit!

Out of the Fat Lane Into A Slimmer, Healthier Life
Without Diets Or Deprivation

Vicki Park

Preface

You never know where or when you may learn something profound about yourself. It can sometimes happen in the most unexpected places. Some years ago I found myself driving down a narrow, winding road behind a huge motor home. It was barely moving. I was on my way to work and I just knew it was going to make me late.

The owner of the motor home was rather thoughtful. To entertain those forced to creep along behind him, he had covered the whole back end with bumper stickers, which were mainly of the "I owe, I owe, it's off to work I go" school of terrible puns. Normally, I'm a sucker for puns. The cornier the better. My husband often threatens to call the imaginary pun police to come get me because I'm always telling some real groaners.

However, that day I was so anxious about getting to work on time that the bumper stickers didn't do much to cheer me. Then I spotted one that didn't just make me smile, it changed my life. It was from that little bumper sticker that I learned the reason I had never been able to stick to a diet.

I always figured the inability to lose weight was some sort of character flaw on my part. I probably hold the record for the world's shortest diets. I would frequently get out of bed promising myself to start a new diet and change my mind by the time I opened my refrigerator door two minutes later. Even if I managed to hang in there for a while, in the long run I always ended up weighing more than when I started.

At the time I saw the bumper sticker, I had "dieted" my way up to 315 pounds. I considered myself a hopeless failure at weight loss. But that little bumper sticker finally explained to me in a few short words why diets had never worked for me. It simply said: A DIET IS THE PUNISHMENT FOR EXCEEDING THE FEED LIMIT! Okay, stop groaning. Maybe you want to call the pun police about that one, but just think about it for a minute. Truer words were never written.

It isn't just me who can relate to that bit of roadside psychology. It applies to all of us who have never been able to stick to a diet. From what some of the experts tell us, that is just about everybody who ever tried.

They also tell us that even if we do manage to lose we probably won't be able to permanently keep it off. We are programmed by news like that to expect failure.

But wait! We have that good old bumper sticker to explain to us why that happens. A DIET IS THE PUNISHMENT FOR EXCEEDING THE FEED LIMIT! There it is in a nutshell. When we diet, we are punishing ourselves. By limiting ourselves to tiny portions of tasteless foods, by subjecting ourselves to weighing and measuring each morsel and by condemning ourselves to constant hunger, we are punishing ourselves for overeating–for exceeding the feed limit. Since no one in their right mind enjoys punishment, few people are willing to keep punishing themselves for long. We are usually back to eating as usual within a very short time. Who can blame us since eating is one of the great pleasures of life?

I have joked about the pun police but they are nothing compared to those imaginary diet police who place us under arrest for overeating and sentence us to rabbit food for life. I named this book *Exceed The Feed Limit*! because the words in the title are true. We don't have to fear failure or punishment by the diet police any more just because we enjoy eating.

Things are changing. There have been exciting developments in the fields of weight loss and nutrition. Researchers now realize that it is possible to lose weight without deprivation or dieting. It can be simply a matter of controlling the amount of fat we eat and the type of food we eat.

When you lower the amount of fat that you eat, you often can, with certain exceptions, eat more food than you could eat on an old-fashioned calorie-based diet and still lose weight. I am living proof. When I stopped dieting I lost 180 pounds. Not only that, my husband Ken lost 90 pounds. We've kept the weight off for six years. Our daughter Ashley has lost the 85 pounds she gained at college too. We never had to give up hearty portions of our favorite dishes–we just learned to enjoy them in a healthier way.

I am not a doctor or nutritionist but I do have something to share that I think can be helpful too–personal experience. By distilling the wisdom I learned from medical experts into a simple system that fit into my busy lifestyle, I finally found a way to lose weight without dieting or deprivation. I had to pass along the good news in hopes that it could help others. As a result I wrote a book called *Live! Don't Diet!*

Live! Don't Diet! has sold more than 120,000 copies and has led to my appearance on TV and radio shows, as well as to stories in newspapers and magazines across the country. The reaction to *Live! Don't Diet!* surpassed my wildest dreams. However, the most exciting thing is not the attention it has received from the media, it is the wonderful letters I have received from people who have told me the book has helped them lose weight and eat healthier too. That gives me joy beyond measure.

Whether or not you have read *Live! Don't Diet!* I hope you'll find *Exceed The Feed Limit!* a helpful addition to your kitchen. You may want to lose weight or perhaps you just want to eat healthier. In either case, I have written it especially for you.

It contains 200 quick and easy low-fat recipes that have helped me, Ken and Ashley lose 355 pounds and keep it off. I hope you'll like my recipes. They are quick, simple and made with ingredients that you don't have to go across town to buy. In fact you probably already have many of the ingredients in your pantry. The recipes are not delicacies that require a gourmet or chef to prepare. They are simple, hearty dishes because that is what we like to eat at our house and these are the recipes I prepare every day.

In addition to my recipes, *Exceed The Feed Limit!* also contains lots of information about eating low-fat, as well as some words that I hope will inspire and motivate you. I hope you will enjoy and benefit from the recipes, tips and techniques I have included. A better life is just a meal away. So come along with me–the best is yet to be!

Section 1

A Little Inspiration

LET'S GET MOTIVATED!

I am not only here to share my recipes and weight loss tips, I am also here to inspire and motivate you. After all, motivation is a major part of successful weight loss. It is very simple–if you aren't motivated, you probably won't succeed. Remember that it's the brain that tells you to open your mouth and shovel that rich, fattening dessert in! It is also the brain that tells you how wonderful you will look and feel when you don't give in to temptation. The trick is to train your brain to think the latter way instead of the former. That's motivation!

It is so important to have some compelling reason you want to lose or improve your eating habits. Maybe it's to live a longer life and to look better and feel better. Heaven knows, there couldn't be any more important reasons. But sometimes it takes more personal reasons. I wanted to be able to have more fun in life and to wear shorts or a bathing suit without embarassment. Call them vain reasons but they worked for me. The mind is the master of the body. That's the reason coaches give pep talks to their teams before a big game. Motivation works. It keeps you focused. So get your mind in gear and go out and win this one for you!

On the next few pages I want to share a few more words to inspire you. Whenever you need a boost to your motivation, go back and re-read them. Also look at the before and after pictures of me on the cover. I am living proof it can be done. The weight I lost made such a dramatic difference in my life yet I didn't have to do anything but make some easy changes in the way I cook and eat. Such a simple thing changed and probably saved my life.

Because I began cooking healthier, Ken also lost the weight he needed to lose and was able to stop taking cholesterol and blood pressure medication. So, you see, it's not just ourselves, it's other members of our family we may be helping. Helping family members improve their health and weight can be a powerful inspiration in itself. So, come on. We'll get and keep your mind on track! Your body has only to follow!

DON'T JUST DREAM IT ... DO IT!

I am a real creature of habit. I really don't like changes in my lifestyle very much. When my daily routine varies very much from the norm, it throws me into a tailspin. I may never retire from the job I have held for almost 30 years because I'm afraid that I could never adjust to a more leisurely routine after years of going to work every day. I'm also afraid I would start putting everything off.

I am a world class procrastinator. I'm like the guy who bought a book titled *Stop Putting Things Off!* but never got around to reading it. If I ever did retire I could probably keep busy finishing up all those half completed craft projects now littering my basement but I would probably end up putting that off too.

I am glad to know I'm not alone in my penchant for procrastination. A friend whose husband shares this same trait used to swear that there was nothing he wouldn't put off. One day she came in with an amazed expression on her face. "Well," she said, "I guess I'll have to eat my words. I have been after Jim for months to fix that shaky old TV antenna on our roof but he never would. Yesterday, during the windstorm, it blew down right in the middle of the football game he was watching. He leapt up, ran to the closet, grabbed a wire coathanger, dragged the TV out onto the front porch, stuck the coathanger into the back of the TV and watched the rest of the game!"

I guess the point here is that sometimes we have to be galvanized into action whether we want to be or not. We may have been told by a doctor that we have to lose weight or that we must change our eating habits for health reasons. We may do it because we need to feel better. Sadly, we may feel we have to do it to keep the affections of someone we love. There can be loads of reasons. In my case, I just didn't want to let fat rob me of the fun and excitement of life anymore. However, as I mentioned I don't like change. I am also a selfish person. While I wanted to be thinner, I obviously didn't want to have to go to much trouble to do it. I didn't like being fat but I also didn't want to punish myself.

People are always saying to me, "You must have had terrific willpower to have lost all that weight." Honestly I never had any willpower and I still don't. If this way had not been the easiest I had ever tried, I still would weigh 315 pounds–or more. I simply learned to cook the things I love to eat in a healthier way. I still cook the same things I always cooked, I still eat a lot of food and I still don't have to spend much time in the kitchen.

More about all that later. I'll give you the details in the section called "The Basics Of Low-fat Weight Loss". Meanwhile, there is another point

I want to make. We all have goals and dreams that we never get around to pursuing. We either decide they are too much trouble or we let other things in life get in our way. Don't let it happen to you. Whether it is weight loss or another goal you have put off pursuing–get started on it now. You never know where it may lead. When I made the decision to try to lose weight again and sat down at my kitchen table to reduce the fat in my recipes, I never dreamed that I would lose 180 pounds or become a cookbook author.

When I was a child we were required to memorize poetry in school. That is so long ago that I barely remember the name of the school I attended, but I do remember part of one of the poems. It was called "Maude Muller," by John Greenleaf Whittier, and the lines were these:

"Of all the sad words of tongue or pen

The saddest are these: It might have been."

I didn't want to come to the end of my days and wonder what life might have been like if I had only gotten my weight under control. Don't let that happen to you either. Whether it's doing something about your weight or some other goal you have put off pursuing–**DON'T JUST DREAM ABOUT IT! DO IT!** You'll be glad you did.

TAKING STOCK:
A BLUEPRINT FOR YOUR FUTURE

What if you lived in a house that you had not cared for as well as you should have? As a result, things are starting to go wrong. The exterior is getting a little shabby and the plumbing is starting to go bad. What if you had the opportunity to remodel your home into a better, more attractive one–at no cost and with very little effort? Anyone who wouldn't jump at the chance to do that would be considered crazy! You have the same opportunity with your body. After all your body is the earthly home your soul inhabits and you should want to make that home a mansion.

There are very few people who couldn't use a little self improvement. We all could do with a little remodeling once in a while. Take stock of yourself. Would you like to be the person you always dreamed you could be? Would you like to live life in a body that is healthier and more attractive? Why settle for just "being" when with so little effort you could be the best that you can be.

It isn't vain to want to look and feel your best. It is only sensible. Just as blueprints are used to remodel a house, you can draw up the blueprints for a new you. Take stock of yourself. What would you like to change? Consider the following questions:

- Are you overweight? Even five pounds can make a difference in the way you look and feel and may affect your life span.

- Are you suffering from the effects of an unhealthy diet? Do you have high blood pressure or cholesterol problems or feel that you are at risk for developing illnesses that may be diet-related?

- Have you let your attitude about life slowly grow more and more negative? Are you seldom enthusiastic about the events going on in your life?

- Have you grown stagnant in your relationships with others–and with yourself?

- Does your appearance need upgrading? Is your wardrobe more of a cover-up than an enhancement?

If the answer to any of the above questions is even "maybe" you could probably benefit from a little personal remodeling. A really good place to start is with your eating habits. It is amazing how the foods we allow our-selves to eat can affect so many facets of our lives. Just think about it. The guilt we face when we overeat or eat things that are bad for us, the weight we may gain, the health problems we may engender, can affect everything we do. Food is a major thread in the physical and emotional fabric of our lives.

By beginning to eat healthier, you may be taking the first baby steps toward a whole new you. As you eat better, you begin to feel better. As you feel better, you want to look better. As you look better, your self-esteem and your enthusiasm for life increases. As your self-esteem and enthusi-asm increases, your relationships with the people in your life may improve. One step leads to another. I speak from experience. That is exactly what happened to me.

Change taken in small steps is so gradual that it seems almost effort-less. It can be a tremendous gift to those you love when you become the best that you can be–but it is really a gift you are giving yourself. When you are looking and feeling your best, you are usually happier and less stressed. You are not only emotionally healthier, you are generally physically healthier as well. Self improvement is literally a gift to yourself that can last a lifetime–a happier and quite possibly a longer lifetime. So get started now remodeling yourself and before long you will be the "you" of your dreams.

IS THERE TIME AND ENERGY FOR FUN IN YOUR LIFE?

I have never seen a tombstone yet that said: "She Kept Her House Perfectly Cleaned" or "She Spent All Of Her Time In The Kitchen." I bet you haven't either. Somehow those things lose their importance in the grand scheme of things.

Of course it is important to keep our homes clean and our families well fed, but often we have a tendency to equate the amount of time we spend on these things with being a worthwhile person. This could be due in large part to the barrage of commercials that imply that a truly worthwhile person has a floor that shines like a mirror and demonstrates love by providing a constant supply of fat-laden homemade goodies. Many of us have become slaves to this concept. As a result, we are too overworked and worn out to enjoy life.

I must admit, I bought into the concept, too. While I never was one to spend much time in the kitchen, I did find myself feeling very guilty if I didn't try to keep my house in perfect condition. I hate even the most routine housework, yet I made myself spend endless hours doing extra household tasks that were noticeable to no one but me. Trying to work full time, raise a teenager and keep a perfect home left me very tired and usually grumpy. Considering that I also weighed 315 pounds, I am amazed that I ever smiled.

One day, it occurred to me that I had let being a super cleaner become so important to me because it gave me back some of the self-esteem that I had allowed fat to take from me. It allowed me to control some aspect of my life. I weighed 315 pounds, so obviously I couldn't control my appetite, but I could control my house. I may have gotten some self-esteem from this, but it didn't make me happy because I really hated doing those household tasks.

Once I started my low-fat lifestyle, began losing weight and gained control over that very important aspect of my life, being a cleaning dynamo didn't seem quite so important anymore. It no longer bothers me if my floors don't sparkle, as long as they are clean. Now, I spend the time I used to spend on extra housekeeping tasks with my husband or my daughter. It is amazing the difference it has made in the atmosphere in our home. We are all happier because Mom isn't so grumpy anymore.

The point of my dime store psychoanalysis is this: if you too have been brainwashed into believing that you must have the perfectly cleaned home or must demonstrate your love by endless hours of baking rich treats for your family, just think about it for a minute. No one is really comfortable in a perfect home–and feeding your family great dishes that are good for them spells loving more than any fat-laden, sugary junk.

Unless you really love extra cleaning or spending all of your time in the kitchen, don't feel guilty about not doing it. Spend that time in doing things with those you love. Memories are not made from perfectly kept homes, they are made from having fun with people we care about. If you do really love cleaning, at least make the arrangements to get "She Kept Her House Perfectly Cleaned" carved on your tombstone. That's the only thing about housework that will last!

I'VE BEEN FAT AND I'VE BEEN THIN

To paraphrase that old line "I've been rich and I've been poor and rich is better," I'd like to say that I've been fat and I've been thinner–and thinner is better. I guess the politically correct term might be weight challenged while the feel good term of the moment for obesity is fluffy, but I wasn't weight challenged or fluffy–I was downright fat!

I know that there are many happy, heavy people who may beg to differ, but having seen the issue from both sides, I have many reasons to personally feel that being thinner is infinitely better. Here's just a few of the reasons:

- I used to catch every cold that came within a city block of me when I was heavy. It probably had more to do with my eating habits than my size, but now that I have lost weight, eat healthy and am more active, I haven't had a cold in years.

- Speaking of being active, when I was heavy, I just didn't have the energy to be very active. Now that I have lost weight, I have more energy than I had as a teenager. It is a great feeling.

- When my husband and I were heavy, a substantial portion of our income went toward buying blood pressure and cholesterol-lowering medications. Because we lost weight and eat healthier, we no longer have to take any of those medications. Now we have better health plus more spending money!

- I used to suffer with chronic knee and ankle pain from carrying around excess weight. Several heavy friends of mine actually had to have knee surgery because of problems associated with overweight. After I lost weight, all of my joint pain ended.

- When I was heavy, I couldn't cross my legs because they were too large. They say that some of life's greatest pleasures are the simplest. For me, finally being able to sit with my legs crossed was such a terrific moment. It may sound silly, but unless you have had the same problem yourself, you can't imagine how uncomfortable it can be to never be able to cross your legs.

- When I was heavy, I stayed drenched with perspiration from May until October. Just thinking of that sticky, awful feeling makes me shudder.

- Once, when I was heavy, it took two brave, strong men to hoist me into a horse-drawn carriage in New Orleans. When I finally got in, I couldn't fit into the seat. A friend once told me she was mega-embarassed when she had to leave a boat because the life vest was too small to fit her.

- I used to envy the cool, comfortable women I would see dressed in shorts during the summer. I wore heavy gabardine slacks, mainly because they covered up a lot. What's more, they were usually black because I thought I looked smaller in black. Talk about hot! Granted, I should have dressed in shorts and not have cared a fig about the opinions of anyone else, but I am ashamed to say that I was superficial when it came to the opinions of others.

- Once, when I attended a meeting, the chairperson announced "Before we get started, I am sure Vicki would like to know where the snack machines are located in the building." I have been lucky. Many heavy people have been the victims of considerably worse remarks.

I could go on and on with examples, but I think you get the idea. These are just some very minor examples of the personal ways being overweight impacted my life. In retrospect, I was very fortunate to not have experienced severe problems. Obviously there could have been some, such as very serious or even life-threatening illness. So many very severe health problems are linked to overweight and to fat in the diet.

If you don't have control of your eating, some of these problems may become your problems if they are not already. I can assure you that the momentary pleasure of unlimited amounts of fattening food is not worth the many problems that being overweight can cause.

HERE'S TO YOUR GOOD HEALTH!

If you have had any exposure to a newspaper or a news program today, I would be willing to bet that you saw a story on the damage that eating too much fat can do to the body. Few days go by without new, alarming revelations about it. Dietary fat has been implicated as the culprit in an enormous number of health problems. We all know about heart disease and a wide variety of cancers, but now scientists are even linking it to such unexpected diseases as certain types of blindness. Apparently there is no part of the body that cannot be damaged by eating too much fat. In fact, it has been noted that most premature deaths caused by illness can be linked to diet–and especially dietary fat.

Of course one of the biggest problems (another bad pun–please excuse me!) too much dietary fat can cause is obesity. If a day passes without a news story on another disease that excessive fat intake can cause, there is sure to be a story on the perils of being overweight. Recent studies have indicated that even being slightly overweight can cut years from your life span. What a terrible thought. Not only are we doomed if we eat too much fat, we also are doomed if we are overweight at all.

Even if you or members of your family are as thin as a rail, the amount of fat that you eat can do great harm to you. The skinniest person I know has terrible cholesterol and blood pressure problems, mainly because she mainlines cheeseburgers and fatty junk foods. I'm sure you know someone just like her. Everyone does. They're the people we love to hate but secretly envy because they seem to be able to eat enormous quantities of the most fattening foods without gaining an ounce. One of their favorite expressions is, "Well, I don't have to worry about what I eat. I can eat anything I want to." This statement is usually delivered with an air of gleeful superiority. I have heard it a million times. Well, it may seem that they are immune but it will probably catch up with them some day. Even people who are a perfect size need to eat healthier or they may be taking years off their life.

Of course, what you drink can be just as important as what you eat. You no doubt recognize the title of this segment as a classic toast, but when toasting your good health, do it with a non-alcoholic drink. Drinking alcohol, especially before or during meals, can lower willpower and make you more susceptible to eating what you want instead of what you know you should have. In other words, that high-fat prime rib or favorite ultra-rich dish in the restaurant may not be so easy to turn down after a little alcohol is in your system. It makes sense. If alcohol lowers other inhibitions, why not those involving food?

Researchers are now saying that it is never too late to improve our health by improving our eating habits. Don't just sit there contemplating whether your spouse will bring a date to your funeral. As the old saying goes–stop digging your grave with your knife and fork! It has never been easier to eat low-fat. The food industry has seen the handwriting on the wall and seldom a day goes by without a great new low-fat product in the grocery store. You can eat healthy and also lose weight with an ease you never dreamed possible.

LOWER THE FAT AND RAISE THE ROOF!

Once, when I weighed 315 pounds, I sat in the car for six hours rather than join my family as they hiked a beautiful trail in the Smoky mountains. While they enjoyed quality time together, I dozed, alone and miserable. That is what fat will do for you. I am not just talking about fat on the body, I am also talking about fat in the body. Even people who are of average weight can feel sluggish and dull when they consume too much fat. It can make even the simple movments of our everyday routine seem tiring.

I have received numerous letters from people of all sizes who tell me how much better they feel now that they have reduced the amount of fat they are consuming. I can certainly relate to that. When I first began limiting the amount of fat I ate, I began to notice how much better I felt. As I began to lose weight, I began to feel even better. My energy level increased dramatically. I feel better today than I did when I was 20. Since I am 50, that is a pretty great feeling.

Not long ago my husband, Ken and I returned to that same mountain trail. This time I hiked every step of the way with him. A major storm had recently uprooted numerous trees on the trail and one blocked it entirely except for a little crawl space formed by some limbs that held it slightly off the ground. As I crawled on my hands and knees under that tree I thought to myself, "You know, Vicki, you were smarter when you sat in the car for six hours!"

I am still not crazy about hiking or any other kind of intense physical exertion. But it is such a thrill to know that I can do it. To me, the biggest benefit of having more energy is felt in more subtle ways. The fact that I can now exercise without agony and get through my daily routine with energy to spare is more important to me than being able to scale a tall mountain or do cartwheels. I am no longer a prisoner of my weight.

LET A READER INSPIRE YOU

I have had the good fortune to hear terrific news from so many people who tell me that my recipes and tips have worked for them. A wonderful young woman named Selina Nobles has graciously allowed me to share several of the letters she has written to me with you. I think you will find them just as inspiring and motivating as I do.

Dear Mrs. Park,

I want to tell you what an answer to my prayers your cookbook has been to me. I have been overweight most of my life and have probably lost several thousand pounds and have gained twice that much back. Several months ago I became more depressed than I have ever been about my weight. I began to pray every night for God to fix whatever was wrong with my body that made me totally incapable of eating normally. He didn't heal my body but instead sent me your book. I have lost 42 pounds and my attitude about myself and my eating habits has completely changed.

I don't look at low-fat eating as a diet–it has simply become my way of life and I have made the adjustment so much easier that I have ever dreamed. Your book has given me a great basis for low-fat cooking and I am beginning to branch out on my own. I want you to know how much my attitude has changed about myself and my life. Even after only a 42 pound loss and knowing I have much more to go, I have made a start and am doing something about my weight instead of watching it just creep up. I feel so much better about myself that I almost can't imagine how I will feel when I reach my goal.

In the past, after losing weight I have always gained it back because I was never able to make the distinction between a diet and changing my eating habits. I have no fear about gaining weight back because, as I said, low-fat is simply the way I eat now. Thank you so much for *Live! Don't Diet!* It is making it possible for me to have my life back.

Sincerely,
Selina Nobles

Dear Mrs. Park,

As of last Thursday my total loss is exactly 80 pounds. Up to this point being a normal size has been a distant and intangible dream. For the first time in years, it is now a tangible reality. There is simply no way I can express my gratitude.

Love,
Selina

Hi Vicki!

I have now lost 103 pounds! I can't believe how my life has changed because of this weight loss. I have started wearing the most incredible clothes. I am going skydiving! Words cannot describe how incredible this change in my life is.

Love you so much,
Selina

Thank you, Selina, for your beautiful letters. I believe they convey so well the real joy we feel when we lose weight we need to lose, whether it is one pound or one hundred.

Section 2

A Lot Of Information

LET'S GET DOWN TO BASICS

I promised you a little inspiration and a lot of information. Now that I've shared some things with you that I hope will motivate and inspire you, let's move on to the information I want to share.

But first, I have another corny joke. Well, it's kind of a joke. It has been a few pages since I have told one so get ready to groan again. It seems that two women were in their local pharmacy looking at the display of weight loss products. One of the women picked up a huge bottle of diet pills. As she read the list of ingredients she remarked to her companion, "I think I'll ask the pharmacist which is the very worst diet pill to take." "Don't bother", said the other woman. "I can answer that. The very worst diet pill to take is a friend who has lost a little weight and wants to tell you about it *over and over and over.*"

I won't do that, I promise. I'm just here to share the information that helped me lose. I'm a counselor by profession and a person who loves to share helpful information with people by nature. This carries over into all parts of my life. If I find a good sale, I'll call everyone I know and tell them about it. My mother often teases me by saying that I should have become a professional shopping consultant.

Well, back to business. First we'll talk about the basics, then we'll get to the tasty and simple low-fat recipes for everything from appetizers to desserts. In this section, the information I want to share will carry you through all aspects of healthier living the low-fat way–from weight loss and exercise information to how to cook, shop and plan low-fat menus. As with most things in life, there are basic guidelines you need to follow to be successful and that's what you'll find in this section. If you have read *Live! Don't Diet!* you may remember a few of these basics, which I also discussed there. However, they are so important that I can't repeat them enough. In addition, this book goes into much greater detail.

I recently heard the term "microwave mentality" used to describe people who want everything quick and easy. I love that expression. While it is probably meant to be derogatory, it fits me in many ways. I have a lot to do besides spending much of my time in the kitchen. Even though I love to eat, I want something that doesn't take hours to prepare. That is why I am so happy with my low-fat lifestyle.

As you read about the basics of low-fat living that you will find here, I think one thing will be quite clear. This way of eating and living is simple. There are not a lot of rules to follow or complicated menus to plan. Grocery shopping and cooking are easier than ever–and so is clean up. All of this would be worth changing to a low-fat lifestyle even if it did not have the wonderful benefits of potential weight loss and better health! So, come on, let's get down to basics.

The Basics Of Low-Fat Weight Loss

As my husband Ken and I watched the Super Bowl last year, the TV camera zoomed in on a huge defensive tackle who appeared to be perfectly square. He seemed at least 6' tall and 6' wide. The announcer, in relating the player's vital statistics, mentioned that he weighed 250 pounds. Ken and I together had lost more than that huge football player weighed! Then I thought about my own 180 pound loss. I realized that I had lost more than most average adult men weigh. I pictured myself bodily picking up a 180 pound man and trying to carry him. I couldn't do it. As a matter of fact, I probably couldn't even pick him up, much less carry him one step. Yet, my body was hauling around that much extra weight for much of my life. I can't believe I didn't keel over years ago.

You may need to lose only a few pounds but think of those pounds in terms of a 10 pound baby or a 40 pound toddler. Most of us have had to carry a sleeping child at one time or another. As much as we love the little darlings, after a few minutes they do get heavy. After a little while, our bodies start protesting with lower back aches, muscle strain and heavy breathing. At least we can put the child down. We can't just put the extra weight down. We have to carry it around endlessly unless we make the decision to do something about it.

Many of us have made that decision to do something about it many times–in my case about 10,000 times. Unfortunately, for the first 9,999 times I tried it the hard way. I tried every diet that came along. I would lose 5 pounds, then gain back 10 pounds. My biggest mistake was thinking about weight loss in terms of DIETING. This is a major blunder that most of us make. We go on a diet, lose the weight and then return to our old lifestyles. Unfortunately, due to the "rabbit food" mentality of many diets, we never even make it to our goal weight. Even if we do, the lost weight returns rapidly once we return to our old eating habits.

It is so important to get rid of the idea of dieting. I cannot stress this strongly enough. The word in itself implies a short-term commitment. No one ever goes on a diet with the intention of remaining on it forever. What we must do is commit ourselves to a lifestyle change to healthier eating. While our main goal may be weight loss, it is best not to even think of it at all. Once you begin eating healthier, the excess weight will often naturally disappear.

Years ago a co-worker of mine was told to eat healthier by her doctor because of cholesterol problems. At lunch time, as I happily waddled off to a high-fat feast, I would always say to her, "Well, Sue, which pasture are you going to graze in today?" I, like many people, thought that healthy eating was condemnation to a lifetime of nothing but fodder. How wrong I was!

Healthy eating is nothing but making simple adjustments to the things we love to eat. I am still able to enjoy all the delicious dishes I have always loved, but now that I have learned to prepare them in a healthy way, I can enjoy them without guilt or fear.

While I am neither a nutritionist or a physician, I have used the wonderful things they learned and shared with the world to lose the weight I could never lose before. Here is what I learned that helped Ken and me finally lose weight and keep it off for more than five years now:

- I had heard that medical experts felt that lowering the fat in our food intake could not only improve health in many cases but could also help in weight loss. I talked to my own doctor and also began reading books from my local bookstore and library on low-fat weight loss. Most experts seemed to feel that keeping the fat intake in the 20-40 fat gram per day range is best for women who wish to lose and in the 30-50 gram range per day for men. I personally decided to keep my own intake in the 25-35 grams per day range. Anyone who is interested in lowering the amount of fat intake should talk to their physician or nutritionist to determine the range that is best for them and should also try to read what the experts say. There are loads of good books on the subject.

- After determining that I would try eating less fat, I purchased several small paperback books that give the fat content in most foods, including those served in chain restaurants. By purchasing several, I was able to keep one at home, at work and in my car. I began reading through them to educate myself on the fat content of my favorite foods. There were some surprises. I was happy to learn that some of the foods that I figured had loads of fat were really not so bad. Of course, the reverse was sometimes true!

- I began reading labels. Almost every packaged food sold commercially has a label that gives the nutritional analysis of the food. I paid particular attention to the number of fat grams per serving.

- I went through my kitchen and removed all the high-fat foods that I knew my family shouldn't eat and replaced them with their low-fat and fat-free equivalents. I resolved that I would simply enjoy these products for their own good taste and not make the mistake of comparing them to the high-fat product they replaced. Making that comparison is self-defeating. So what if the fat-free version doesn't taste quite as rich as the old high-fat original! I'm just grateful that I can enjoy lower-fat and no-fat versions of everything from sour cream to potato chips without guilt and without the fear that all that fat will someday kill me.

- I took all of my favorite recipes and began working on them to remove as much fat as possible while keeping all of the good taste. In most cases it was simply a matter of using a leaner cut of meat, a low-fat equivalent of a high-fat ingredient or a little extra spice.

- I resolved that I would not count calories. Calorie counting is too reminiscent of the old dieting mentality. I simply decided to eat until I was comfortably full. Eating lots of fiber-rich foods is a good way to get full and stay that way. Beans, grains and vegetables are especially filling.

- I tried to reduce my sugar intake as much as possible, because sugar makes me hungry. I'm not the only one. A friend of mine won't even chew regular chewing gum because the sugar in it makes her hungry. It is self-defeating to fill up on a delicious low-fat meal then make myself hungry all over again with a sugary dessert. I learned to make sugar-free and fat-free desserts and to eat commercially prepared fat-free cookies and cakes only sparingly since they are still often high in sugar.

- I trained myself to wait a few minutes before helping myself to seconds at mealtime. Often we don't realize we how full we are until we stop eating for a moment.

- I determined that I would forever forget the word diet. I also resolved to not think about the fact that I was making any sort of "change" in my lifestyle. After all I was in my forties and pretty set in my ways. The idea of change didn't really appeal to me. I wanted to lose weight but I didn't want to have to change my life much to do it! I simply began using my low-fat and fat-free ingredients to prepare the dishes I had always prepared and always will prepare. It was simply a matter of using the healthier ingredients I now had on hand to make the dishes I loved. Because it is so painless, it has been so easy for me to maintain my healthier life and my weight loss. I know that I can prepare a low fat version of practically any dish that I want to eat.

A friend of mine, who lost 70 pounds through low-fat eating recently said to me, "Vicki, wouldn't it have been wonderful if doctors had learned about low-fat weight loss years ago. Just think of the heartache, the frustration and the years of letting fat ruin our lives that we could have been spared." Yes, it would have been wonderful, but I am just glad that they learned about it before I killed myself with fat.

THE BASICS OF EXERCISE

When I weighed 315 pounds, my attitude toward exercise was rather like that of my young relative. As a small child, he was, like me, a classic couch potato. His greatest form of exercise was pressing the buttons on the TV remote control. One day his father was particularly disturbed because he wanted to watch TV while the other children were playing ball. "Son," his dad exclaimed, "We are definitely going to have to get you on a good exercise program!" "Yipee!" the little boy replied. "I'm going to be on TV!"

I can relate to that. When I weighed 315 pounds I never did anything that required more than necessary movement if I could help it. As the old joke goes, the only exercise I ever got was pushing my luck! When I started eating healthy, I felt that if I also tried to begin an exercise program, I would be changing my lifestyle too much at once and would probably quickly quit. Therefore, I put exercising off. I didn't do any real exercise until I had lost over 100 pounds. I am not proud of that fact but in my case change had to come just a little at a time. I now realize I should have started exercising sooner.

We've already talked about making changes gradually. I started my healthier lifestyle by first changing the way I cooked. Then, in time came an exercise video with some easy walking movements. Now I have added workouts on a recumbent exercise bicycle and a treadmill to my routine. I try to do about 30-45 total minutes of exercise at least every other day. By taking little baby steps toward healthy eating and a healthy exercise program, I have been able to build up to a lifestyle that I would have quit in a heartbeat if I had started it all at once. I admit I should have started sooner but at least I finally got my act together. I am still no great fan of exercise but I do it because I know what it can do. Regular exercise can not only help us lose weight and keep it off. It can also help the body fight disease and reduce stress. Experts now say that it can possibly even extend your life. It's kind of like saving money. You might hate to do it, but the end results sure are nice.

Aerobic exercise is the most effective way to strengthen the heart and also contributes to both losing weight and keeping it off. There are excellent aerobic exercises for every taste and age. Brisk walking, either outdoors or on a treadmill, is an excellent aerobic exercise, as is cycling, running, jogging and stair climbing. Which ever exercise you choose, start slowly and build up. If you plan to buy exercise equipment such as a treadmill, stationary bicycle, stair climber or ski machine, spend some time trying them out in a store or health club before buying. Also question other people about their experiences with home exercise equipment. I bought my recumbent bicycle after a friend told me about hers. When she told me that it allows her to sit back in a comfortable seat and read while cycling, I knew I had to have one. That is definitely my kind of exercise!

For an inexpensive source of help in exercising, you may want to invest a few dollars in an exercise video. They range from very gentle workouts to really strenuous routines. A good way to find one that is right for you is to check out the selection at your local library or video rental store. You can try out the ones that seem right for you before buying.

Even the simple routines of daily life can be turned into effective exercise. Instead of casually strolling down the mall or to the mailbox, pick up your step and get some exercise out of it. If you work at a desk, get up and briskly walk around the office as frequently as possible. No matter what you are doing, put some pep into it and you will get the benefits of exercising your body.

Strength training is also important. Those exercises that tone the abdominals and other muscle groups aren't just for firming up, they are also helpful in giving muscles strength to protect us from some types of injury. No matter what kinds of exercise you are considering, your own personal program should be planned by you and your physician. You should begin any change in eating habits or exercise only with the advice and consent of your doctor. Food and exercise needs can vary considerably depending on the individual. Your health care professional can help you decide the perfect plan for you.

THE BASICS OF LOW-FAT MENU PLANNING

Planning meals is tough. If we prepare the same meals all of the time, our families often complain of eating the same old thing. If we get adventurous and serve new dishes, they want their familiar comfort foods back. The recipes and the menus in *Exceed The Feed Limit!* are for low-fat versions of old favorites and for new dishes that make use of ingredients that are popular with everyone. These are the dishes and the menus I prepared for my family while we were losing our weight and that I still prepare all of the time. Speaking of family, these are recipes that can be enjoyed by all members of the family. Everyone needs to eat healthier.

I freely admit to being a person who doesn't like to spend much time in the kitchen. I just don't have the time since I still work at the job I have held for years in addition to doing housework and writing cookbooks. Even if I had lots of time I wouldn't want to spend it in the kitchen. I love to eat but lots of cooking and kitchen clean-up just isn't for me. I'm not too crazy about grocery shopping either. That's why the recipes and menus you'll find here are for very quick and simple dishes containing common ingredients.

On the following pages are a few suggestions for breakfast, lunch and dinner. I hope you will find them helpful. Happy cooking!

WHAT'S FOR BREAKFAST???

I am often asked what I eat for breakfast. As a matter of fact, the only question I am asked more frequently is if I have had a facelift, since I formerly had three chins and now I have just one. The answer to that, in case you wondered, is no. I need one but I am a world class chicken! The skin has a marvelous elasticity. If it didn't, I would be kicking flab out of the way with every step. But back to the subject of breakfast. Before I began my low-fat lifestyle, I never ate breakfast at all. I just made up for it later in the day by consuming everything in sight. It was only when I began to eat healthy that I realized how important it is to eat breakfast. I once read that eating breakfast gets the metabolism going strong again after it has slowed down during sleep. That sounds reasonable to me. The morning meal also satisfies our appetites after a night of fasting. If we skip breakfast, it can be more than 16 hours between dinner and lunch the next day. We tend to go wild after that long without food.

Now I never miss breakfast. However, since I must be at my job by 8:00 A.M., I tend to eat the same easy things every work day and save the more elaborate morning meals for the weekend. The recipes for some of my favorite weekend breakfast treats are on the following pages. Listed below are some of my regular work day breakfasts:

- Oatmeal doctored with sugar substitute, fat-free liquid margarine and cinnamon. I sometimes add chopped peaches or raisins.
- Bagels, English muffins or several slices of toast with reduced calorie preserves and fat-free cream cheese or fat-free liquid margarine.
- Ready to eat fat-free, low-sugar cereal and sliced fruit.
- Commercially prepared low-fat toaster waffles or pancakes with liquid fat-free margarine and sugar-free maple syrup.
- Sweet roll taste-alikes or pancake taste-alikes (see recipe index).
- A sandwich made from several slices of 98% fat-free ham (deli-sliced) and fat-free Cheddar cheese on toast or an English muffin.

It is also important to drink something with every meal. At breakfast, I usually have fat-free, sugar-free hot chocolate or an orange-flavored, sugar-free beverage. This tastes a lot like orange juice and is vitamin enriched but has practically no calories. I love fruit juice, which is fat-free but quite high in calories. I am ashamed to say it but I would rather save my calories for things to eat, not things to drink!

LET'S DO LUNCH

Whether we are at home or at work, it is easy to have a low-fat, filling lunch. Since most of us are too busy to cook at lunch time, sandwiches, salads and soups are often quick and simple to prepare. They are staples for many of us, especially if we have to pack a lunch for ourselves, our spouses and our children to eat at work or school.

It is terrific that there is such a fantastic selection of low-fat and fat-free sandwich ingredients, salad dressings and soups in the grocery store these days. Thin-sliced deli-style meats such as ham and turkey paired with fat-free cheese on hearty whole-grain bread are a wonderful lunch time treat, especially when dressed with a spicy mustard. It is fun to haunt the condiments aisle in the market to look at some of the unique and delicious mustards that are now available. You can even doctor fat-free mayonnaise with herbs or spices to concoct your own gourmet sandwich spreads. One neat trick is to add low-fat or fat-free dry salad dressing mix to the mayo. This makes a wonderful sandwich spread, salad dressing or dip.

I love great big sandwiches and a good way to add bulk to them is by adding lots of lettuce, tomato or sprouts. If you haven't tried alfalfa sprouts on a sandwich, do it. They are available in most grocery stores and add a terrific taste. If you have to eat on the job, you still don't have to limit your choices to cold sandwiches. A friend of mine puts a couple of fat-free wieners in a thermos then covers them with hot, low-fat onion or chicken soup. At lunch, she eats the soup, then makes herself hot dogs with the wieners. She also buys the big bags of pre-chopped salad ingredients available in most grocery stores and often makes herself a big salad in a sealable plastic bag. She adds some deli-sliced ham or turkey, a little fat-free cheese and has herself a lovely chef's salad with just a few minutes work. Before adding the salad ingredients to the bag, she pours in her dressing. It remains at the bottom of the bag until lunch time, when she shakes the bag to distribute it. That way it doesn't wilt the greens. She eats from the bag, then throws it away. No empty bowl to have to take home!

Many offices provide microwave ovens for the use of their employees, which really opens up the possibilities for quick, hot lunches. From frozen commercially-prepared low-fat meals to leftovers from the night before, the microwave allows us to eat what we please. It also makes possible break time treats such as low-fat popcorn or even nachos.

I work in an office that provides a microwave and refrigerator for the use of employees, but to be honest, I seldom make use of them because I like to eat out at lunch. Most fast food and full service restaurants now provide low-fat menu selections that make it easy to dine out any time of day. Many chain restaurants even have pamphlets giving the nutritional information on all of their foods that are available if you ask. Some even print it on the menu. Of course, books listing the fat grams in foods also usually include chain restaurants. Even those restaurants that do not have low-fat menu items are usually very accommodating if you ask them to prepare your selection in a low-fat manner.

Some offices provide cafeterias for their employees. Many are very responsive to requests for low-fat selections. I was very honored when I was told that a group of employees gave a copy of my book *Live! Don't Diet!* to their cafeteria manager and requested that she prepare dishes from it. She now regularly offers low-fat selections and even posts the fat grams in the day's selections.

Just as with breakfast and dinner, you have complete freedom to choose delicious, low-fat hot or cold meals at lunch. You can enjoy a homemade treat or eat out without the least deprivation and with the knowledge that you are treating your body right! What could be easier or more gratifying?

The Age-Old Question: What's For Dinner?

I imagine that thousands of years ago cave-dwelling cooks stood over their fires at the last minute and pondered what to fix for dinner, just as I do practically every night. I am the type person who never knows what I plan to serve until I get home from work and see what is in my refrigerator. Fortunately, most of my low-fat recipes are so easy they can be made in minutes.

For those of you who like to plan your meals, I have put together a few suggested menus from some of the recipes in this book. As for me, I'll probably still throw things together at the last minute. Organizational skills are one type of self-improvement that I'm too disorganized to ever learn! I'm the same way with cooking. I have good intentions about planning meals in advance but never get around to it.

I have read that the more dishes that are served as part of a meal, the more we tend to eat. That sounds like a perfect reason to prepare fewer dishes. I'm open to any justification for cooking less! That's why I usually serve just a main course with one or two vegetables or a salad.

Onion Baked Steak*
Fat-Free Mashed Potatoes*
Steamed Carrots

Chicken Picante*
Steamed Rice
Mexican Corn*

Steak In A Stew*
Delicious Layered Slaw*
Warm French Bread

Rich Ravioli Casserole*
Green Beans
Kind Of Greek Salad*

Quick And Tender Turkey*
My Favorite Sweet Potatoes*
English Peas

Lemon-Herb Chicken*
Easy Baked Rice*
Sautéed Broccoli*

Slow Cooker Oriental Beef*
Steamed Rice
Jellied Fresh Fruit Salad*

American Dinner Pie*
Snappy Cabbage*
Cornbread

Hearty White Chili*
Crunchy Apple Salad*
Custard Cornbread*

Crispy Oven Chicken*
Barbecued Potatoes*
Cole Slaw

Tasty Tamale Pie*
Mexican Spinach Salad*

Shortcut Lasagna*
Mixed Green Salad

Busy Day Ham And Dumplings*
Steamed Broccoli
Mixed Green Salad

Country-Style Pork*
Autumn Fruited Rice*
Squash Casserole*

*Denotes Recipes In This Book

THE BASICS OF LOW-FAT SHOPPING

Before I wised up to the benefits of eating low-fat, my favorite meal was a big charcoal-broiled ribeye steak, a baked potato dripping with butter and a salad topped with loads of creamy dressing, followed by a huge piece of cheesecake. No wonder I weighed 315 pounds. Actually, I can still enjoy this meal and not have to worry about it. Now I eat a sensibly-sized sirloin with the visible fat removed and a large baked potato with fat-free liquid margarine and fat-free sour cream. My salad is still topped with creamy dressing and I still have cheesecake, although now the dressing and cheesecake are fat-free. This meal is just as good to me as the high-fat version used to be because I know I can have it without harming my health or my weight.

There are those among you who may be saying, "The low-fat versions just aren't as tasty! I'll never be able to get used to fat-free sour cream or cheese." Don't let yourself think this way. It is terribly self-defeating. Those low-fat versions of my favorite high-fat foods enabled me to continue eating my favorite meals–the ones that caused me to weigh 315 pounds–while losing 180 pounds. I could still have cheesy lasagna, rich casseroles and creamy desserts. I didn't have to give them up for the rest of my life. I certainly believe the slight difference in taste is worth it! Besides, in a very short time the low-fat versions will begin to taste better to you than the high-fat ones.

If you think about it, fat has no taste. It just has an oily richness that acts as a conveyor of the flavors of the other ingredients in a dish. That's right! The flavors are in the other ingredients, not the fat. By giving up the fat you are not giving up flavor. You are only allowing yourself to enjoy the true, delicious taste of your foods.

It can truly become an adventure to go grocery shopping when you are living a low-fat lifestyle. Every day more and more great low-fat products are appearing on the shelves, thanks to the demand of health conscious consumers. I recently came home from grocery shopping and told my husband, "I have got to get a life! The most exciting thing that happened to me today was discovering a delicious new fat-free, 10 calorie per serving cheese spread at the store!" I was just kidding, but it really is fun to discover new products that we can enjoy. After all, much of life is centered around food. Just because we are living a healthy lifestyle doesn't mean we don't love to eat!

When you shop for groceries there are some things you definitely need to remember. I have said it before and will say it over and over–LEARN TO READ THE NUTRITIONAL DATA ON LABELS! Pay particular attention to the amount of fat in each serving. If you have special dietary needs, due to health problems, you may also need to monitor the sodium content and the saturated fat content. Even if you do not have special needs, you may wish to monitor the sodium content, particularly if you retain water easily.

While I don't count calories, I do pay attention to the calories per serving on labels. If one brand is lower in calories than another, I will buy that brand. I also try to avoid purchasing snacks and desserts that have a zillion calories per serving despite their low fat content because I know myself well enough to know that one serving of them is never enough for me. Consuming a half gallon of fat-free ice cream at 90 calories per half-cup will not help us lose weight!

On the following pages, I would like to share with you some of the ingredients that allowed me to lose 180 pounds and Ken to lose 90 pounds without deprivation. These are simply some of the basic foods that are important not only in losing weight, but in living a healthy lifestyle. As you live your own healthier lifestyle, you will discover more and more foods that you and your family can enjoy, but this may help you. Let's get out the grocery cart and get started!

Beef

Many people have the misconception that beef is loaded with fat but that isn't necessarily true. As with all meats, you simply have to eat the lower-fat cuts, remove all visible fat and cut back on portions. The difference in the amount of fat in the different cuts of beef can be astonishing. A 3-ounce serving of prime rib can have a whopping 30 grams of fat, while a 3-ounce serving of top round roast can have as few as 6 grams.

When buying beef, always buy top round or top sirloin, because those cuts are lowest in fat. Be sure to also remove any visible fat remaining. If buying ground beef, ask the butcher to freshly grind top round trimmed of all fat. In many grocery stores, ultra-lean ground beef is sold already packaged. Be sure that the amount of fat per serving is listed on the label and it is below 10 grams per serving. Many stores market specially prepared ground beef that has as little as 7 grams of fat per serving.

Since low-fat cuts of beef and low-fat ground beef do not have enough fat to keep them from sticking when sautéed, it is important to lightly spray your skillet with no-stick cooking spray. Low-fat cuts of beef may also be less tender, so you may wish to marinate them before cooking or sprinkle them with commercially prepared meat tenderizer.

If you are preparing ground beef for a casserole, soup or sauce, it is important to remove any fat remaining after cooking by blotting the meat with paper towels. You may also want to put the cooked ground beef in a colander and run hot water over it, then pat it dry. I have done this for a number of years now and have never had any problems with my plumbing result from it, but if you have delicate plumbing, you may need to skip this step.

If you are serving beef or any meat, learn to make it a supporting player in your meal, not the star attraction. Serve it with lots of vegetables on the side, or better still, make it part of a casserole, soup or pasta sauce. You will be surprised at how far a little meat will go when it is combined with other ingredients. Six ounces of meat, either ground or cut into small bite-sized pieces, will serve a whole family. You will still get a bit of meat in each bite. After all, it's the flavor and texture of the meat that counts. It doesn't take huge chunks of it. When I began cooking low-fat, I reduced the ground beef in my chili from 2 pounds to 6 ounces. I simply added more beans, onions and tomatoes to make up for it. It was actually better. I made similar adjustments in all of my recipes containing meat. I really got many more compliments from my family after I changed the recipes!

PORK

I never expected that pork could be part of a low-fat lifestyle, but we eat it regularly at my house. Like beef, pork can vary from very high in fat to very low in fat. Here again the important point is to read labels and make sure you are buying pork and pork products that are low in fat. Pork tenderloin, trimmed of all visible fat, contains only 4 fat grams in a 3-ounce serving. On the other hand, spareribs can contain 26 grams of fat in 3 ounces and pork shoulder can contain 13 grams in the same size serving. Since I only want to use the cut that is lowest in fat, I always buy tenderloin. It can be roasted whole, sliced into chops or cutlets, cubed for kebobs and stews or cut into thin slivers for stir-frying. I even slice it into long strips to barbecue like spareribs on occasion

More low-fat and no-fat pork products are becoming available every day. It is possible to buy ham and wieners that have practically no fat, as well as low-fat smoked sausage. Fat-free cold cuts, such as salami and bologna are also available. We have hot dogs and ham sandwiches at our house regularly. Along with the low-fat dairy products, the growing availability of low-fat meats has made it so easy to eat like a normal person. We don't have to sacrifice a thing!

POULTRY

Surprisingly, chicken and turkey breast are similar in fat content to the leanest cuts of beef and pork. That may especially interest the people who think that they can only eat chicken if they are eating low-fat. However, it is good to serve chicken and turkey often, since they can be prepared in so many terrific ways. In fact, many recipes featuring pork can be used interchangeably with those containing chicken or turkey.

It is best to use only the breast meat of chicken or turkey since it is considerably lower in fat than the dark meat. A 3-ounce portion of breast meat contains about 3 fat grams. Never eat the skin. There is a lot of fat in poultry skin. Many food experts do feel that it doesn't matter whether the skin is removed before or after cooking.

I usually buy boneless, skinless chicken breasts since they are quick and easy to work with, but the bone-in breasts work equally well in most recipes. The availability of turkey cutlets and boneless roasts cut from the breast also makes regularly serving turkey so easy. It is not just a holiday treat anymore.

If you are buying a fresh or frozen turkey or turkey breast, be sure to notice if the label states whether or not it has been pre-basted. Some turkeys are injected with oil to make the meat more moist. Others are injected with broth. The solution used to baste the turkey may raise the fat content of the meat considerably. Choose only those that have been pre-basted with broth or with nothing.

Ground turkey is another product we need to purchase selectively. Some people like to use it in place of ground beef. Make sure the ground turkey you buy is 100% breast meat only. Some ground turkey even contains skin and is high in fat. If you cannot find 100% pure ground turkey breast, have the butcher grind it for you.

Precooked, low-fat turkey breast pieces and ham pieces, weighing 1-2 pounds are available in most grocery stores, as are precooked chicken breasts. Since I like to spend as little time in the kitchen as possible, I keep these on hand to use in casseroles and stir-fried dishes, as well as in sandwiches. Using precooked turkey and chicken breasts can cut down considerably on time when you don't want to have to cook the meat from scratch. If you must be careful about sodium, look for low-sodium brands, since processed meats are often quite high in sodium. Speaking of processed meats, both turkey and chicken-based low-fat versions of popular sandwich meats such as ham, salami, bologna and wieners are on the market.

Chicken and turkey are not only delicious hot, they are equally good cold. After all, who doesn't love a wonderful chicken salad or sliced turkey sandwich? For versatility and taste, chicken and turkey are a terrific part of a healthy and wonderful low-fat lifestyle.

SEAFOOD

Remember this corny joke: "I'm on the seafood diet–I eat all the food I see!" I can relate to that, even if it is a joke. In years gone by that was the only diet I could ever stick to! Well, all joking aside, seafood can be a wonderful addition to our low-fat menus. As always, you need to read labels carefully since some types of fish are much higher in fat than others. Cod, flounder, grouper, haddock, perch, pike, pollock and snapper only average 1 gram of fat in a 3-ounce serving while mackerel can contain up to 12 grams.

Practically all varieties of shellfish are very low in fat. Lobster, crabs and scallops have only 1 gram in a 3-ounce serving, while shrimp, oysters and mussels have as many as 2 grams per serving. Since fish or seafood is especially delicious grilled, sautéed or steamed, it is easy to prepare ultra low-fat seafood main dishes. However, even that old favorite, fried seafood can be made in a delicious low-fat way by using our oven-frying technique or by frying it in only 1 tablespoon of oil.

If you think the old days of drawn butter or tartar sauce served along with your favorite seafood are behind you if you are eating low-fat, think again. Liquid fat-free margarine with a little lemon makes a terrific drawn butter-style dipping sauce, while delicious fat-free tartar sauce is available in stores. It can also be made at home.

Many grocery stores now feature fresh seafood counters. They have every kind of fresh fish and shellfish you can imagine. Not only do they sell great seafood, they will tell you the best ways to prepare it and may even steam it for you if you ask. My grocery store's seafood counter features a section of special spices, seasonings and sauces to use in preparing fish and shellfish. Some of the special seasonings are even good on vegetables or in dips or salad dressings. As I like to say—experiment!

CHEESES

Hooray for the makers of fat-free and low-fat cheeses! From fat-free cottage cheese in rich lasagna to fat-free cream cheese in silky cheesecake to fat-free Cheddar in gooey casseroles, these wonderful products are among the most important because they enable us to enjoy so many dishes that were previously taboo to those wanting to lose weight or eat healthy. After all, many cheeses have a tremendous 9 fat grams per ounce—and who can eat just one ounce?

Some years ago, I bought a package of fat-free shredded Cheddar cheese at the grocery. As the cashier totaled my purchases, she picked up the package of cheese and said "Is this stuff any good?" "Yes, if you like to eat pencil erasers," I replied, only half in jest. At the time I didn't know how to use it properly. Many people still don't, which is one reason they sometimes complain that they don't like it.

With the exception of fat-free Parmesan cheese, many types of fat-free cheese do not come out well when used to top a casserole or dish that requires lengthy cooking. They get hard. It is best to add these cheeses just before serving and let the heat of the dish melt them. Briefly topping the dish with a piece of foil or plastic wrap can hold in the heat and help the melting process. Shredded fat-free cheese works best when it is layered or mixed with other ingredients in a casserole. Then it acts and tastes much like regular shredded Cheddar.

Some people I know like to have the best of both worlds. They will use fat-free shredded cheese in a casserole, but will use a tablespoon or two of finely shredded regular cheese as a topping or in combination with the fat-free cheese. When divided between 4 servings of a casserole or other entree, this only adds a few fat grams, so you might like to try doing this yourself.

Today, you can find a fat-free version of almost any cheese from cream cheese to mozzarella. If you haven't tried fat-free cheese recently, I suggest you try it again. Many of them are now quite delicious. Some of the processed fat-free cheeses are especially good and melt really well. Try several brands. You may find you like one better than another. If you plan to eat a fat-free cheese in a salad or sandwich or with crackers, I suggest you let it come to room temperature first. This enhances the flavor and texture.

Personally, I am eternally grateful to the makers of fat-free cheese. So what if it isn't always quite as rich and delicious as the high-fat version. I have grown to love it because it allows me to enjoy many of my very favorite dishes without fat or fear.

Sour Cream

Creamy dips, gooey casseroles, rich sauces. Where would these treats be without sour cream? At 45 fat grams per cup, sour cream is both the curse and the blessing of many wonderful dishes. That is why it is so terrific that we can enjoy sour cream and all of the dishes it so wonderfully enhances without the fat. Fat-free sour cream is a real boon to the weight and health conscious.

Once I made plain old California dip with fat-free sour cream and dehydrated onion soup mix, which also has no fat. I took it to a social gathering, along with fat-free chips. I thought I had made enough for a huge crowd but it was gone in minutes. People could not get enough of it. Two small children ate about a pint each before their Mom pulled them away. This not only shows the great taste of fat-free foods but also how readily children will eat them. Only small babies need much fat in their diet. If we begin to train our children to enjoy low-fat foods early in life, they will no doubt lead healthier lives.

Fat-free sour cream is an especially welcome product because it can replace some of the creaminess and rich taste that fat used to add to our foods. For example, I use fat-free sour cream instead of butter and whole milk in preparing packaged macaroni and cheese. Like many packaged mixes, the macaroni and cheese contains very little fat until you add the butter and whole milk at home. The sour cream is a great replacement.

Eggs And Egg Substitutes

A medium egg contains 5 fat grams. Practically all of the fat is in the yolk. While nutritionists recommend limiting eggs to three per week, people with high cholesterol may need to limit them even further, depending upon the advice of their physician or nutritionist. While it is best to eat high-fiber fruits and breads or whole-grain cereals for breakfast, if you feel that you must eat eggs, try scrambling several egg whites with a little yellow food color added. That way you can enjoy eggs without any fat. Use no-stick cooking spray to keep the eggs from sticking. Serve with several low-fat ham slices or low-fat smoked sausage and toast. If you enjoy stuffed eggs for lunches or picnics, try stuffing the cooked whites with seasoned fat-free cream cheese, chicken salad or tuna salad.

Fat-free egg substitutes are a terrific way to enjoy eggs without the fat and without the trouble of separating the white from the yolk. Egg substitutes are ready to use right out of the carton. If you hate to clean up, that means no shells to have to throw away or extra bowls to wash. If you use egg substitutes exclusively, that also means having more room in the refrigerator since there are no large egg cartons taking up space.

"But I want real eggs!" you may be saying. Most egg substitutes are real eggs. They are made from egg whites. They are indistinguishable from whole eggs when used to prepare baked goods. They also make very tasty scrambled eggs and omelets. As an added bonus, most brands have only 30-40 calories per 1/4 cup serving compared to 79 in a whole egg. Try several brands to find the one you like best.

OILS, COOKING SPRAYS AND MARGARINE

There is no way around it, cooking oils are pure fat and have an average 12-14 fat grams per tablespoon. That makes their use limited on a low-fat lifestyle, unless you want to blow all of your daily fat allowance on a few tablespoons of oil for frying. Not me. I want to use my fat grams for real food! If you must, you can prepare pan fried foods by cooking several servings with 1 tablespoon of oil. However, you can use no-stick cooking sprays to fry or sauté without any oil or butter. Just keep the heat fairly low. Better still, use the oven-frying technique that I use in several of the recipes in this book. Just lightly spray the pan with cooking spray, add the food, which is also lightly sprayed and bake at a medium-high temperature. Cooking sprays are available in a variety of flavors including butter-flavor and olive oil-flavor. Just remember that cooking sprays also contain oil and don't go overboard when using them. Most cooking sprays contain about 1 fat gram in a 1 1/4 -second application. This is enough to coat a skillet or casserole dish.

When I began eating low-fat one of the things I missed most was butter and margarine. Butter and margarine have 11-12 fat grams per tablespoon. Even reduced-fat margarines contain an average 5 grams per tablespoon. Then, several years ago ultra-low fat and fat-free margarines began appearing on the shelves. That was a great day for me. While the original products took some getting used to, they are getting better and better. Some of the new fat-free liquid margerines are almost as tasty as the real thing and are almost calorie-free.

MILK

We have always been told how good milk is for us, yet a 1-cup serving of whole milk contains 8 fat grams. It also contains 150 calories. As the public becomes more health conscious, whole milk is becoming less popular. Since it is so high in fat, you can see why. Many consumers now use 2% milk instead. However 2% milk still contains 5 fat grams and has 121 calories in a 1-cup serving. Even 1% milk has 3 fat grams per cup. Why not have the pleasures of milk without any of the fat? Learn to use skim milk. Once you do, you won't know the difference. As a matter of fact, lots of people who have made the change say that even 1% milk now tastes unpleasantly oily to them and whole milk is like drinking cream.

Some brands of skim milk are better than others. Try them till you find the one you like best. Some of them are virtually indistinguishable from whole milk in appearance and are quite delicious. Adding a little non-fat dry milk powder or evaporated skim milk to the carton can make them even more like whole milk.

Non-fat dry milk and evaporated skim milk are also good to use in cooking when you want a richer milk flavor. They have no fat, yet can make cream sauces and other recipes containing milk seem almost decadently rich.

Buttermilk is also a terrific way to add great flavor to foods. Despite its name, low-fat buttermilk is commonly available. It can also perk up a variety of foods, from soups to salad dressings. If you don't use a lot of buttermilk, you might prefer powdered low-fat buttermilk.

MAYONNAISE AND SALAD DRESSING

In the past, the most complaints I heard about the taste of a low-fat food was about mayonnaise. Practically everybody hated it. In truth, it used to taste a lot like wallpaper paste must taste– gummy and bland. But as with many low-fat and fat-free versions of our favorite high-fat foods, the quality has improved dramatically.

Quite frankly, I didn't use fat-free mayonnaise for a number of years, having tried it and found it terrible. I preferred instead to use fat-free Ranch salad dressing in recipes that called for mayonnaise. However, about a year ago I tried fat-free mayonnaise again and found it to be much better. I use it all the time now in all of the same ways I formerly used the high-fat version. It is fun to use it by the heaping spoonfuls without guilt.

I really don't know how we could ever be so crazy about real mayonnaise to start with. Not only does it have 11 fat grams and 100 calories in a tablespoon, but the primary ingredients are oil and eggs. That doesn't sound too appetizing, does it? Well, despite its drawbacks, it does taste wonderful and fortunately the current fat-free versions come closer than ever to capturing its taste. If you still can't get used to it, try the next best thing, the reduced-fat version. You can find at least one national brand that has only 3 fat grams per tablespoon.

While low-fat and fat-free salad dressings have always been quite good, they also continue to improve in taste. Commercially prepared low-fat and fat-free dressings are available bottled and as dried packaged mixes that you prepare at home. The dried mixes are really versatile. They can be added to fat-free mayonnaise to make a great dip or sandwich spread.

CEREALS

Cereals are a vital part of healthy eating–and not just at breakfast. Cereal makes a really great snack too. As with most foods, there are some really healthy cereals and some really unhealthy ones. It is important to shop carefully. A number of cereals are fairly low in fat but still high in sugar. Try to avoid these. Choose cereals that are not only low in fat but low in sugar or sugar-free.

If you are really interested in eating healthy, some of the no-frills cereals are the best choices. Basic cereals, such as shredded wheat and bran-based cereals are full of fiber and nutrients. As we know, fiber is vital to good health and also helps us keep that full feeling that is so important when we are trying to lose weight.

In addition to being so good for us, the basic cereals have another benefit. They are usually less expensive than the cereals that have added fruits or other frills. They are also easier to find in generic brands, which can help cut costs even further. If you want fruit, you can add it yourself at home. You can even flavor plain cereal up with some spices. A little cinnamon or nutmeg, along with a sprinkle of granulated sugar substitute can made a basic cereal seem more special. At our house, cereal often substitutes for a snack or dessert.

When buying cereals, don't pass the hot cereals up. They are also an extremely important addition to a low-fat lifestyle. Not only are they healthful, they are a real comfort food. Nothing is more satisfying than starting or ending the day with a big bowl of hot cereal. I love to dress it up with fruit, cinnamon, granulated sugar substitute and fat-free liquid margarine. My favorite hot cereal is oatmeal but I also love cream of wheat. When buying oatmeal, get the quick-cooking variety rather than the instant kind that comes in packets. I personally find that the quick-cooking kind has a much more appealing texture than the instant since it retains more of the whole-grain consistency that makes it so good for you. Cream of wheat and multi-grain hot cereals are also great choices for a quick, warming start to a busy day.

CONDIMENTS

If vegetables, breads and grains are the heart of a low-fat lifestyle, condiments and spices are its soul. Consider this: when you season your foods with butter or oils, you are adding nothing but a greasy, slick taste. In contrast, condiments such as salsas, relishes, jams and preserves add sparkle and interest without any fat. There is nothing like the zesty taste of a chunky salsa served with Mexican food, or the marvelous pure fruit flavor of preserves spread on warm bread.

Check out all the various sections of your grocery where condiments are found. Don't forget the jam, jellies and syrups, the sauces and gravies, the pickles and relishes. An amazing number of them are fat-free or low-fat. It is fun to see just how many of these wonderful treats there are. Eating can never get dull!

While the stores are full of enough condiments to keep you happy forever, there is something very gratifying about making your own from time to time. Summer, when vegetables and fruits are plentiful and inexpensive, is the ideal time to treat yourself to homemade relishes or jams. They can be made in minutes and many of them can be successfully frozen or canned for later use.

I like to use aspartame-based sugar substitute in my homemade condiments instead of sugar. This removes a significant amount of calories. I am ashamed to say that I have been known to eat a whole jar of homemade preserves in one day. Since they contain nothing but fruit, sugar substitute and pectin, I can do it without feeling guilty. Of course, my family gets mad at me for eating them up, since they love them too.

I prefer to freeze homemade condiments made with sugar substitutes, when I make them in quantity. However, the makers of sugar substitutes and the makers of canning products are beginning to come out with recipes using sugar substitutes in canned goods. If you like to can your condiments, but don't want to use sugar, you might consult the recipe books put out by the major canning product makers.

While they are not technically considered condiments, herbs and spices also lend zest to your recipes. If fact, many food experts say that adding them to your food is an ideal way to make up for the fat you have taken out. The spice section of the grocery is full of familiar and not so familiar spices, as well as other marvelous flavoring agents, including extracts and seasoning blends. Remember to also check out the produce section. Fresh herbs are often available in season.

There are a million ways to use condiments and spices to add thrill to your meals. A spoonful of relish is terrific with dried beans or sliced ham. It can also be added to fat-free mayonnaise to make a spicy salad dressing. Spicy salsas are turning up in everything from main dishes to dips. Jams and jellies are not just for breakfast anymore. They are finding their way into everything from appetizers to desserts.

While fancy restaurants wouldn't be caught dead with a ketchup bottle on the table, many neighborhood eateries keep an array of condiments on every table. The restaurants do it to save the server steps. Since I am generally the server in my house, I like to save steps too. I keep everyday condiments that aren't refrigerated, like mustard, ketchup, steak sauce and hot sauce in a little basket in my cupboard. That way they can be whisked out at mealtime.

Whether you prefer the comforting flavors of these everyday condiments or the more exotic tastes of condiments from around the world, they make your low-fat lifestyle an adventure. That is definitely not the case with dull old butter or oil. Now, aren't you glad they are out of your life!

BREADS

I have always loved bread. When I was a very chubby child, my Mom would try in vain to keep me from pigging out. Once, as I stuffed another roll in my mouth, Mom said reprovingly, "Vicki, three rolls!" "No, Mom," I said, patting my fat little tummy, "just one great big roll." As I grew older that one great big roll that was my stomach did grow into three, or maybe four. Amazing as it may be, bread helped me lose that tummy and go from a size 52 to size 8.

Most breads are surprisingly low in fat. They are also very filling and very comforting. With the exception of croissants and some specialty breads, even most commercially prepared breads have little more than 1/2 to 1 gram of fat per slice. However, as always, be sure to read the nutritional information on the package before purchasing. It is best to eat whole-grain breads. The dense, chewy texture of whole grain breads makes them especially satisfying, as well as more nutritious. If you would like two slices of bread for the calorie cost of one, you'll want to try the reduced-calorie breads. It is also possible to buy reduced-calorie buns and rolls. Most breads are great served plain, but a little fat-free or low-fat margarine or low-sugar jam can make them extra-special.

While most of us may be too busy to prepare time-consuming home-made breads, even making a simple quick bread from scratch can give you a great sense of satisfaction, a delicious treat to eat, and, as an added bonus, a heavenly aroma coming from your kitchen! Even if you have just a minute, you can make fresh bread for your family.

One of the most popular members of the bread family is the bagel. Once a specialty of the big city, every crossroads now has a shop where fresh bagels are prepared daily. Even convenience stores have a supply in their freezer. Since they are extremely low in fat and very filling, they are great for healthy eating. But beware. Some of them can contain over 400 calories each–so don't get carried away!

English muffins are also wonderful. Like bagels, they now come in every flavor under the sun and can provide a great breakfast or snack. English muffins and bagels are also really versatile. Whether you eat them plain, use them for sandwiches or for instant pizza, they can add heartiness and terrific taste to our low-fat menus.

To round out our shopping tour of the bread department, don't forget the tortillas. In many stores it is possible to find packaged fresh tortillas.

The taste of the fresh tortillas is especially wonderful. If you have the time one day, you might even like to try making your own. They are not difficult and are worth the effort. Both corn and flour tortillas are really jacks of all trades. Serve either along with your main course just as you would any bread.

Corn tortillas, of course, are also essential for such wonderful treats as tacos and enchiladas They can also be used to make homemade tortilla chips. Flour tortillas are just as versatile. They can be used for a multitude of purposes from burritos to dumplings. A dampened flour tortilla pressed into a pie plate can even pinch-hit for pie crust. While fat-free corn and flour tortillas are available, most regular tortillas are still very low in fat. Tortillas can also be found in both the refrigerated and frozen foods section of your grocery store.

Vegetables, Fruits And Grains

When I was a child my Mom would tease me about being a "bottomless pit" because she could never fill me up. I just loved to eat. That is how I eventually ended up weighing 315 pounds. Well, I guess I'm still a bottomless pit. I still love to eat. The big difference is that I have learned what to eat. I used to fill up on junk food. I still fill up on things that taste good but the big difference is that these things are also good for me. Vegetables, fruits and grains are by far the most essential foods to those of us who want to lose weight and eat healthy. They are not only nutritious but are also very filling. They are, for the most part, fiber-rich and foods that are high in fiber keep us satisfied. Because I fill up on them, I'm not tempted to fall off the wagon.

Fresh vegetables and fruits are no longer just seasonal treats. During our winter, they are imported from countries south of the equator where it is the summer growing season. On the iciest days we can have fresh asparagus, watermelon and strawberries as well as exotic fruits and vegetables that are totally new to us. It is fun to buy new vegetables and fruits which may be unfamiliar and experiment with them.

With the availability of the microwave oven and electronic steamers, fresh vegetable preparation has never been easier. Some stores even package them already trimmed, cleaned and ready for cooking. Frozen vegetables and unsweetened frozen fruits are also convenient options. The ultimate in convenience is canned vegetables and fruits. Try to buy low-sodium canned vegetables or rinse them well since they are often high in sodium. Always buy juice-packed canned fruits rather than those in sugar-sweetened syrup.

While all vegetables are mega-important, some, such as beans, potatoes, brown rice and other whole grains are particularly vital. They are "power foods"–high in satisfying carbohydrates and fiber, yet extremely low in fat. "But pigging out on a potato just isn't as much fun as pigging out on chocolate cake!" you may be saying. Nonsense! What does pigging out on chocolate cake get you except fatter and more depressed? You can eat a whole pound of tasty oven-fried, fat-free French fries for less calories than a little piece of chocolate cake. A pound of French fries is not only fun but will fill you up and keep you full. The cake won't do anything but make you want more. Which would you rather be–full, fit and fabulous or just plain fatter by the day? The foods you feed yourself will make all the difference.

Seasoning is very important in making our vegetables taste special without fat. The new liquid fat-free margarines are wonderful on vegetables and a little low-fat deli-sliced ham adds a delightful smoky taste to green vegetables and dried beans. Chicken bouillon is also great to season many vegetables. Don't forget gravy! Make your own fat-free gravy with flour, beef or chicken bouillon and skim milk or water. I usually opt for the commercially prepared gravies from the grocery. Many are very low in fat.

Load up your shopping cart with as many vegetables, fruits and grains as your refrigerator or cupboard will hold. With the exception of the avocado, they are all virtually fat-free. Make them the sun around which your low-fat world revolves. You may be rewarded with better health, more energy and the figure of your dreams!

DESSERTS

Desserts can be the most wonderful and the most terrible things in the world. Like a really gorgeous person who is terribly shallow, desserts look magnificent while hiding the fact that they often have no nutritional value. In fact, they could also be compared to a really gorgeous person who is also a hit-man since they might eventually kill you if you aren't careful. Okay, maybe I'm being overly dramatic but you know what I mean. They are too often loaded with fat and sugar, which over time can lead your body into deep trouble.

Since I am a sugar addict, I try to make desserts that are totally sugar-free or very low in sugar. As I have mentioned before, a little sugar just makes me want more. Even if cookies, ice cream or cake are fat-free, they can be loaded with tons of empty sugar calories. As much as we would like to think otherwise, you can't eat unlimited amounts of that stuff and lose weight. While fat-free and sugar free ice cream can still carry quite a caloric wallop if eaten in unlimited amounts, some of the aspartame-sweetened fruit flavored popsicles now on the market contain as little as 15 calories each. You could eat a whole box of these in one day and not be in much trouble.

The ideal solution is to eat desserts that are fat-free and sweetened with sugar substitute, even though we still need to limit these to sensible amounts. Sugar-free, fat-free puddings and gelatins can be used to make a variety of delicious desserts, as can fresh and canned fruits. Speaking of fruit, don't ignore fresh fruit as a dessert or snack. It is more filling than pudding, pie or cake and is more nutritionally valuable as well. A melange of fruit and melon chunks makes a most attractive and delicious dessert, even for company. One of the most memorable desserts I ever had was a gorgeous assortment of fresh mixed fruits served in a stemmed goblet and topped at the last minute with sparkling club soda. Create beautiful, healthy desserts and congratulate yourself on being both gorgeous and intelligent!

THE BASICS OF LOW-FAT COOKING

My daughter, Ashley, likes to joke that I should have named my first book *Live! Don't Fry It!* instead of *Live! Don't Diet!* While I have to give her points for that one, it isn't quite true. You can still enjoy the crisp taste of fried foods when you are eating low-fat. It's just that you fry them in a healthier way. Almost any method of cooking can be used to prepare low-fat treats but some of the most delightful and familiar flavors can be created by oven-frying and sautéing since many of our favorite comfort foods before we started watching our fat intake were fried.

Microwaving and steaming are also great ways to enjoy the delicious taste of vegetables with little time or trouble. On the next few pages, I would like to share with you the basics of these tried and true cooking techniques.

"Frying" The Low-Fat Way

Some time in the very, very distant future, anthropologists will be digging around in the relics of our era and will come across one of our cookbooks. They will be mystified by the fact that the seemingly intelligent and sophisticated people of our day actually cooked food by throwing it into a vat of boiling fat until it was brown and hard. This (along with trying to figure out the purpose of a man's necktie!) will completely baffle them. Actually it is already starting to baffle many people here and now. Frying not only completely hides the natural taste of the food, it is unhealthy and messy. That last reason alone is reason enough to stop frying. Nothing is worse that having to clean grease out of dishes and off of walls.

Okay, so my pep talk above is not convincing. You and I love the taste of fried foods and don't want to give them up. There are several ways to enjoy a reasonable facsimile of fried foods without the fat or the mess. I am a really lazy cook so I prefer oven-frying. It is not messy at all and you don't have to watch the food constantly. A baking sheet (lined with foil if you want to really cut down on clean up) is coated with no-stick cooking spray. The food is added in a single layer and is given a light coating of cooking spray as well. It is then baked at 400-425 degrees. The food needs to be turned half way through the cooking time, which will vary depending on the size and type of food. Vegetables, chicken and fish can be breaded before oven-frying. Dip them briefly into 1/4 cup water mixed with 1/4 cup fat-free egg substitute, then into crumbs. Dry seasoned bread crumbs, corn flake crumbs and crushed dry stuffing crumbs all make good coatings. If you want just a bit of oil, add from 1 teaspoon to 1 tablespoon of vegetable oil to the egg mixture. When divided by several portions it will only add a few fat grams to each serving.

Sautéing and stir-frying are also forms of frying that are particularly great for cooking healthy. The foods are quickly cooked in a skillet or wok coated with no-stick cooking spray. Stir-fried foods are usually cut into small pieces of uniform size so they cook in minutes. Both sautéing and stir-frying are excellent ways to keep delicious taste and texture in food without added fat. However, don't think that the stir-fried dishes and sautéed dishes available in restaurants are low in fat. Many of them are cooked in lots of oil. When eating out ask that your sautéed and stir-fried entrees be prepared with very little or no fat added.

QUICK-COOKING VEGETABLES AND GRAINS BY STEAMING OR MICROWAVING

While the time-honored way of cooking vegetables in boiling water is okay, it is not the most nutritious nor the quickest method. Vital nutrients can be lost in the cooking water and vegetables can come out soggy and limp if boiled too long. In addition to sautéing and stir-frying, steaming and microwaving are terrific ways to cook vegetables. Since they are not submersed in water, the nutrients remain in the food, which also retains texture and taste. Steaming and microwaving are also exceptionally quick, which is a terrific bonus.

Food can be easily steamed with a deep, covered pot and an inexpensive steam rack. However, electric steamers that are controlled by a timer are very affordable. Because they turn themselves off, they do not have to be watched. This is a real plus since you can leave the kitchen without having to worry about overcooking the food. You can select a basic electric steamer or one that has various compartments for steaming more than one food at a time.

Although most homes now have microwave ovens, statistics indicate that they are mainly used to reheat meals or to make popcorn. If you don't use your microwave to cook vegetables, you should really try it. Microwaving is probably the simplest and best way to cook many vegetables. They don't have to be watched, they can't overcook if you time them correctly and they retain their nutrients. Of course, they also taste wonderful when correctly cooked in the microwave.

To steam or microwave vegetables, the pieces should be of fairly uniform size. If you plan to steam your food on the stovetop, select a deep pot with a lid. Add several inches of water, put the food in a steamer basket and place the basket in the pot. Make sure the water does not touch the food. Cover the pot and place over medium heat. Start counting the cooking time when wisps of steam can be seen rising from the pot. Do not let all of the water boil away. Add more if needed.

Microwaving is even more simple. Place the food in a covered microwave-proof dish along with several tablespoons of water and set the timer. Both the microwave and the electric steamer do practically everything but wash the dish for you.

If you cook vegetables the old-fashioned way in boiling water, ham or chicken bouillon cubes are great seasonings to add to the water during cooking. However, if you microwave or steam, the food is not submersed in the water. Therefore, they are best seasoned after cooking with a little granulated bouillon powder, fat-free margarine or a sauce. If you use fat-free margarine, the liquid kind works especially well. You may also wish to add additional seasoning along with the margarine. Garlic or other herbs, powdered crab spices and lemon juice are also flavorful additions.

Vegetable Steaming And Microwaving Chart

Times shown are for trimmed and cut up vegetables cooked tender-crisp. Time may vary depending on the wattage of your microwave or on whether you use an electric or stovetop steamer.

Vegetable	Amount	Steamed	Microwaved
Artichokes	1 pound	30 minutes	6-7 minutes
Asparagus	1 pound	8 minutes	6-7 minutes
Beets	1 pound	30 minutes	8 minutes
Broccoli	1 pound	10-15 minutes	8 minutes
Brussels Sprouts	1 pound	15 minutes	8 minutes
Cabbage	1 head	15 minutes	10 minutes
Carrots	1 pound	15 minutes	10 minutes
Cauliflower	1 head	10 minutes	10 minutes
Corn	4 ears	8-10 minutes	7 minutes
Eggplant	1 pound	10 minutes	7 minutes
Green Beans	1 pound	12 minutes	10 minutes
Green Peas	1 pound	10 minutes	7 minutes
Green Peppers	1 pound	10 minutes	6 minutes
Onions	1 pound	15 minutes	7 minutes
Potatoes	2 potatoes	30 minutes	7 minutes

Section 3

The Recipes

COME FEAST ALONG WITH ME

Now we get to the meat and potatoes of low-fat living–the recipes. Okay, so that's another bad pun, but those of you who aren't familiar with low-fat eating may really be under the impression that meat and potatoes are bad for you, especially if you are trying to lose weight. They aren't bad for you at all. You just have to learn how to prepare them properly. If you look at the following recipes and the recipes in *Live! Don't Diet!*, you will see that they are for real food. There is no pureed broccoli or boiled codfish. I couldn't eat that way for the rest of my life and neither can you.

These are more of the recipes that my husband Ken and I enjoyed while losing a total of 270 pounds. They not only helped us lose it, they help us keep it off because they are the recipes we live with day in and day out. There is good reason that we find them so easy to live with. Unlike dieting, which requires major deprivation, much lengthy preparation and the purchase of special ingredients, living a low-fat lifestyle allows us to eat like normal people, only healthier. We can have pizza or cheesecake or our favorite gooey casseroles. It is wonderful to be able to eat this way and still lose weight and maintain our good health.

In addition, you will be amazed at how much easier you will find preparing low-fat meals. If you are like me, you don't have a lot of time to spend in the kitchen so you will particularly like the fact that these low-fat dishes are quick and easy. There are no exotic, hard to find ingredients to buy and many of the dishes can be prepared in a very short time.

I have deliberately not used brand names in my ingredients list because brand names vary widely throughout the country. Even major food producers sell the same products under different labels in different areas. Nothing is more frustrating than looking for a brand called for in a recipe only to find that it is not available. The important thing is to read the label and make sure the brand you use is fat-free or low in fat.

I like to think of my recipes as road maps. In other words, they will get you where you are going. Prepared according to directions, they will result in tasty, filling, low-fat dishes. However, some of you may like to take little detours off the beaten path, so change the recipes to suit yourself. Feel free to do whatever you want, as long as any ingredient you add is low in fat. After all, they are just recipes, not something carved in stone.

I have listed only the fat grams with each recipe. I personally don't like to see the calorie content. That reminds me too much of a diet. Since

I don't count calories, they are not of great concern to me if the recipe is a healthy, low-fat one. However, some people want to know the calorie content of their meals. For those who want this information, I have listed it at the end of the recipe section.

These are not just my recipes, now they are your recipes. You can impress your family and friends with just how tasty eating healthy can be–and just think of the thanks you'll get when you tell them you are cooking low-fat because you care about them and their good health. So you have friends or family who would rather fall dead than eat something healthy? Well, don't tell them that what they are eating is low in fat. They'll probably never know the difference and you will know you are helping them. So, come feast along with me!

BREAKFAST RECIPES

BREAKFAST SWEET ROLL TASTE-ALIKES

I have a real weakness for pastries. I am often tempted to leap the bakery counter, grab a few dozen goodies and stuff them into my mouth. However, I control myself because I know I can make something at home to satisfy my craving. While some of the pastries sold commercially may be relatively low in fat, they are still often loaded with sugar and calories. Since I can seldom eat just one, I prefer make my own reduced-calorie version at home.

The fat-free cinnamon roll recipe in *Live! Don't Diet!* has seen me through many tough times, especially after shopping. Grocery stores all seem to have bakery departments these days. I think they pump the heavenly aroma of cinnamon and sugar into the air to lure us to buy lots of goodies. This usually sends me into a frenzy that can only be satisfied by a sweet treat. If I don't have time or inclination to make my healthier homemade version, I'll make what I call a taste-alike. Maybe it doesn't taste exactly the same as the real thing, but it's close enough. You can do the same at breakfast or at any time you crave a pastry. Just think for a moment–what is a pastry? It is usually a form of yeast roll topped by a gooey, sweet filling and a sugary glaze. You can get much the same taste sensation by using plain old reduced-calorie bread as your base. After all, the real sweet roll dough is just another variation of basic yeast and flour–in other words, bread. Okay, so we're not talking haute cuisine here but it does the trick. It will help satisfy that craving for the pastry you think you can't live without. Try some of these toppings for pastry taste-alikes.

- To make a fruit pastry taste-alike, spread a slice of reduced-calorie bread with your favorite reduced-sugar preserves. To make the glaze, blend several packets of aspartame-based sugar substitute with a few drops of water or fruit juice and drizzle over the top. For real overkill, squirt on some fat-free whipped topping.

- To make a cheese Danish taste-alike, spread a slice of reduced-calorie bread with the Cheesy Breakfast Burrito filling (see index) and drizzle on sugar substitute glaze.
- To make a cinnamon roll taste-alike, lightly spray your bread with fat-free, butter-flavored spray or squirt on liquid fat-free margarine. Sprinkle on a few raisins, then granulated aspartame-based sugar substitute and cinnamon to taste. Top with the sugar substitute glaze.
- To make a real monster taste-alike pastry, spread the bread with the Cheesy Breakfast Burrito filling, add your favorite jam or preserves, top with the sugar substitute glaze and add a bit of fat-free whipped topping.

The possibilities for making sweet roll taste-alikes are as limitless as your imagination. Experiment to your heart's content. The next time you are driven to contemplate buying a dozen of every sweet roll in the bakery case at your grocery, smile smugly to yourself and pass on by. You know that you can have your very own version at home without the guilt.

Cheesy Breakfast Burrito

We are all familiar with the breakfast burritos served at our favorite fast food restaurants. They are easy to make at home. One advantage to eating a breakfast burrito is that they are portable if you are in a hurry. The filling can be made in quantity and kept in the refrigerator. These burritos could also serve as a dessert in the evening. The filling of a breakfast burrito can change to suit your mood or what you have on hand. Scrambled egg substitute with a bit of minced low-fat ham and fat-free shredded Cheddar cheese is also good.

For each burrito:
1 fat-free flour tortilla
2 tablespoons fat-free cream cheese, softened
1 tablespoon fat-free sour cream
3 packets granulated aspartame-based sugar substitute
2 teaspoons low-sugar jam or preserves

Combine the cream cheese, sour cream and sugar substitute. Heat the tortilla in the microwave oven for approximately 10 seconds to soften. Spread the filling down the center of the tortilla, leaving 1" without filling at the top and bottom. Spoon the jam over the filling. Fold the unfilled top and bottom of the tortilla over the filling and roll the tortilla up, so that the filling is completely enclosed. Heat for another 10 seconds in the microwave oven, if desired.

1 serving
0 fat grams per serving

Cottage Cheese Pancakes

It amazes me that cottage cheese can be the primary ingredient in pancakes. I like this recipe because the cottage cheese adds protein. Also, a half cup of fat-free cottage cheese only has 80 calories, while a half cup of flour has about 200 calories. As I often say, I don't count calories but if I can reduce the calories in a recipe, I will. In this recipe, the 1½ cups of cottage cheese has 240 calories, in contrast to 600 calories in the 1½ cups of flour that a recipe for regular pancakes might contain.

½ cup fat-free egg substitute
1½ cups fat-free cottage cheese
¼ cup all-purpose flour
1 teaspoon sugar
No-stick cooking spray

Combine the egg substitute and cottage cheese. Gradually add the flour and sugar. Bake on a griddle that has been coated with no-stick cooking spray.

Variation: Add grated orange peel, grated apple, blueberries or sliced banana to the uncooked pancakes just after the batter is poured on the griddle.

8 pancakes
0 grams of fat per serving

Ham And Cheese Breakfast Casserole

This is a dish that is equally good for breakfast, lunch or dinner. As an added bonus it can be prepared the day before and refrigerated so that the only thing left to do is put it in the oven an hour before mealtime. Fresh fruit is a good accompaniment for the morning meal, while a vegetable salad goes well if it is served at dinner. Be sure to read the labels on the packaged croutons at your store. The brand I use has 8 fat grams per cup.

2 cups packaged garlic and cheese-flavored croutons
1 cup fat-free Cheddar cheese, shredded
4 ounces 98% fat-free ham, finely minced
1 medium onion, finely minced
2 cups skim milk
1 cup fat-free egg substitute
Light salt and pepper to taste

Combine the croutons, cheese, ham and onion. Place in a 8" x 8" baking dish that has been coated with no-stick cooking spray. Mix the milk, egg substitute, salt and pepper together and pour over the crouton mixture in the baking dish. Bake at 325 degrees for 50 minutes or until a knife inserted into the center comes out clean.

4 servings
5 fat grams per serving

Pancake Taste-Alikes

Not only is it easy to prepare homemade fat-free pancakes, many commercially prepared varieties in the frozen food section of the grocery are quite low in fat. However, sometimes we don't have time to make homemade pancakes and there are none in the freezer. This usually occurs at my house about the time all the pancake mix manufacturers choose to run advertisements on television featuring an actor attacking mounds of pancakes dripping with syrup and butter. When this happens, it makes me wish I could reach right into the TV and grab those pancakes right off the actor's plate. Instead, I'll just fool my mouth by making a stack of pancake taste-alikes.

Remember what I told you about sweet rolls? Right! They are just a variation on the same yeast and flour mixture that bread is made from. The same is essentially true of pancakes. The main ingredients are flour and a leavening agent, just like bread. Therefore, I just whip out my trusty loaf of reduced-calorie bread and make believe the slices are pancakes. Believe me, it works! My brain may know they aren't real pancakes, but my taste buds are satisfied. Here are a few pancake taste-alikes I rely on:

- Warm several slices of reduced-calorie bread for a few seconds in the microwave. Pour on liquid fat-free margarine and sugar-free syrup.

- For banana pancake taste-alikes, thinly slice ½ of a medium banana and mound it on reduced-calorie bread slices. Sprinkle the banana with a little cinnamon and granulated sugar substitute, pop it into the microwave briefly to warm it, then top with the liquid fat-free margarine and sugar-free syrup. This also works well using cooked apple slices instead of banana.

Sometimes I yearn for more elaborate pancakes. Remember all of those forbidden treats that pancake houses serve? Pancakes topped with sugar, fresh strawberries and whipped cream.

Pancakes rolled around link sausages. I could go on forever since they have a million variations on the good old pancake–all loaded with fat and sugar. Everyone has their own personal favorites.

With a little creativity, it is easy to make our own low-fat version of almost any pancake house specialty, using our homemade pancakes, frozen pancakes or our pancake taste-alike, bread.

Potato-Crusted Breakfast Pie

If your family is accustomed to weekday breakfasts of cold cereal, they will be delighted if you serve this as a special weekend breakfast.

The crust:
2 large, potatoes, peeled and shredded
1 tablespoon all-purpose flour
¼ cup fat-free egg substitute
Light salt and pepper to taste
No-stick cooking spray

The filling:
1 cup fat-free Cheddar cheese, shredded
2 cups fat-free cottage cheese
4 ounces 98% fat-free ham, cubed
½ cup fat-free egg substitute
Light salt and pepper to taste

Prepare the crust by combining the potatoes, flour, egg substitute, salt and pepper. Press into a pie pan that has been coated with no-stick cooking spray. Bake, unfilled, for 15 minutes at 400 degrees. While the potato crust is baking, combine all of the filling ingredients. Remove the crust from the oven and top with the filling. Lower the oven temperature to 350 degrees and bake an additional 30 minutes.

4 servings
2 fat grams per serving

APPETIZERS

Baked Bean Dip

Surprisingly, most brands of baked beans are low in fat, despite the pork cooked with them. Just be sure to discard the pork and also check the label to make sure the brand you use is low in fat.

2 15-ounce cans fat-free vegetarian-style baked beans
1 medium onion, finely minced
1 green bell pepper, finely minced
2 teaspoons imitation bacon bits

Puree the baked beans in a blender or food processor. Add the remaining ingredients. May be served warm or at room temperature.

8 servings
1 fat gram per serving

Chunky Bean Spread

A popular restaurant near my home serves a similar spread to diners as they await their meal.

1 15-ounce can red beans, rinsed and drained
3 tablespoons sweet pickle relish
½ medium onion, finely minced
3 tablespoons fat-free mayonnaise
3 tablespoons fat-free sour cream

Combine all of the ingredients. Serve chilled as a spread with fat-free crackers, melba toast, or rye-crisp or serve on a bed of lettuce as a salad.

4 servings
0 fat grams per serving

Creamy Salsa Spread

This is good spread on crackers or as a dip with fat-free potato chips, pretzels or raw vegetables.

1 cup fat-free mayonnaise
1 cup fat-free sour cream
1 12-ounce jar mild or medium chunky salsa
½ medium onion, finely minced

Combine all ingredients. Serve chilled.

24 servings
0 fat grams per serving

Don't Give Up The Chip

A variation on the cinnamon and sugar sprinkled chips that many Mexican fast food restaurants offer as dessert.

10 fat-free flour tortillas
Butter-flavored no-stick cooking spray
Cinnamon to taste
Granulated aspartame-based sugar substitute to taste
Honey or sugar-free maple-flavored syrup

Cut each tortilla into 8 wedges. Place them in a single layer on a baking sheet that has been coated with no-stick cooking spray. Lightly spray the tops of the wedges with no-stick cooking spray. Sprinkle each one with cinnamon and sugar substitute to taste. Bake at 400 degrees for about 5 minutes or until the chips are lightly browned and crisp. Serve with honey or sugar-free maple-flavored syrup.

10 servings
0 fat grams per serving

Heavenly Fruit And Cheese Spread

Dried fruit and cheese make an interesting and appealing combination.

1 cup fat-free Cheddar cheese, shredded
½ cup dried apricots, finely chopped
½ cup pitted dates, chopped
½ cup golden raisins
½ cup boiling water
1 8-ounce package fat-free cream cheese, softened
⅓ cup skim milk

Allow the Cheddar cheese to come to room temperature. Combine the apricots, dates and raisins. Pour the boiling water over them and set aside. In a separate bowl, combine the cream cheese, the Cheddar cheese and milk. Drain the fruit and add it to the cheese mixture. Serve with fat-free wheat crackers.

8 servings
0 fat grams per serving

Herbed Cream Cheese Spread

2 8-ounce packages fat-free cream cheese, softened
2 teaspoons garlic powder or 2 cloves garlic, minced
½ teaspoon dried oregano
¼ teaspoon dried dillweed
½ teaspoon dried basil
2 tablespoons dehydrated minced onion flakes

Combine the cream cheese, garlic, oregano, dillweed, basil and onion flakes. Serve chilled.

8 servings
0 fat grams per serving

Snappy Crackers

These crackers are not only a tasty snack, but are also terrific served as a topping for soup or salad.

No-stick butter-flavored cooking spray
1 16-ounce package oyster crackers, fat-free if available
1 envelope dry Ranch salad dressing mix

Coat a baking sheet with low sides with cooking spray. Place a layer of crackers on the baking sheet. Lightly coat the crackers with the cooking spray. Stir the crackers and lightly spray again. Sprinkle the crackers with the salad dressing mix and stir to coat. Bake the crackers for 45 minutes at 275 degrees, or until they are lightly browned. Store in an airtight container.

36 crackers per serving
0 fat grams per serving

Tangy Shrimp Spread

2 8-ounce packages fat-free cream cheese, softened
1 7-ounce can shrimp, rinsed and drained
½ medium onion, finely minced
No-stick cooking spray
½ cup bottled cocktail sauce

Combine the softened cream cheese, shrimp and onion. Pack into a small mold or bowl that has been coated with no-stick cooking spray. Chill until firm. Unmold on a serving plate that has been lined with lettuce. Spoon the cocktail sauce over the shrimp mold. Serve with fat-free crackers.

8 servings
1 fat gram per serving

SOUPS

Almost Effortless Ravioli Stew

Surprisingly, one of the most popular brands of commercially prepared canned cheese ravioli is now fat-free. This hearty stew, made with canned ravioli, is popular with children and adults as well. It can be made in minutes, which is a definite bonus.

1 medium onion, chopped
1 bell pepper, chopped
No-stick cooking spray
2 15-ounce cans Italian-style tomato sauce
1 15-ounce can sliced mushrooms, drained
2 15-ounce cans fat-free cheese ravioli
Fat-free Parmesan cheese

Sauté the onion and bell pepper in a skillet that has been coated with no-stick cooking spray. Place the onions, green pepper, tomato sauce and mushrooms in a large saucepan. Add the ravioli. Simmer for 15 minutes. Top individual portions with Parmesan cheese.

8 servings
0 fat grams per serving

Chunky Potato Soup

This is a recipe that can easily be changed to suit your taste. Use chopped broccoli instead of spinach if you like. A little 98% fat-free chopped ham or some sliced fat-free wieners can also be added.

1 large onion, chopped
2 stalks celery, chopped
No-stick cooking spray
2 15-ounce cans low-sodium, fat-free chicken broth
4 medium potatoes, peeled and chopped
1 10-ounce package frozen chopped spinach
2 cups skim milk
⅓ cup all-purpose flour
Light salt and pepper to taste (optional)

Sauté the onion and celery until tender in a large saucepan that has been coated with no-stick cooking spray. Add the chicken broth, potatoes and spinach. Bring to a boil, then lower the heat and simmer for 30 minutes or until the potatoes are tender. In a mixing bowl, gradually add the flour to the skim milk and stir until the flour is dissolved. Gradually add the milk to the simmering soup, stirring constantly. Simmer for 10 more minutes or until slightly thickened. Add light salt and pepper, if desired.

8 servings
0 fat grams per serving

Hearty White Chili

Serve topped with fat-free sour cream and chopped onion. Complete the white color scheme if you like by adding a little fat-free shredded mozzarella cheese as a topping. On the other hand, if you would like to add a little color, sprinkle on fat-free shredded Cheddar cheese and some chopped green onion, including the green tops. Cornbread is a hearty and delicious bread to offer on the side.

1 medium onion, finely chopped
3 15-ounce cans Great Northern beans
2 cups cooked boneless, skinless chicken breast, diced
1 15-ounce can low-sodium chicken broth
1 small can chopped chili peppers, mild or medium
2 teaspoons garlic powder
2 teaspoons cumin
Light salt and pepper to taste (optional)

Toppings:
Fat-free sour cream
Chopped onion or green onion, including green tops
Fat-free shredded mozzarella or Cheddar cheese

In a saucepan, combine the onions, beans, chicken, chicken broth, chili peppers, garlic powder, cumin, light salt and pepper to taste (optional). Simmer for 15 minutes. Ladle into individual soup bowls and add toppings.

4 servings
2 fat grams per serving

Smoky Pea Soup

I never really paid much attention to the packages of dried split peas I saw in the dried bean section at my local grocery store until my Mom served me a bowl of delicious split pea soup one chilly day. Now it's a favorite at my house, especially when served with hot cornbread.

8 cups water
2 cups dried split peas, soaked overnight and drained
1 15-ounce can low-sodium chicken broth
6 carrots, thinly sliced
1 medium onion, chopped
3 stalks celery, chopped
5 fat-free wieners, sliced
½ teaspoon liquid smoke
Light salt and pepper to taste (optional)

In a large saucepan, combine the water, split peas and chicken broth. Bring to a boil, lower the heat and simmer, covered, for 1 hour. Add the carrots, onion, celery, wieners, light salt and pepper. Simmer 30 additional minutes.

8 servings
1 fat gram per serving

Terrific Taco Soup

One evening when I was serving a thick, chili-flavored bean soup for dinner, I had some shredded lettuce on hand that I needed to use. Instead of making salad, I topped the soup with the lettuce and other Mexican-style taco toppings. It tasted somewhat like tacos, but was much easier to eat!

3 15-ounce cans chili beans
2 15-ounce cans Mexican-style chunky tomato sauce
1 medium onion, chopped
1 bell pepper, chopped
6 ounces browned ground round, rinsed and patted dry
6 fat-free corn tortillas
No-stick cooking spray
½ head iceberg lettuce, finely shredded
1 cup fat-free sour cream
1 mild onion, finely chopped
1 cup fat-free Cheddar cheese, shredded
1 cup mild or medium salsa

Combine the chili beans, tomato sauce, onion, bell pepper and ground round. Simmer for 30 minutes, or until the onion and the bell pepper are tender. Meanwhile cut each tortilla into 8 wedges and place on a baking sheet that has been coated with no-stick cooking spray. Bake at 350 degrees for 15 minutes, or until crisp. Ladle the soup into individual soup bowls. Top each portion with shredded lettuce, sour cream, chopped onion, shredded cheese and salsa. Serve with the tortilla wedges.

6 servings
4 fat grams per serving

Vegetable Soup With A Kick

Some people prefer meatless vegetable soup, while others like meat in it. This recipe is flexible. I use chicken, but 6 ounces of browned ground round that has been rinsed and patted dry is also good. It is equally delicious without any meat. Don't forget the cornbread! It is a must when you are serving vegetable soup.

2 cups cooked boneless, skinless chicken breast meat, diced
2 large onions, chopped
2 large potatoes, peeled and cubed
4 carrots, thinly sliced
1 48-ounce can vegetable juice
1 15-ounce can tomatoes with chili peppers, undrained
2 10-ounce packages frozen baby lima beans, thawed
2 15-ounce cans whole kernel corn, drained
Louisiana hot sauce to taste (optional)
Chopped raw onion (optional)

Combine the chicken, onions, potatoes, carrots, vegetable juice, tomatoes, lima beans and corn in a slow cooker. Cook for 10-12 hours on low. Top individual portions with Louisiana hot sauce to taste and chopped raw onion, if desired.

12 servings
2 fat grams per serving

Warm, Cozy Cream Of Tomato Soup

This is a comfort food from my childhood. My mother still makes it regularly for me–only now she makes a fat-free version.

2 medium onions, finely chopped
No-stick cooking spray
6 tablespoons all-purpose flour
4 cups skim milk
2 15-ounce cans tomatoes, chopped
Light salt and pepper to taste (optional)

In a large saucepan coated with no-stick cooking spray, sauté the onion. When tender, add the flour. Gradually stir in the milk. When the mixture is slightly thickened, add the tomatoes and their juice. Add light salt and pepper to taste (optional).

4 servings
0 fat grams per serving

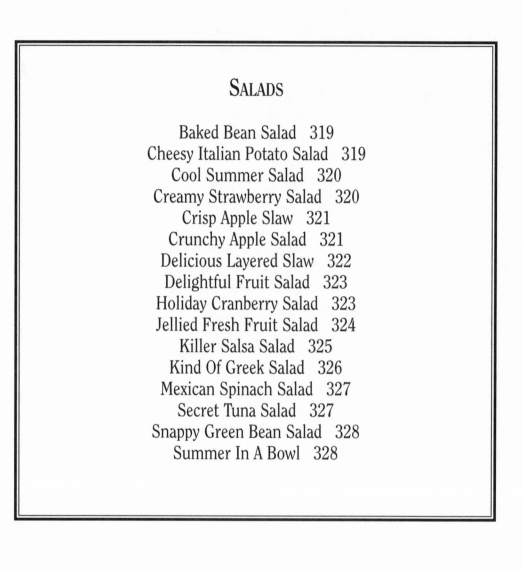

SALADS

Baked Bean Salad

1 head iceberg lettuce, shredded
2 16-ounce cans vegetarian-style baked beans, drained
1 mild onion, chopped
4 ounces 98% fat-free ham, chopped
1 cup fat-free Cheddar cheese, shredded
Fat-free Thousand Island or Ranch salad dressing

Arrange a bed of shredded lettuce on 4 dinner plates. Meanwhile, heat the baked beans until warmed through. Top the lettuce with beans, followed by salad dressing to taste. Add chopped onion, chopped ham and shredded Cheddar cheese.

4 servings
1 fat gram per serving

Cheesy Italian Potato Salad

4 large potatoes, peeled, cubed and boiled
1 medium onion, finely chopped
2 stalks celery, finely chopped
1 cup fat-free cottage cheese
½ cup fat-free sour cream
1 teaspoon garlic powder
1 teaspoon dried oregano
Light salt and pepper to taste (optional)
1 cup fat-free mozzarella cheese

Combine all of the ingredients. Gently toss to coat the vegetables. Serve chilled.

8 servings
0 fat grams per serving

Cool Summer Salad

1 head green cabbage, finely shredded
8 ounces 98% fat-free ham, chopped
1 medium onion, chopped
2 carrots, shredded
1 cup fat-free Swiss or mozzarella cheese
1 ounce bleu cheese, crumbled
1 cup fat-free mayonnaise
Light salt and pepper to taste (optional)

Combine the cabbage, ham, onion, carrots and Swiss or mozzarella cheese. In a mixing bowl, combine the bleu cheese and mayonnaise. Add to the cabbage mixture and toss to combine. Add light salt and pepper to taste (optional). Chill for at least 15 minutes to combine the flavors.

4 servings
3 fat grams per serving

Creamy Strawberry Salad

1 15-ounce can juice-packed crushed pineapple
1 large (8-serving) size fat-free, sugar-free strawberry gelatin
2 cups low-fat buttermilk
1 8-ounce carton fat-free whipped topping

Place the pineapple and juice in a saucepan and bring to a boil over medium heat. Add the gelatin and stir until it is completely dissolved. Let the dissolved gelatin cool to room temperature. When cool, add the buttermilk. Place the mixture in the refrigerator and chill until slightly thickened. Add the whipped topping and fold in gently. Chill until firm.

10 servings
0 fat grams per serving

Crisp Apple Slaw

1 head green cabbage, finely chopped or shredded
4 unpeeled red apples, cored and coarsely chopped
4 tablespoons dark raisins
1 cup fat-free mayonnaise
6 packets aspartame-based sugar substitute
⅓ cup lemon juice

Combine the cabbage, apples and raisins. In a separate mixing bowl, combine the mayonnaise, sugar substitute and lemon juice. Add the dressing to the cabbage mixture and toss to coat. Serve chilled.

10 servings
0 fat grams per serving

Crunchy Apple Salad

This salad is delicious served with ham or turkey.

3 large red apples, cored and cut into bite-size pieces
3 large green apples, cored and cut into bite-size pieces
3 large stalks celery, coarsely chopped
¼ cup raisins
½ cup fat-free mayonnaise
3 packets aspartame-based sugar substitute
2 tablespoons lemon juice

Combine the apples, celery and raisins in a serving bowl. In a separate bowl, combine the mayonnaise, sugar substitute and lemon juice. Add the mayonnaise mixture to the apple mixture and toss gently. Serve chilled.

8 servings
0 fat grams per serving

Delicious Layered Slaw

Layered salads, prepared in advance, frosted with a mayonnaise-based dressing, and tossed at serving time have been popular for quite a while. It is easy to see why. They are easy to prepare, pretty and very tasty. The concept works equally well with cole slaw.

1 head green cabbage, shredded
3 medium potatoes, peeled, cubed and boiled
1 10-ounce package frozen English peas, thawed, rinsed
  and drained
1 medium onion, chopped
4 hard-boiled eggs, whites only, chopped
1 bell pepper, chopped
1 cup fat-free mayonnaise
2 tablespoons cider vinegar
2 packets sugar substitute

In a clear glass serving dish, place a layer of cabbage, a layer of potatoes, a layer of peas, a layer of chopped onion, a layer of egg whites and a layer of green pepper. Repeat the layers. In a mixing bowl, combine the mayonnaise, vinegar and sugar substitute. Spread the mixture over the slaw. Cover and refrigerate until serving time. Before serving, toss the ingredients to combine.

8 servings
0 fat grams per serving

Delightful Frozen Fruit Salad

1 8-ounce package fat-free cream cheese, softened
½ cup skim milk
4 packets aspartame-based sugar substitute
1 15-ounce can juice-packed fruit cocktail, undrained

Combine the cream cheese, skim milk and sugar substitute. Add the fruit cocktail. Place the mixture in a serving dish and freeze until firm. Allow to stand at room temperature for about 10 minutes before serving,

8 servings
0 fat grams per serving

Holiday Cranberry Salad

1 large (8-serving size) box sugar-free strawberry gelatin
1½ cups boiling water
1 8-ounce can juice-packed crushed pineapple,
   drained, juice reserved
½ cup unsweetened orange juice
2 cups fresh cranberries
1 medium apple, peeled, cored and sliced

Place the gelatin in a large mixing bowl. Add the boiling water and stir until dissolved. Add the reserved pineapple juice and the orange juice. Chill until it is slightly thickened. Meanwhile, chop the cranberries and apple in a blender or food processor. Add the fruits to the gelatin mixture and place in a serving dish or mold. Chill until firm.

12 servings
0 fat grams per serving

Jellied Fresh Fruit Salad

This is a very refreshing and pretty salad. For maximum effect, serve unmolded on a bed of leaf lettuce or in a clear class serving dish.

1 large (8-serving size) box fat-free, sugar-free
   orange gelatin
3 cups water, divided
1 8-ounce can juice-packed pineapple tidbits, juice reserved
1 grapefruit, peeled, seeded and sectioned
2 oranges, peeled, seeded and sectioned
2 ripe bananas, thinly sliced
1 cup fresh strawberries, sliced

Place the gelatin in a large mixing bowl. In a saucepan, bring 2 cups of water to a boil. Add the boiling water to the gelatin and stir until the gelatin is completely dissolved. Combine the remaining 1 cup water and the reserved pineapple juice. Add to the gelatin. Refrigerate until the mixture is slightly thickened. Chop the grapefruit and orange sections into bite-size pieces. Add the pineapple, grapefruit, oranges, bananas and pineapple. Pour the mixture into a serving dish or mold and chill until firm.

12 servings
0 fat grams per serving

Killer Salsa Salad

Well, maybe it's not a killer but it will bowl diners over with its delicious spicy taste. Top with a dollop of fat-free sour cream and a sprinkle of finely chopped green onion. Fat-free tortilla chips are terrific served along with this salad.

1 15-ounce can stewed tomatoes
2 tablespoons cider vinegar
½ cup finely minced onion
1 bell pepper, finely minced
½ cup celery, finely minced
1 small can mild, medium or hot chopped chili
   peppers, drained
1 teaspoon Louisiana hot sauce
1 small (4-serving size) box sugar-free lemon gelatin

In a saucepan, combine the stewed tomatoes, vinegar, onion, bell pepper, celery, chili peppers and hot sauce. Bring the mixture to a boil over medium heat. Add the gelatin and stir until it has dissolved. Pour into a mold or serving dish and refrigerate until firm.

6 servings
0 fat grams per serving

Kind Of Greek Salad

Cottage cheese is a pretty good substitute for the feta cheese normally found in Greek salads. If you can't do without the feta, go ahead and use it in moderation. One ounce contains only 6 fat grams.

1 head iceberg lettuce, shredded
1 mild onion, sliced into thin rings
1 cucumber, thinly sliced
1 tomato, cut into wedges
½ cup fat-free cottage cheese
Fat-free Italian salad dressing
4 tablespoons fat-free Parmesan cheese, grated
Coarsely ground black pepper

Place a bed of shredded lettuce on individual salad plates. Scatter onion rings, cucumber slices and tomato wedges over lettuce. Top with a tablespoon of cottage cheese, then with Italian salad dressing. Sprinkle a tablespoon of Parmesan cheese and a bit of coarsely ground black pepper over the salad.

4 servings
0 fat grams per serving

Mexican Spinach Salad

1 1-pound bag fresh spinach, washed, stems removed
  and torninto bite-size pieces
1 medium onion, thinly sliced
1 cup sliced fresh mushrooms
1 cup fat-free Cheddar cheese, shredded
½ cup fat-free vinaigrette salad dressing
1 teaspoon chili powder
½ teaspoon cumin

Combine the spinach, onion, mushrooms and cheese. Combine the salad dressing, chili powder and cumin. Toss with the spinach mixture. Serve chilled.

4 servings
0 fat grams per serving

Secret Tuna Salad

My Mom has a friend who gave her a great secret tip for making terrific tuna or chicken salad. Add a potato!

1 large baking potato, peeled and boiled
2 7-ounce cans white chunk tuna, water-packed
2 stalks celery, finely chopped
3 tablespoons sweet pickle relish
3 tablespoons fat-free mayonnaise
1 tablespoons prepared mustard

Refrigerate the potato until it is cold, then grate into a mixing bowl. Add the tuna, celery, pickle relish, mayonnaise and mustard. Mix gently until thoroughly combined.

8 servings
1 fat gram per serving

Snappy Green Bean Salad

3 15-ounce cans cut green beans, drained
2 medium potatoes, peeled, cubed and boiled
1 medium onion, chopped
$\frac{1}{2}$ cup fat-free mayonnaise
$\frac{1}{2}$ cup fat-free Italian salad dressing
Light salt and pepper to taste (optional)

Combine the green beans, potatoes, and onion. In a separate bowl, combine the mayonnaise, Italian dressing and light salt and pepper to taste (optional). Combine the vegetables and the dressing. Serve chilled.

8 servings
0 fat grams per serving

Summer In A Bowl

$\frac{1}{2}$ medium watermelon, seeded and cubed
1 cantaloupe, seeded and cubed
1 15-ounce can juice-packed pineapple tidbits,
    juice reserved
2 cups seedless red or green grapes
1 pint strawberries, hulled and sliced
4 fresh peaches, peeled, seeded and sliced
1 12-ounce can apricot nectar
2 tablespoons almond extract
6 packets aspartame-based sugar substitute

In a large serving bowl, combine the fruit. In a separate bowl, combine the apricot nectar, almond extract and sugar substitute. Add the apricot mixture to the fruit and toss gently. Allow to chill for several hours in the refrigerator.

12 servings
0 fat grams per serving

BEEF MAIN DISHES

Acapulco Rice

Combining ground beef with rice and lots of vegetables is a good way to make a little meat go a long way.

3 stalks celery, chopped
1 pound fresh mushrooms, sliced
No-stick cooking spray
4 cups cooked rice
1 15-ounce can diced tomatoes with chilies, undrained
1 1-ounce package dehydrated onion soup mix
6 ounces brown ground round, rinsed and patted dry
1 cup fat-free sour cream
1 cup fat-free Cheddar cheese, shredded

Sauté the celery and mushrooms in a skillet that has been coated with no-stick cooking spray. When the vegetables are tender, add the rice, tomatoes, onion soup mix and ground round. In a casserole dish that has been coated with no-stick cooking spray, place ½ of the rice mixture. Spread the sour cream over the rice, then add the cheese. Top with the remaining rice mixture. Bake for 30 minutes at 350 degrees.

4 servings
3 fat grams per serving

Baked Beef And Pasta Supreme

There are loads of different shaped pastas on the market. Most of them can be used interchangeably in this recipe. Children especially might like wheel-shaped pasta or shell-shaped pasta. Tri-colored pasta would also be fun to use for a change.

1 12-ounce package small pasta shells, cooked and drained
6 ounces browned ground round, rinsed and patted dry
1 cup fat-free cottage cheese
1 cup fat-free mozzarella
1 tablespoon Italian seasoning blend
Light salt and pepper to taste (optional)
No-stick cooking spray
1 28-ounce jar commercially prepared fat-free
  spaghetti sauce
1 15-ounce can sliced mushrooms, drained
1 1-ounce package dehydrated onion soup mix
1 tablespoon grated fat-free Parmesan cheese

Combine the pasta shells, ground round, cottage cheese, mozzarella and Italian seasoning blend. Add light salt and pepper if desired. Place the mixture in a casserole dish that has been coated with no-stick cooking spray. Combine the spaghetti sauce, mushrooms and onion soup mix. Pour over the pasta. Bake at 350 degrees for 30 minutes. Top with the grated Parmesan cheese just before serving.

4 servings
4 fat grams per serving

Barbecue Pie

The wonderful zesty taste of barbecue has a natural affinity for cornbread.

1 large onion coarsely chopped
1 large green bell pepper, coarsely chopped
No-stick cooking spray
6 ounces browned ground round, rinsed and patted dry
1 cup fat-free barbecue sauce
1 cup cornmeal mix
½ cup fat-free cottage cheese
1 cup fat-free Cheddar, shredded
¼ cup fat-free egg substitute
1 cup water

Sauté the onion and green bell pepper in a skillet that has been coated with no-stick cooking spray. When the vegetables are tender, add the ground round and the barbecue sauce. Place the mixture in a casserole dish that has also been coated with no-stick cooking spray. Combine the cornmeal mix, cottage cheese, Cheddar cheese, egg substitute and water. Pour this mixture over the beef mixture. Bake for 30 minutes at 350 degrees.

4 servings
5 fat grams per serving

Chili Mountain

Children love this dish not only because it is different, but also because it contains many childhood favorites–macaroni, chili and cheese. Adults love it for the same reason. It is also fun when you have guests for a casual dinner. You can set out the ingredients and let guests build their own mountain.

3 15-ounce cans chili-style beans
2 15-ounce cans chunky Mexican-style tomato sauce
6 ounces browned ground round, rinsed and drained
1 16-ounce package elbow macaroni, prepared
  according to package directions
Finely shredded iceberg lettuce
1 onion, finely minced
1 cup fat-free sour cream
½ cup commercially prepared bottled salsa, hot or mild
1 cup fat-free Cheddar cheese, shredded

Combine the chili beans, tomato sauce and ground round in a saucepan. Simmer for 10 minutes. Meanwhile place a portion of the macaroni on 4 dinner plates. Top with the chili, followed by shredded lettuce, minced onion, sour cream, salsa and cheese.

4 servings
4 fat grams per serving

Country-Style Butterbean Pie

If you prefer, other beans, such as Great Northern beans or kidney beans can be used in this recipe. You can even combine a variety of your favorites.

4 cups cooked large white butterbeans
1 medium onion, coarsely chopped
1 medium potato, peeled and chopped
6 ounces browned ground round, rinsed and patted dry
1 15-ounce can tomato sauce
No-stick cooking spray
1 cup cornmeal mix
¼ cup fat-free egg substitute
1 cup water
1 tablespoon fat-free sour cream

Combine the butterbeans, onion, potato, ground round and tomato sauce. Place this mixture in a baking dish that has been coated with no-stick cooking spray. Combine the cornmeal mix, egg substitute, water and sour cream. Pour this mixture over the butterbean mixture. Bake for 45 minutes at 350 degrees.

4 servings
3 fat grams per serving

Creamy Pasta Casserole

1 12-ounce package elbow macaroni, prepared according to
   package directions
½ cup fat-free egg substitute, divided
1 cup skim milk
Light salt and pepper to taste (optional)
No-stick cooking spray
1 cup fat-free cottage cheese
¼ cup fat-free Parmesan cheese
2 cups commercially prepared fat-free spaghetti sauce
6 ounces browned ground round, rinsed and patted dry
1 15-ounce can mushrooms, drained

In a mixing bowl, combine the macaroni, ¼ cup egg substitute and the skim milk. Add the light salt and pepper, if desired. Place the mixture in a baking dish that has been coated with no-stick cooking spray. Combine the cottage cheese, Parmesan cheese and the remaining ¼ cup egg substitute. Pour this mixture over the pasta layer. Combine the spaghetti sauce, ground round and mushrooms. Spoon gently over the cottage cheese layer. Bake for 30 minutes at 350 degrees.

4 servings
3 fat grams per serving

Crunchy Potato-Beef Casserole

This recipe will be a hit with the meat and potatoes fans in the family.

2 large onions, chopped
1 large green pepper, chopped
No-stick cooking spray
6 ounces browned ground round, rinsed and patted dry
1 15-ounce can tomato sauce
1 1-ounce package dehydrated onion soup mix
1 package refrigerated or frozen shredded potatoes

Sauté the onion and green pepper in a skillet that has been coated with no-stick cooking spray. When the vegetables are tender, add the ground round, the tomato sauce and the onion soup mix. Place the mixture in a baking dish that has been coated with no-stick cooking spray. Top the meat mixture with the shredded potatoes. Lightly spray the potatoes with no-stick cooking spray. Bake for 30 minutes at 425 degrees.

4 servings
4 fat grams per serving

Dinnertime Sloppy Joes

Sloppy Joes are very good and very popular sandwiches. This dish goes a step further and serves them open-faced as an entree. Good with mashed potatoes and cole slaw on the side.

1 medium onion, chopped
No-stick cooking spray.
6 ounces browned ground round, rinsed and patted dry
1 10¾-ounce can low-fat beef gravy
1 15-ounce can mushrooms, drained
1 tablespoon ketchup
2 tablespoons fat-free sour cream
1 teaspoon garlic powder
4 reduced-calorie hamburger buns, split and toasted

Sauté the onion in a skillet that has been coated with no-stick cooking spray. When it is tender, add the ground round, beef gravy, mushrooms, ketchup, sour cream and garlic powder. Simmer until warmed through. Place two hamburger bun halves on each dinner plate. Top each half with the hamburger mixture.

4 servings
2 fat grams per serving

Extra-Easy Baked Eye Of Round Roast

1 2-pound eye of round roast, all visible fat removed
1 10¾-ounce can 97% fat-free cream of mushroom soup
½ cup water
1 1-ounce package dehydrated onion soup mix
1 teaspoon garlic powder

Place a large piece of aluminum foil in a medium-sized baking dish. Place the roast in the center of the foil. Pull the sides of the foil up so that they surround the roast. Combine the mushroom soup, water, garlic powder and onion soup mix. Pour over the roast. Pull the aluminum foil up over the top and ends of the roast and fold so that the gravy cannot leak out. Bake the roast for 2 hours at 350 degrees. It will be well done.

8 servings, 6 fat grams per serving

Gourmet Steak

1 pound eye of round roast, all visible fat removed
1 teaspoon garlic powder
1 teaspoon Worcestershire sauce
No-stick cooking spray
6 green onions, including tops, chopped
1 15-ounce can sliced mushrooms, drained
1 10½-ounce can low-fat beef gravy

Cut the eye of round into 4 4-ounce steaks. Sprinkle each steak with garlic powder and Worcestershire sauce. Sauté the beef in a skillet that has been coated with no-stick cooking spray until done to your preference. Meanwhile, combine the green onions, mushrooms and beef gravy in a small saucepan and simmer for 5 minutes. Place each steak on a dinner plate and top with several tablespoons of the gravy.

4 servings, 6 fat grams per serving

Onion Baked Steak

The flavors of onions and beef compliment each other beautifully. The same can be said for onions and potatoes. This recipe can't help but please everyone since it combines all of these great tastes.

4 4-ounce top round steaks, trimmed of all visible fat
No-stick cooking spray
4 medium potatoes, peeled and cubed
1 10¾-ounce can condensed French onion soup
½ soup can water

Sauté the steaks in a skillet that has been coated with no-stick cooking spray for 5 minutes per side. When they are browned, remove them to a baking dish that has also been coated with no-stick cooking spray. Place the potatoes around the meat. Combine the onion soup and water. Pour the soup over the meat and potatoes. Cover and bake at 350 degrees for 45 minutes.

4 servings
5 fat grams per serving

Pizza Macaroni-Style

You and your family will like this unique twist on that old standby, pizza. Serve with a mixed green salad and Italian bread.

1 16-ounce package elbow macaroni, prepared according to package directions
No-stick cooking spray
1 cup skim milk
½ cup fat-free egg substitute
Light salt and pepper to taste
1 28-ounce can fat-free spaghetti sauce
6 ounces browned ground round, rinsed and patted dry
1 medium onion finely chopped
1 green pepper, finely chopped
1 cup fresh mushrooms, sliced
1 cup fat-free mozzarella cheese, shredded
4 tablespoons fat-free Parmesan cheese, grated

Spread the macaroni in a 9" x 13" baking dish that has been coated with no-stick cooking spray. Combine the milk, egg substitute, salt and pepper. Pour the mixture over the macaroni. Bake for 10 minutes at 350 degrees. Remove from the oven and spread the spaghetti sauce over the macaroni. Top with the ground round, onion and green pepper. Bake for 20 additional minutes. Remove from the oven and top with the mozzarella and Parmesan cheese. Serve immediately.

8 servings
3 fat grams per serving

Ken's Quick Stuffed Peppers

My husband Ken thought up this recipe one day when he found about a zillion bell peppers in our refrigerator. I think he wanted them out of the way, so he suggested I make low-fat stuffed peppers. They have been a regular meal on our menu ever since.

4 large bell peppers
1 box instant long grain and wild rice mix, made according
    to package directions, omitting margarine
6 ounces browned ground round, rinsed and drained
1 medium onion, chopped
1 15-ounce can tomato sauce
3 packets sugar substitute
1 tablespoon cider vinegar

Cut the bell peppers in half lengthwise, removing stems, pith and seeds. In a mixing bowl, combine the rice, ground round and onion. Spoon the rice mixture into the 8 pepper halves. Press the mixture down to tightly stuff the pepper. Place the pepper halves in a microwave-proof baking dish. Combine the tomato sauce, sugar substitute and vinegar. Pour over the stuffed peppers. Cover the baking dish loosely with plastic wrap. Microwave for 10 minutes on high. Let stand 5 minutes.

4 servings
4 fat grams per serving

Slow Cooker Oriental Beef

We usually equate oriental recipes with quick cooking since so many of them are stir-fried. This recipe is just the opposite. It cooks all day! It's even easier than stir-frying because it doesn't have to be watched.

1 pound top round, cut into cubes
1 large onion, chopped
1 6-ounce can tomato paste
½ cup water
1 8-ounce can juice packed pineapple tidbits, undrained
1 8-ounce can sliced water chestnuts, drained
¼ cup cider vinegar
3 packets sugar substitute
Hot, cooked rice

Place the meat, onion and water chestnuts in a slow cooker. In a mixing bowl, combine the tomato paste, water and undrained pineapple tidbits. Pour over the beef. Cook for 8-10 hours on low. Shortly before serving, add the vinegar and sugar substitute. Serve over rice.

4 servings
4 fat grams per serving

Spaghetti With A Difference

We usually think of serving spaghetti with a tomato-based sauce. However beef gravy makes a different and very good spaghetti sauce.

2 medium onions, coarsely chopped
No-stick cooking spray
2 10½-ounce cans low-fat beef gravy
1 15-ounce can sliced mushrooms, drained
6 ounces browned ground round, rinsed and patted dry
1 teaspoon garlic powder
1 16-ounce package angel hair pasta, prepared according to
   package directions

Sauté the onion in a skillet that has been coated with no-stick cooking spray. When the onion is tender, add the beef gravy, mushrooms, ground round and garlic powder. Simmer for 10 minutes. Meanwhile, place a portion on the cooked spaghetti on each dinner plate. Top the spaghetti with the heated sauce.

6 servings
4 fat grams per serving

Steak In A Stew

A cross between a steak dinner and beef stew which my family enjoys. This recipe can be simplified even more by using canned whole potatoes. They lose much of their canned taste in the cooking process.

4 4-ounce slices eye of round, all visible fat removed
No-stick cooking spray
4 medium baking potatoes, peeled and cubed
4 medium carrots, peeled and cut into 2" pieces
1 15-ounce can English peas, drained
1 15-ounce can sliced mushrooms, drained
1 10½-ounce can low-fat beef gravy
½ cup water
1 teaspoon garlic powder
Light salt and pepper to taste (optional)

Sauté the beef slices in a skillet that has been coated with no-stick cooking spray for 5 minutes per side. Remove to a baking dish that has also been coated with no-stick cooking spray. Arrange the vegetables around the meat. Combine the gravy, water, garlic powder, salt and pepper. Pour over the meat and vegetables. Cover and bake for 1 hour at 350 degrees.

4 servings
5 fat grams per serving

Steak Teriyaki

This teriyaki recipe has a different twist. It contains orange juice instead of pineapple juice. It can also be served with fruit, such as mandarin orange sections or pineapple tidbits, added to the sauce.

4 4-ounce cube steaks (top round)
No-stick cooking spray
1 cup unsweetened orange juice
2 tablespoons light soy sauce, low-sodium if desired
1 teaspoon garlic powder
1 tablespoon cornstarch
3 packets sugar substitute

Sauté the cube steaks in a skillet that has been coated with no-stick cooking spray. When cooked to your personal preference, remove to a platter. Combine the orange juice, soy sauce, garlic powder and cornstarch. Place the sauce ingredients in the skillet and cook over low heat until thickened, stirring frequently. Add the sugar substitute. Return the meat to the skillet and heat briefly.

4 servings
5 fat grams per serving

Tasty Tamale Pie

Cornmeal mixture:
4 cups water, divided
1½ cups cornmeal
1 tablespoon chili powder
1 teaspoon cumin
Light salt to taste

Filling:
6 ounces browned ground round, rinsed and patted dry
1 6-ounce can tomato paste
1 tablespoon each chili powder and cumin
1 cup water
1 medium onion, finely minced
1 15-ounce can whole kernel corn
No-stick cooking spray
1 15-ounce can chunky Mexican-style tomato sauce

Combine the cornmeal, chili powder, cumin and light salt. Slowly add 1½ cups cold water. Gradually add this mixture to the boiling water. Stir until thickened. For the filling, combine the ground round, tomato paste, spices, water, onion and corn. Pour half of the hot cornmeal mixture into a 9" x 13" baking dish that has been coated with no-stick cooking spray. When it has cooled slightly top with the filling ingredients. Pour the remaining cornmeal mixture over the filling. Cover and bake for 30 minutes at 350 degrees. Top portions with the heated tomato sauce.

12 servings
2 fat grams per serving

Chicken Main Dishes

Barbecued Chicken Casserole

Everyone in my family loves this because they are crazy about barbecue. I love it because it is a meal in one dish and cooks itself while I'm at work. Cole slaw makes a good accompaniment.

4 medium potatoes, peeled and cubed
2 medium onions, coarsely chopped
4 4-ounce chicken breast halves, boned and skinned, cut into bite-sized pieces
1 cup fat-free bottled barbecue sauce
1 1-ounce package dehydrated onion soup mix
½ cup water

Place the potatoes and onions in the bottom of a slow cooker. Place the chicken on top of the vegetables. Combine the barbecue sauce, onion soup mix and water. Pour over the vegetables and chicken. Cook on low for 8-10 hours. This may also be cooked in the oven, covered, for 1 hour at 350 degrees.

4 servings
4 fat grams per serving

Basic Lemon-Herb Broiled Chicken

1 tablespoon lemon juice
1 tablespoon vegetable oil
1 teaspoon garlic powder
1 teaspoon dried parsley flakes
1 teaspoon Worcestershire sauce
4 4-ounce chicken breast halves, skinned and boned
No-stick cooking spray
Light salt and pepper to taste (optional)

Combine the lemon juice, oil, garlic powder, parsley flakes and Worcestershire sauce. Place the chicken breasts in a baking dish that has been coated with no-stick cooking spray. Brush each breast with the basting sauce. Broil 7 minutes then turn and brush with the sauce. Broil an additional 7 minutes. Watch carefully. The exact cooking time will depend on the size and thickness of the chicken pieces.

4 servings
6 fat grams per serving

Chicken Italian

While real pepperoni has too much fat, 97% fat-free smoked sausage is close enough in taste to be an acceptable substitute, either on pizza or in this recipe.

No-stick cooking spray
4 4-ounce chicken breast halves, skinned and boned
1 onion, cut into wedges
½ pound 97% fat-free smoked sausage, thinly sliced
2 cups commercially prepared fat-free spaghetti sauce

Sauté the chicken breasts in a skillet that has been coated with no-stick cooking spray for 6 minutes on each side. Remove the chicken from the skillet. Sauté the onion and the smoked sausage until the sausage is lightly browned. Return the chicken to the skillet and add the spaghetti sauce. Simmer for 10 minutes.

4 servings
6 fat grams per serving

Chunky Chicken Hash

This is a not only a meal in one dish, it is a good way to use up some of the vegetables you have left in the refrigerator. Just add them to the basic recipe.

2 cups cooked chicken breast, cubed
4 medium potatoes, peeled, cubed and boiled
1 medium onion, coarsely chopped
1 10¾-ounce can 97% fat-free cream of mushroom soup
1 cup fat-free sour cream
Light salt and pepper to taste (optional)
No-stick cooking spray

Combine the chicken, potatoes, onion, mushroom soup, sour cream, light salt and pepper. Pour into a casserole dish that has been coated with no-stick cooking spray. Bake for 40 minutes, covered, at 350 degrees.

4 servings
5 fat grams per serving

Creamy Chicken Casserole

1 10-ounce package frozen chopped spinach, cooked
   and drained
$\frac{1}{4}$ cup fat-free egg substitute
1 cup fat-free cottage cheese
$\frac{1}{2}$ cup fat-free Parmesan cheese
1 cup fat-free mozzarella cheese, shredded
1 12-ounce package medium noodles, prepared according to
   package directions
1 cup fat-free sour cream
Light salt and pepper to taste (optional)
1 cup cooked chicken breast, chopped
No-stick cooking spray

Combine the spinach, egg substitute, cottage cheese, Parmesan cheese and mozzarella cheese. In a separate bowl, combine the cooked noodles, sour cream and chicken. Add light salt and pepper if desired. In a casserole dish that has been coated with no-stick cooking spray, place half of the noodles followed by half of the cheese mixture, then the remaining noodles, followed by the remaining cheese mixture. Bake, covered, for 30 minutes at 350 degrees.

4 servings
2 fat grams per serving

Crispy Oven Chicken

This is a different variation on that stand-by, oven-fried chicken. It is special enough to serve to company.

1 cup fat-free sour cream
1 tablespoon lemon juice
½ teaspoon garlic powder
Light salt and pepper to taste (optional)
6 4-ounce chicken breast halves, skinned and boned
2 cups packaged herb-seasoned stuffing crumbs
No-stick cooking spray

Combine the sour cream, lemon juice, and garlic powder. If desired add the light salt and pepper. Coat each chicken breast half with the mixture. After coating, roll each breast in the stuffing crumbs. If the crumbs are large, you may wish to crush them slightly before rolling the chicken in them. Place the chicken in a baking dish that has been coated with no-stick cooking spray. Lightly spray each breast with the cooking spray. Bake, uncovered, for 30 minutes at 400 degrees, until well browned. Do not overcook.

6 servings
5 fat grams per serving

Ham And Cheese Chicken

While the French call their classic dish Chicken Cordon Bleu, this variation, as well as the original, are basically combinations of those All-American favorites, ham, cheese and chicken.

4 4-ounce chicken breast halves, boned and skinned
No-stick cooking spray
Light salt and pepper to taste (optional)
4 extra-thin slices deli-style 97% fat-free ham
4 ¾-ounce slices fat-free Swiss or Cheddar cheese

Sauté the chicken in a skillet that has been coated with no-stick cooking spray for about 6 minutes each side. When the chicken is cooked, top with a slice of cheese and a slice of ham. Cover briefly to melt the cheese. Serve immediately.

4 servings
4 fat grams per serving

Helen's And Linda's Chicken Picante

My friend Helen Davis has lost 75 pounds since she began watching her fat intake. She got this super quick and easy recipe from her sister, Linda Mendel.

4 4-ounce boneless, skinless, chicken breast halves
   cut into bite-size pieces
No-stick cooking spray
1 20-ounce jar chunky picante sauce, mild or medium
Hot, cooked rice

Place the chicken in a baking dish that has been coated with no-stick cooking spray. Pour the picante sauce over the chicken. Bake, covered for 30 minutes at 350 degrees. Serve over hot, cooked rice.

4 servings
4 fat grams per serving

Mexican Grilled Chicken

1 teaspoon cider vinegar
¼ cup water
1 teaspoon ground chili powder
1 teaspoon ground cumin
1 teaspoon garlic powder
4 4-ounce chicken breasts, skinned and boned

Combine the vinegar, water, chili powder, cumin and garlic powder. Brush the chicken on both sides with the mixture. Grill for approximately 20 minutes.

4 servings
4 fat grams per serving

Pasta Jambalaya

A new way to enjoy the spicy flavors of the Louisiana classic, Jambalaya. Fresh shrimp can also be added, if desired, for an even more authentic version.

No-stick cooking spray
1 medium onion, coarsely chopped
1 bell pepper, coarsely chopped
3 stalks celery, coarsely chopped
1 cup cooked chicken breast, cubed
½ pound 97% fat-free smoked sausage, sliced
½ cup 98% fat-free ham, cubed
1 15-ounce can tomato sauce
1 tablespoon Cajun-style seasoning, commercially
   prepared or homemade (see recipe index)
1 12-ounce package angel hair pasta, prepared
   according to package directions

In a skillet that has been coated with no-stick cooking spray, sauté the onion, green pepper and celery until tender-crisp. Add the chicken, smoked sausage and ham and continue cooking for several minutes until the meats are slightly browned. Add the tomato sauce and the Cajun seasoning. Serve over angel hair pasta.

6 servings
5 fat grams per serving

Peachy Chicken Deluxe

I love the taste of fruit with chicken. Somehow their flavors seem to complement each other. Chinese Sweet and Sour Chicken is not the only way to enjoy the taste of chicken with fruit. This recipe is another.

No-stick cooking spray
6 4-ounce chicken breast halves, skinned and boned
1 onion, coarsely chopped
1 bell pepper, coarsely chopped
1 15-ounce can sliced peaches, packed in juice,
   juice reserved
¼ cup soy sauce
2 tablespoons lemon juice
1 tablespoon cornstarch
½ cup water

Sauté the chicken breasts in a skillet that has been coated with no-stick cooking spray for 6 minutes on each side. When they are cooked throughout and lightly brown, remove them from the skillet. In the same skillet, sauté the onion and peppers until they are tender-crisp. Remove the onion and peppers from the skillet. Drain the juice from the peaches into the skillet. Add the soy sauce and lemon juice. Combine the water and cornstarch and add to the skillet. Stir over low heat until the sauce has thickened. Add the sliced peaches to the sauce, as well as the reserved chicken and vegetables. Continue cooking for 5 minutes.

6 servings
4 fat grams per serving

Piquant Barbecued Chicken

We usually think of the traditional tomato-based sauce when we think of barbecue. However, this spicy sauce is just as good in its own way. Try it for a change.

1 tablespoon vegetable oil
2 tablespoons lemon juice
1 teaspoon dry mustard
1 tablespoon Worcestershire sauce
1 teaspoon garlic powder
¼ teaspoon Louisiana-style hot sauce
6 4-ounce chicken breasts, skinned and boned
No-stick cooking spray

Combine the oil, lemon juice, dry mustard, Worcestershire sauce, garlic powder and hot sauce. Place the chicken breasts on a grill that has been coated with no-stick cooking spray. Brush with the sauce. Grill for about 6 minutes per side, basting frequently with the sauce. Do not overcook.

6 servings
6 fat grams per serving

Quick And Tender Roast Turkey

I often buy the precooked, boneless roast turkey breast sold in 1-2 pound pieces in the grocery. This recipe gives it a little more home-cooked taste with almost no effort.

1 10¾-ounce can 97% fat-free cream of chicken soup
½ soup can water
1 2-pound precooked, fat-free, boneless roast turkey
   breast piece
No-stick cooking spray

Combine the soup and water. Slice the turkey breast into ¼" slices. Place the sliced turkey in a baking dish that has been coated with no-stick cooking spray. Pour the soup mixture over the turkey. Bake, covered, for 30 minutes at 350 degrees.

8 servings
3 fat grams per serving

Rich And Creamy Chicken Bake

1 10¾-ounce can 97% fat-free cream of mushroom soup
1-ounce package dehydrated onion soup mix
4 4-ounce chicken breast halves, skinned and boned
No-stick cooking spray

Combine the mushroom soup and dehydrated onion soup mix. Place the chicken breasts in a baking dish that has been coated with no-stick cooking spray. Spread the mixed soups over the chicken. Cover and bake for 30 minutes at 350 degrees.

4 servings
4 fat grams per serving

Roasted Deviled Chicken Breasts

1 tablespoon lemon juice
2 tablespoons liquid fat-free margarine
1 teaspoon prepared mustard
¼ teaspoon ground red pepper
1 teaspoon garlic powder
6 4-ounce chicken breasts halves, skinned and boned
No-stick cooking spray

Combine the lemon juice, liquid margarine, mustard, red pepper and garlic powder. Place the chicken breasts in a baking dish that has been coated with no-stick cooking spray. Brush the breasts with the basting mixture. Roast, covered, at 350 degrees for 20 minutes, or until juices run clear when pierced with a fork.

6 servings
4 fat grams per serving

Slow Cooker Mushroom Chicken

This recipe is so easy that you can decide to prepare it five minutes before you leave for work in the morning. It will cook by itself and be ready for you to serve by dinnertime.

4 4-ounce chicken breast halves, skinned and boned
1 8-ounce can sliced mushrooms, drained
1 10¾-ounce can 97% fat-free cream of chicken soup
Light salt and pepper to taste (optional)

Place the chicken in the slow cooker. Top with the mushrooms. Spread the chicken soup over all, adding light salt and pepper, if desired. Cook on low for 8-10 hours.

4 servings
5 fat grams per serving

Slow Cooker Cranberry Chicken

2 medium onions, cut into wedges
6 carrots, peeled and cut into 2" pieces
6 4-ounce chicken breasts, boned and skinned
1 15-ounce can whole berry cranberry sauce
½ cup fat-free French salad dressing
1 tablespoon lemon juice

Place the vegetables in the bottom of a slow cooker. Top with the chicken breasts. Combine the cranberry sauce and the French dressing. Pour the mixture over the chicken and vegetables. Cook on low for 8-10 hours.

6 servings
4 fat grams per serving

Spectacular Stuffed Chicken Breasts

A special dish that is good to serve to company. If you want to simplify, it is a good replacement for traditional turkey and stuffing at a holiday meal.

6 4-ounce chicken breast halves, boned and skinned
1 box cornbread stuffing mix, prepared according to package
   directions, omitting margarine
No-stick cooking spray
1 10¾-ounce can 97% fat-free cream of mushroom soup
½ cup water
1 8-ounce can sliced mushrooms, drained

Place each chicken breast between two sheets of waxed paper. Using a meat mallet or heavy, flat object, flatten the chicken. Place several tablespoons of the stuffing mixture on one side of each breast and roll up. Place seam side down in a baking dish that has been coated with no-stick cooking spray. Combine the mushroom soup, water and mushrooms. Pour the soup mixture over the chicken. Bake, covered, for 45 minutes at 350 degrees.

6 servings
5 fat grams per serving

Turkey Divan Casserole

Traditional Turkey Divan is made with whole spears of broccoli topped with sliced turkey and a rich, creamy sauce. I really like this version better. Of course, chicken can easily be substituted for the turkey.

3 cups cooked white rice
2 10-ounce boxes frozen, chopped broccoli, cooked
1 medium onion, finely chopped
2 cups cooked turkey breast, cubed
No-stick cooking spray
1 10¾-ounce can 97% fat-free cream of mushroom soup
1 cup fat-free sour cream
Light salt and pepper to taste (optional)

Combine the rice, broccoli, onion and turkey in a casserole dish that has been coated with no-stick cooking spray. Combine the soup and sour cream. Add the light salt and pepper to the soup mixture, if desired. Combine the soup with the rice mixture. Cover and bake for 30 minutes at 350 degrees.

6 servings
4 fat grams per serving

Uptown Chicken Hollandaise

Hollandaise sauce is probably the most lethal sauce in the world, since its main ingredients are melted butter and egg yolks. This dish is crowned with a fat-free version of Hollandaise that is still very good–yet totally healthy.

4 4-ounce chicken breast halves, skinned and boned
No-stick cooking spray
¾ cup fat-free mayonnaise
2 teaspoons lemon juice
¼ cup skim milk
4 English muffin halves, toasted

Sauté the chicken breasts in a skillet that has been coated with no-stick cooking spray for about 6 minutes per side. When they are browned and thoroughly cooked, remove them from the skillet. In a saucepan over low heat, combine the mayonnaise, lemon juice and skim milk. Place each chicken breast on a toasted English muffin half on a dinner plate. When the sauce is warm, spoon several tablespoons over each chicken breast.

4 servings
4 fat grams per serving

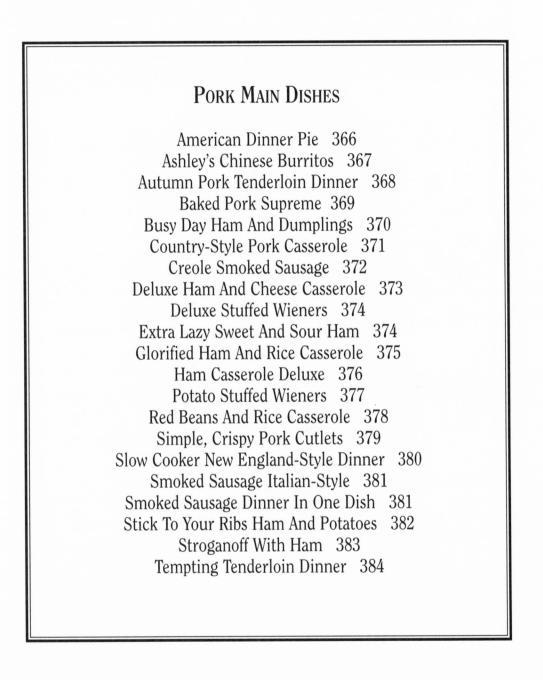

Pork Main Dishes

American Dinner Pie

The traditional English dish, Shepherd's Pie, contains beef and gravy topped with a blanket of mashed potatoes. This recipe uses the American favorites wieners and baked beans to create our own down home version.

1 pound fat-free wieners, cut into slices
2 15-ounce cans fat-free baked beans
1 medium onion, chopped
½ cup ketchup
No-stick cooking spray
2 cups prepared fat-free mashed potatoes
½ cup fat-free sour cream
1 cup fat-free Cheddar cheese

Combine the wieners, baked beans, onions and ketchup. Place in a baking dish that has been coated with no-stick cooking spray. Combine the mashed potatoes, sour cream and Cheddar cheese. Spread the potatoes over the bean mixture. Bake for 30 minutes at 350 degrees.

6 servings
0 fat grams per serving

Ashley's Chinese Burritos

My daughter Ashley has always enjoyed Mo Shu Pork in Chinese restaurants. The authentic version involves Chinese pancakes wrapped around a mixture of Chinese vegetables and meat. This is a quick and easy version to make at home using flour tortillas–a real international combination!

8 ounces pork tenderloin, all fat removed
No-stick cooking spray
2 cups cabbage, finely shredded
1 medium onion, thinly sliced
1 8-ounce can sliced mushrooms, drained
1 tablespoon light soy sauce
½ teaspoon Chinese sesame oil
1 13½-ounce package fat-free flour tortillas
1 cup fat-free barbecue sauce

Cut the pork tenderloin into matchstick-size pieces. Sauté in a skillet that has been coated with no-stick cooking spray. When the pork is lightly browned, remove from the skillet and sauté the cabbage and onions until tender-crisp. Return the pork to the skillet and add the mushrooms, soy sauce and sesame oil. Meanwhile, puncture the plastic bag containing the flour tortillas and microwave them on medium for about 1 minute, or until they are pliable. Brush each tortilla with barbecue sauce. Place several tablespoons of the pork and vegetable mixture on one side of each tortilla, then roll up. Serve immediately.

5 servings
1 fat gram per serving

Autumn Pork Tenderloin Dinner

Autumn and winter are perfect times to enjoy this flavorful recipe. It will warm the heart and soul on a cold evening.

4 3-ounce slices pork tenderloin, all fat removed
No-stick cooking spray
4 medium sweet potatoes, peeled and cut into 1" chunks
4 cooking apples, peeled and sliced
1 cup water
2 tablespoons soy sauce
1 tablespoon sugar

Place the pork slices between two pieces of waxed paper and flatten with a meat mallet or other flat, heavy object. Sauté the pork in a skillet that has been coated with no-stick cooking spray for 6 minutes per side. Arrange the pork slices, the sweet potatoes and the apples in a baking dish that has also been coated with no-stick cooking spray. Combine the water, soy sauce and sugar in a measuring cup. Pour over the pork and vegetables. Bake, covered, for 40 minutes at 350 degrees or until the sweet potatoes are tender.

4 servings
4 fat grams per serving

Baked Pork Supreme

I really like letting the oven do most of the work in this recipe. As you know, my motto is "make it simple, fix it quick and get out of the kitchen!"

4 3-ounce slices pork tenderloin, all fat removed
No-stick cooking spray
½ cup uncooked rice
1 medium onion, sliced
1 green pepper, sliced
1 15-ounce can tomatoes, chopped and drained
   (juice reserved)
Hot water
Light salt and pepper to taste (optional)

Place the pork slices between two pieces of waxed paper and flatten with a meat mallet or other heavy, flat object. Brown the slices on both sides over medium heat in a skillet that has been coated with no-stick cooking spray. Meanwhile, place the rice in a baking dish that has also been coated with no-stick cooking spray. Place the browned pork slices on the rice. Top each pork slice with onion and green pepper slices. Scatter the chopped tomatoes over the top. In a measuring cup, add enough hot water to the reserved tomato juice to equal 2 cups. Add light salt and pepper, if desired. Pour the water and tomato juice over the ingredients in the baking dish. Bake, tightly covered, at 350 degrees for 1 hour, or until the rice is tender.

4 servings
3 fat grams per serving

Busy Day Ham And Dumplings

I've had lots of positive comments about the chicken and dumplings recipe in *Live! Don't Diet!* This recipe uses the same surprise ingredient–flour tortillas. If you can't find the fat-free flour tortillas, most regular flour tortillas are still very low in fat and can be used.

6 cups water
1 ham or chicken bouillon cube
8 ounces 98% fat-free ham
1 13½-ounce package fat-free flour tortillas
1 10¾-ounce can 97% fat-free cream of mushroom soup (optional)
1 8-ounce can sliced mushrooms, drained (optional)

Combine the water, ham or chicken bouillon and ham in a medium saucepan. Bring to a boil over medium heat. Meanwhile cut the tortillas into 1" squares. Drop the tortilla squares slowly in to the boiling liquid. Stir frequently while adding the tortillas to keep them from sticking together. Lower the heat and simmer for about 15 minutes. Check frequently. When the dumplings are no longer doughy, add the mushroom soup and the mushrooms, if desired.

4 servings
2 fat grams per serving

Country-Style Pork Casserole

Sauerkraut seems to have a natural affinity for pork. The sweetness of the apples in this recipe mellows the usually sharp tang of the sauerkraut.

4 3-ounce slices pork tenderloin, all fat removed
No-stick cooking spray
2 cooking apples, peeled and sliced
1 medium onion, chopped
1 15-ounce can sauerkraut, drained
1 8-ounce can tomato sauce

Place the pork slices between two pieces of waxed paper and flatten with a meat mallet or other flat, heavy object. Sauté the pork in a skillet that has been coated with no-stick cooking spray for 6 minutes per side. In a mixing bowl, combine the apples, onion, sauerkraut and tomato sauce. Place the sauerkraut mixture in a casserole dish that has been coated with no-stick cooking spray. Place the pork on top of the sauerkraut. Bake, covered, for 40 minutes at 350 degrees.

4 servings
3 fat grams per serving

Creole Smoked Sausage

1 cup diced celery
1 medium bell pepper, coarsely chopped
1 medium onion, coarsely chopped
No-stick cooking spray
1 pound 97% fat-free smoked sausage, cut into 20 pieces
1 15-ounce can tomato sauce
1 15-ounce can tomatoes, chopped, with their juice
1 teaspoon garlic powder
Louisiana-style hot sauce to taste
1 tablespoon cornstarch

Sauté the celery, bell pepper and onion until tender in a skillet that has been coated with no-stick cooking spray. Remove the vegetables and sauté the sausage until lightly browned in the same skillet. Return the vegetables to the skillet. In a mixing bowl, combine the tomato sauce, tomatoes, garlic powder, hot sauce and cornstarch. Pour the sauce over the smoked sausage and vegetables in the skillet and simmer several minutes until the sauce has thickened.

4 servings
3 fat grams per serving

Deluxe Ham And Cheese Casserole

Who doesn't like ham and cheese? This recipe combines ham with two cheeses—and sour cream. Eating low-fat has never been better!

1 8-ounce can sliced mushrooms, drained
4 green onions, including tops, chopped
1 cup fat-free cottage cheese
1 cup fat-free sour cream
Light salt and pepper to taste (optional)
8 ounces 98% fat-free ham, cubed
1 cup fat-free Cheddar cheese, shredded
1 8-ounce package noodles, prepared according to
    package directions
No-stick cooking spray

Combine the mushrooms, green onions, cottage cheese, sour cream, light salt, pepper, ham, Cheddar cheese and noodles. Pour into a casserole dish that has been coated with no-stick cooking spray. Bake at 350 degrees. for 30 minutes.

4 servings
2 fat grams per serving

Deluxe Stuffed Wieners

This is an interesting and fun way to prepare wieners for a change. Great with slaw and baked beans.

1 package cornbread stuffing mix, prepared according to
    package directions, omitting margarine
1 pound fat-free wieners
5 tablespoons ketchup
No-stick cooking spray

Split each wiener almost in half lengthwise. Fill the split with several spoonfuls of the prepared stuffing. Top with ketchup. Bake for 20 minutes at 350 degrees.

5 servings
0 fat grams per serving

Extra-Lazy Sweet And Sour Ham

8 ounces precooked 98% fat-free ham, cut into matchstick-
    size pieces
1 large onion, cut into wedges
1 large bell pepper, cut into cubes
No-stick cooking spray
1 8-ounce can juice-packed pineapple tidbits
1 jar commercially-prepared, fat-free sweet and sour sauce
Hot, cooked rice

In a skillet that has been coated with no-stick cooking spray, sauté the ham, onion and bell pepper until the vegetables are tender-crisp. Add the pineapple and juice to the skillet, followed by the sweet and sour sauce. Simmer briefly. Serve over hot, cooked rice.

4 servings
1 fat gram per serving

Glorified Ham And Rice Casserole

2 cups cooked rice
2 10-ounce boxes frozen English peas, cooked according
    to package directions
8 ounces 98% fat-free ham, cubed
1 medium onion, coarsely chopped
1 teaspoon garlic powder
3 tablespoons fat-free grated Parmesan cheese
½ cup fat-free sour cream
½ cup fat-free mayonnaise
1 teaspoon lemon juice
Light salt and pepper to taste (optional)
No-stick cooking spray

Combine the rice, peas, ham and onion. In a separate mixing bowl, combine the garlic powder, Parmesan cheese, sour cream, mayonnaise, lemon juice. Add light salt and pepper to taste, if desired. Combine the sour cream mixture with the rice mixture. Place the mixture in a casserole dish that has been coated with no-stick cooking spray. Bake for 30 minutes at 350 degrees.

4 servings
2 fat grams per serving

Ham Casserole Deluxe

You probably wonder if we eat ham around my house every night, since I am including so many ham recipes. We really don't, but I do serve it often. I have always enjoyed ham, and since it is possible to buy it almost fat-free and precooked, it is a mainstay around my house for sandwiches, main courses and salads.

2 cups cooked rice
2 10-ounce packages chopped spinach, cooked and drained
1 medium onion, finely minced
1 8-ounce can sliced mushrooms, drained
8 ounces precooked 98% fat-free ham, diced
1 cup fat-free sour cream
¼ cup fat-free liquid margarine
1 1-ounce package dehydrated onion soup mix
Light salt and pepper to taste (optional)
No-stick cooking spray

Combine the rice, spinach, onion, mushrooms, ham, sour cream, liquid margarine, onion soup mix, light salt and pepper. Place the mixture in casserole dish that has been coated with no-stick cooking spray. Bake for 30 minutes at 350 degrees.

4 servings
2 fat grams per serving

Potato Stuffed Wieners

My mother made these for me as a child. I guess my inner child still loves them because I still like to make them. If you don't have leftover mashed potatoes, use instant mashed potatoes made according to package directions, omitting the margarine and using skim milk. Add 1 tablespoon fat-free sour cream to the potatoes. Use slightly less milk than the directions call for. The potatoes need to be fairly stiff.

1 cup leftover fat-free mashed potatoes
2 teaspoons dehydrated minced onion
¼ cup fat-free Cheddar cheese, shredded
1 pound fat-free wieners
No-stick cooking spray

Combine the mashed potatoes, onion and cheese. Cut each wiener almost in half lengthwise. Fill the slit in the wiener with about 2 tablespoons of the potato mixture. Place the wieners in a baking dish that has been coated with no-stick cooking spray. Bake for 20 minutes at 350 degrees.

5 servings
0 fat grams per serving

Red Beans And Rice Casserole

If you love the taste of red beans and rice, you'll like this casserole. Using canned beans may not be authentic, but it sure helps when you decide you would like to make this dish at the last minute.

4 cups cooked white rice
2 15-ounce cans red beans or kidney beans, rinsed
    and drained
1 medium onion, chopped
1 medium bell pepper, chopped
½ pound 97% fat-free smoked sausage, thinly sliced
1 15-ounce can chunky tomato sauce,
Light salt and pepper to taste (optional)
Louisiana hot sauce to taste
No-stick cooking spray

Combine the rice, beans, onion, bell pepper, smoked sausage, tomato sauce, light salt, pepper and hot sauce. Place in a casserole dish that has been coated with no-stick cooking spray. Bake, covered, for 1 hour at 350 degrees.

4 servings
1 fat gram per serving

Simple, Crispy Pork Cutlets

4 3-ounce slices pork tenderloin, all fat removed
¼ cup fat-free egg substitute
¼ cup water
1 teaspoon vegetable oil
1 cup cornflake crumbs
1 teaspoon garlic powder
Light salt and pepper to taste (optional)
No-stick cooking spray

Place the slices of pork between two sheets of waxed paper. Using a meat mallet or other heavy, flat object, flatten each slice. In a shallow dish, combine the egg substitute, water and oil. In another shallow dish, combine the cornflake crumbs and garlic powder. Add light salt and pepper, if desired. Dip each flattened slice of pork into the egg mixture, then into the crumbs. Place each coated slice in a baking dish that has been coated with no-stick cooking spray. Bake for 30 minutes or until browned at 400 degrees. Check frequently. Do not overcook.

4 servings
3 fat grams per serving

Slow Cooker New England-Style Dinner

This recipe replaces the corned beef in the traditional New England boiled dinner with ham and adds the convenience of slow cooking instead of boiling. The sauce may not exactly be traditional either, but it is good.

1 medium cabbage, cut into 4 large wedges
4 medium potatoes, peeled and cut into wedges
4 medium onions, peeled and cut into wedges
4 large carrots, scraped and cut into 2" pieces
4 4-ounce slices 98% fat-free ham
½ cup water

Sauce:
1 cup fat-free sour cream
2 tablespoons skim milk
Horseradish to taste

Place the cabbage, potatoes, onions and carrots in a slow cooker. Top with the ham slices. Pour the water over all and bake on low for 8-10 hours. Combine the sauce ingredients in a small saucepan and warm briefly. Serve along with the ham and vegetables.

4 servings
2 fat grams per serving

Smoked Sausage Italian-Style

My husband, Ken, has always loved Italian sausages cooked with peppers and onions. Since we began our low-fat lifestyle his favorite is a now much leaner variation.

1 pound 97% fat-free smoked sausage, sliced
No-stick cooking spray
1 medium onion, sliced
1 bell pepper, sliced

Sauté the sausage slices in a skillet that has been coated with no-stick cooking spray. When they are lightly brown, add the onions and pepper. Continue cooking until the vegetables are tender-crisp.

6 servings
1 fat gram per serving

Smoked Sausage Dinner In One Dish

1 pound 97% fat-free smoked sausage
3 medium potatoes, peeled and sliced
2 medium onions, chopped
4 carrots, scraped and cut into 2" pieces
15-ounce can chunky tomato sauce
No-stick cooking spray

Combine the smoked sausage, vegetables and tomato sauce in a casserole dish that has been coated with no-stick cooking spray. Bake, covered, for 45 minutes at 350 degrees, or until the vegetables are tender.

4 servings
2 fat grams per serving

Stick To Your Ribs Ham And Potatoes

2 cups instant potato flakes
2 cups boiling water
½ cup fat-free egg substitute
1 cup packaged seasoned, dry breadcrumbs
3 tablespoons dehydrated minced onion
Light salt and pepper to taste (optional)
No-stick cooking spray
8 ounces 98% fat-free precooked ham, diced
1 medium onion, chopped
1 10-ounce package frozen chopped broccoli, cooked
    and drained
1 cup fat-free sour cream

Combine the instant potato flakes and the boiling water. When cool, add the egg substitute, breadcrumbs, dehydrated minced onion and the light salt and pepper. Spread the mixture in a 8" x 8" baking dish that has been coated with no-stick cooking spray. Combine the ham, onion, broccoli and sour cream. Spread over the potato mixture. Bake for 30 minutes at 350 degrees.

4 servings
2 fat grams per serving

Stroganoff With Ham

When we think of stroganoff, we usually think of beef as the main ingredient. However, ham is a very good change of pace. Serve over rice or noodles.

1 pound fresh mushrooms, sliced
1 medium onion, sliced
No-stick cooking spray
8 ounces 98% fat-free ham, cut into matchstick-sized pieces
1 teaspoon garlic powder
1 cup fat-free sour cream
1 teaspoon Worcestershire sauce
Light salt and pepper to taste (optional)
1 8-ounce package noodles, prepared according to package
　directions

Sauté the mushrooms and onions in a skillet that has been coated with no-stick cooking spray. When they are tender, add the ham and continue cooking briefly. When the ham is slightly browned, add the garlic powder, sour cream, Worcestershire sauce and light salt and pepper, if desired. Serve on a bed of noodles or rice.

4 servings
3 fat grams per serving

Tempting Tenderloin Bake

It's hard to imagine life without pork. Thanks to pork tenderloin, we don't have to even think about doing without it. A 3-ounce serving of lean pork tenderloin has only 4 fat grams.

4 3-ounce slices pork tenderloin, all fat removed
No-stick cooking spray
1 medium onion, chopped
½ cup ketchup
¼ cup water
1 teaspoon garlic powder
3 tablespoons lemon juice
1 teaspoon dry mustard

Place the pork tenderloin slices between two sheets of waxed paper and flatten with a meat mallet or other flat, heavy object. Sauté the slices in a skillet that has been coated with no-stick cooking spray for 5 minutes per side or until lightly browned. Place the pork in a baking dish that has also been coated with no-stick cooking spray. Sprinkle the chopped onion over the pork. In a mixing bowl, combine the ketchup, water, garlic powder, lemon juice and dry mustard. Pour the sauce over the pork. Cover and bake for 30 minutes at 350 degrees.

4 servings
4 fat grams per serving

Seafood Main Dishes

Baked Fish In A Hurry

This is another one of those recipes that is great to make when preparation time is at a premium or when the pantry is almost bare–like mine becomes when I have put off going to the grocery store too many times.

6 4-ounce boneless perch or flounder fillets
1 10¾-ounce can 97% fat-free cream of mushroom soup
1 tablespoon dried parsley flakes
No-stick cooking spray

Place the fish in a baking dish that has been coated with no-stick cooking spray. Pour the soup over the fish and sprinkle with the parsley flakes. Cover and bake for 30 minutes at 350 degrees.

4 servings
3 fat grams per serving

Chinese-Style Sesame Shrimp

Stir-frying is a great way to cook. It doesn't take much oil and the ingredients retain their fresh texture and color. Those of us who want to get out of the kitchen fast love it because it is so quick–and doesn't mess up a lot of pots and pans!

1 tablespoon vegetable oil
No-stick cooking spray
1 pound fresh or thawed frozen shrimp, peeled and deveined
1 tablespoon sesame seeds
1 medium onion, cut into wedges
2 tablespoons reduced-sodium soy sauce
$\frac{1}{4}$ teaspoon ground ginger
$\frac{1}{4}$ teaspoon garlic powder
Hot, cooked rice

Add the oil to a wok or skill that has been coated with no-stick cooking spray. Heat the oil, then add the shrimp, onions, and sesame seeds. Cook over medium heat until the shrimp have turned pink. Do not overcook. Add the soy sauce, ginger and garlic powder. Serve with hot, cooked rice.

6 servings
5 fat grams per serving

Crispy Sesame Broiled Scallops

Scallops are the perfect seafood—no bones to worry about, like fish, no shells to peel off, like shrimp—just tender nuggets of wonderful flavor that cook in an instant.

1 pound scallops
1 tablespoon vegetable oil
½ cup commercially prepared seasoned dry breadcrumbs
1 tablespoon sesame seeds
Light salt and pepper to taste (optional)
No-stick cooking spray

Place the scallops and oil in a mixing bowl. Stir gently until all of the scallops are lightly coated. Drain off any excess oil. Place the breadcrumbs, sesame seeds, light salt and pepper in a zip-top plastic bag. Add the scallops a few at a time and shake gently to coat with the breadcrumb mixture. Place the scallops on a baking sheet that has been coated with no-stick cooking spray. Lightly coat the scallops with cooking spray. Broil 5" from the heat source for 3-4 minutes or until browned. Turn and broil for 3-4 more minutes. Watch carefully to prevent overcooking.

4 servings
8 fat grams per serving

Crunchy Tuna Casserole

Don't scream! Yes, I know you are probably not too excited about another tuna casserole recipe, but this one is different enough your family will love it.

2 8-ounce cans water-packed light chunk tuna
3 stalks celery, finely minced
1 medium onion, finely minced
1 8-ounce can sliced water chestnuts, drained
1 cup herb seasoned stuffing mix
1 cup fat-free mayonnaise
½ cup fat-free sour cream
2 tablespoons lemon juice
1 cup fat-free Cheddar cheese, shredded
Light salt and pepper to taste (optional)
No-stick cooking spray

Combine the tuna, celery, onion, water chestnuts, stuffing mix, mayonnaise, sour cream, lemon juice, cheese, salt and pepper in a baking dish that has been coated with no-stick cooking spray. Bake for 30 minutes at 350 degrees.

6 servings
1 fat gram per serving

Mandarin-Style Baked Snapper Fillets

Other low-fat fish fillets can be substituted for the snapper, if desired.

4 6-ounce snapper fillets
No-stick cooking spray
1 teaspoon vegetable oil
3 tablespoons water
1 tablespoon cornstarch
3 tablespoons reduced-sodium soy sauce
1 tablespoon vinegar
1 8-ounce can sliced water chestnuts, drained
Sugar substitute to equal 2 tablespoons sugar

Place the fillets in a baking dish that has been coated with no-stick cooking spray. Brush the fish lightly with oil and bake for 20 minutes at 350 degrees or until it flakes easily with a fork. Meanwhile, combine the water and cornstarch in a saucepan. Add the soy sauce, vinegar and water chestnuts. Bring to a boil, reduce the heat and simmer until thickened. Remove from the heat and add the sugar substitute. When the fish is done, remove to individual plates and top with the sauce.

4 servings
3 fat grams per serving

Oven-Baked Shrimp Jambalaya Casserole

This recipe combines some of the great spicy flavors that make it easy to eat low-fat. Louisiana hot sauce has become a mainstay around our house. It can add zip to just about anything. I even heard that there are folks who put it on ice cream!

1 pound salad-size frozen shrimp, thawed
3 cups cooked white rice
1 12-ounce package frozen sliced okra, thawed
1 15-ounce can tomatoes, chopped
1 8-ounce can tomato sauce
6 green onions, including tops, chopped
Light salt and pepper to taste (optional)
Red pepper to taste
1 teaspoon garlic powder
Louisiana hot sauce to taste
No-stick cooking spray

Combine the shrimp, rice, okra, tomatoes, tomato sauce, green onions, light salt and pepper, red pepper, garlic powder. and hot sauce. Place the mixture in a baking dish that has been coated with no-stick cooking spray. Bake for 30 minutes at 350 degrees or until the shrimp are pink.

6 servings
2 fat grams per serving

Oven-Fried Fish With Creamy Garlic Butter Sauce

4 6-ounce boneless perch or flounder fillets
1 tablespoon vegetable oil
1 cup cornflake crumbs
Light salt and pepper to taste (optional)
No-stick cooking spray

Sauce:
1 cup fat-free sour cream
¼ cup liquid fat-free margarine
1 teaspoon garlic powder
Light salt and pepper to taste (optional)
1 teaspoon dried parsley flakes

Lightly brush each fillet on both sides with oil. Combine the cornflake crumbs with the light salt and pepper to taste. Roll each fillet in the crumbs to coat. Place the fillets on a baking sheet that has been coated with no-stick cooking spray. Lightly spray the fillets with the cooking spray. Bake for 20 minutes at 425 degrees. Turn and bake for 10 minutes or until the fillets are browned and flake easily with a fork. Combine the sauce ingredients in a saucepan. Place over low heat, stirring frequently. When the sauce is warm, spoon over the fillets.

4 servings
2 fat grams per serving

Quick And Spicy Fish Fillets

One of the best parts of shrimp cocktail is the tangy horse-radish-flavored cocktail sauce that usually accompanies it. This basic sauce adds it's own special zip to baked fish as well.

4 6-ounce perch or flounder fillets
No-stick cooking spray
1 15-ounce can tomato sauce
1 tablespoon horseradish (or to taste)
1 tablespoon lemon juice
1 teaspoon Worcestershire sauce

Place the fish fillets in a baking dish that has been coated with no-stick cooking spray. Combine the tomato sauce, horse-radish, lemon juice and Worcestershire sauce. Pour over the fish and bake, covered, for 30 minutes at 350 degrees. The fish is done when it flakes easily with a fork.

4 servings
2 fat grams per serving

Saucy Shrimp And Pasta Au Gratin

Surprisingly, many brands of packaged macaroni and cheese are low in fat. Buy one of the low-fat brands and omit the butter and whole milk.

1 box low-fat macaroni and cheese (with powdered cheese sauce packet)
½ cup fat-free sour cream
1 teaspoon garlic powder
2 tablespoons dehydrated onion flakes
½ teaspoon red pepper
Light salt to taste
1 cup fat-free Cheddar cheese, shredded
1 cup cooked fresh or frozen shrimp or 1 8-ounce can shrimp
2 ounces precooked 98% fat-free ham finely minced
No-stick cooking spray

Cook the macaroni according to package directions. Drain the macaroni but allow several tablespoons of water to remain. Slowly add the powdered cheese sauce that comes with the boxed mix, stirring constantly to prevent lumps. Add the sour cream, garlic powder, onion flakes, red pepper, light salt and shredded Cheddar cheese. Add the shrimp and ham and combine thoroughly. Pour the mixture into a baking dish that has been coated with no-stick cooking spray. Bake for 30 minutes at 325 degrees.

4 servings
2 fat grams per serving

Scallop Sauté

Scallops are my favorite seafood. They are bite-size, mild in flavor and are relatively inexpensive compared to other shell-fish, at least in most parts of the country. They are also just plain good!

1 pound scallops
3 tablespoons lemon juice
1 teaspoon garlic powder
1 teaspoon dried parsley flakes
1 teaspoon vegetable oil
No-stick cooking spray

Combine the scallops, lemon juice, garlic powder and parsley flakes. Add the vegetable oil to a skillet that has been coated with no-stick cooking spray. Sauté the scallops over medium heat for 5-7 minutes or until they are lightly browned.

4 servings
2 fat grams per serving

Shrimp Stroganoff

I never get tired of the rich taste of stroganoff sauce but just in case you do, the addition of tomato sauce gives this dish a little different taste.

1 pound fresh shrimp or thawed frozen shrimp, peeled
  and deveined
No-stick cooking spray
1 15-ounce can tomato sauce
1 cup fat-free sour cream
2 tablespoons dehydrated minced onion
1 8-ounce can sliced mushrooms, drained
Light salt and pepper to taste (optional)
Hot, cooked rice

Sauté the shrimp in a skillet that has been coated with no-stick cooking spray for about 3 minutes or until pink. Do not overcook. Add the tomato sauce, sour cream, onion, mushrooms, light salt and pepper. Simmer briefly until warmed through. Serve over hot, cooked rice.

4 servings
3 fat grams per serving

Sunday Salmon Loaf

Read labels carefully when buying canned salmon. Some brands are quite high in fat, while others are much lower.

1 16-ounce can skinless, boneless pink salmon, flaked
1 cup soft bread crumbs, made from reduced-calorie bread
1½ cups skim milk
½ cup fat-free egg substitute
¼ cup liquid fat-free margarine
Light salt and pepper to taste (optional)
No-stick cooking spray

Combine the salmon and the bread crumbs. Add the milk, egg substitute, liquid fat-free margarine, light salt and pepper. Combine thoroughly. Place the mixture in a 9" x 5" loaf pan. Bake for 1 hour at 350 degrees.

4 servings
4 fat grams per serving

Tempting Baked Fish

1 cup fat-free sour cream
1 tablespoon prepared mustard
1 teaspoon dehydrated onion flakes
4 6-ounce perch or flounder fillets
1 cup dry breadcrumbs
No-stick cooking spray

Combine the sour cream, mustard and onion flakes. Spread both sides of each fish fillet with the mixture, then coat with the breadcrumbs. Place the coated fillets in a baking dish that has been coated with no-stick cooking spray. Bake for 20 minutes at 400 degrees or until the fish is lightly browned and flakes easily with a fork.

4 servings
3 fat grams per serving

Tuna-Rice Casserole

This is a versatile recipe. If you are not in the mood for tuna, chicken breast or low-fat ham works equally well.

3 cups cooked white rice
1 8-ounce can water-packed light tuna, drained and flaked
1 cup fat-free sour cream
¼ cup liquid fat-free margarine
1 1-ounce package dehydrated onion soup mix
1 medium onion, finely minced
Pepper to taste (optional)
No-stick cooking spray

Combine the rice, tuna, sour cream, margarine, onion soup mix, onion and pepper. Place the mixture in a baking dish that has been coated with no-stick cooking spray. Bake for 30 minutes at 350 degrees.

4 servings
1 fat gram per serving

Zesty Fish Scampi

Shrimp Scampi is a flavorful dish found on the menu of many seafood restaurants. While it is a delicious way to prepare shrimp, even at home, there are times when we don't really want to blow the grocery budget on shrimp. Using a mild, low-fat fish can provide the flavor without the cost.

4 4-ounce fillets of your favorite mild, low-fat fish
No-stick cooking spray
½ cup fat-free Italian salad dressing
½ teaspoon coarsely ground black pepper
1 teaspoon dried parsley flakes

Place the fillets in a baking dish that has been coated with no-stick cooking spray. Combine the Italian dressing, pepper and parsley flakes. Pour over the fish. Cover and bake for 30 minutes at 325 degrees. The fish will be done when it flakes easily with a fork.

4 servings
Fat grams per serving will vary
depending on fish used.
The sauce contains no fat

MEATLESS MAIN DISHES

Baked Egg Foo Young

I used to love ordering Egg Foo Young in Chinese restaurants but those delicious patties soak up oil like a sponge. The baked version is fat-free and infinitely better for you.

1 large onion, finely chopped
1 large bell pepper, finely chopped
No-stick cooking spray
1 15-ounce can bamboo shoots, drained
2 cups fat-free egg substitute
1 tablespoon cornstarch
Light salt and pepper to taste (optional)

Sauce:
1 10½-ounce can low-fat beef gravy
1 tablespoon low-sodium soy sauce

Sauté the onion and pepper in a skillet that has been coated with no-stick cooking spray. When tender, add the bean sprouts and continue cooking 5 minutes. Remove the vegetables from the heat and allow them to cool. Meanwhile, in a mixing bowl, combine the egg substitute, cornstarch, salt and pepper. Add the cooled vegetables to the egg mixture. Pour into a baking dish that has been coated with no-stick cooking spray. Bake for 30 minutes at 350 degrees or until a knife inserted into the center comes out clean. In a saucepan, combine the sauce ingredients and heat until warm. To serve, cut the Egg Foo Young into 4 servings and place one on each dinner plate. Top with a portion of the sauce.

4 servings
1 fat gram per serving

Baked Lasagna With Cream Sauce

Traditional lasagna with hearty tomato sauce is great but this version with cream sauce is just as tasty and satisfying.

2 cups skim milk
½ cup fat-free sour cream
4 tablespoons cornstarch
Light salt and pepper to taste (optional)
1 10-ounce package frozen chopped spinach, cooked and
   squeezed dry
2 cups fat-free cottage cheese
1 cup fat-free mozzarella, shredded
¼ cup fat-free Parmesan cheese, grated
1 tablespoon garlic powder
¼ cup fat-free egg substitute
1 8-ounce package lasagna noodles, cooked according
   to package directions
No-stick cooking spray

Combine the milk, sour cream, cornstarch, light salt and pepper. Place in a saucepan and cook over low heat, stirring often, until thickened. In a mixing bowl, combine the spinach, cottage cheese, mozzarella cheese, Parmesan cheese, garlic powder and egg substitute. In a 9" x 13" baking dish that has been coated with no-stick cooking spray, spread a thin layer of the cream sauce. Top with 3 of the cooked lasagna noodles, followed by ⅓ of the sauce and ½ of the cheese mixture. Top the cheese mixture with 3 more noodles, ⅓ cup of the cream sauce, the remaining cheese mixture and the last 3 noodles. Spread the final ⅓ of the cream sauce on top. Cover with foil and bake for 30 minutes at 350 degrees. Let stand 10 minutes.

8 servings
1 fat gram per serving

Creamy Fettuccini

This recipe is a country cousin of that rich Italian specialty Fettuccini Alfredo. Serve with a mixed green salad and Italian bread.

16-ounce package fettuccini noodles, cooked according to
   package directions
1 15-ounce can sliced mushrooms, drained
1 15-ounce can tomatoes, chopped and drained
1 cup fat-free sour cream
¼ cup liquid fat-free margarine
½ cup fat-free grated Parmesan cheese
1 teaspoon garlic powder
1 tablespoon lemon juice
Light salt and pepper to taste (optional)
1 tablespoon dried parsley flakes

In a saucepan, combine the cooked noodles, mushrooms, chopped tomatoes, sour cream, liquid margarine, Parmesan cheese, garlic powder, lemon juice, light salt and pepper and parsley flakes. Simmer briefly until heated through. Top with additional Parmesan cheese if desired.

4 servings
1 fat gram per serving

Easy Cheesy Pie

Not only is this savory pie easy to put together, it also makes its own crust. The crust does best if you use a glass pie plate instead of a metal one.

2 cups fat-free Cheddar cheese, shredded
1 medium onion, chopped
1 8-ounce can sliced mushrooms, drained
No-stick cooking spray
2 cups skim milk
1 cup fat-free egg substitute
½ teaspoon red pepper
Light salt and pepper to taste (optional)
½ cup all-purpose flour
2 teaspoons baking powder

Combine the cheese, onion and mushrooms in a pie plate that has been coated with no-stick cooking spray. Combine the milk, egg substitute, red pepper, light salt, pepper, flour and baking powder and stir until well blended. Pour the milk mixture over the cheese and vegetables. Bake for 45 minutes at 350 degrees. The pie will be done when a knife inserted into the center comes out clean.

4 servings
0 fat grams per serving

Old-Fashioned Potato Dumplings

I have heard older people reminiscing about eating potato dumplings during the Great Depression. They were popular because they were inexpensive, yet very filling and very good. That's still the reason to enjoy them today. Canned or home-made chicken broth can be used in place of the water and bouillon. Just make sure it is low-fat.

4 large baking potatoes, peeled and cubed
6 cups water
2 packets chicken or ham bouillon, low-sodium if possible
1 13½-ounce package flour tortillas, cut into 1" squares
1 10¾-ounce can 97% fat-free cream of mushroom soup
½ cup fat-free sour cream
Light salt and pepper to taste (optional)

Place the potatoes, water and bouillon in a saucepan over medium heat. Bring to a boil, reduce the heat, cover and let simmer for about 30 minutes or until the potatoes are easily pierced with a knife. When the potatoes are tender, slowly add the tortilla squares a few at the time, stirring frequently. Add additional water if needed. Simmer for approximately 10 minutes or until the dumplings are tender. Add the mushroom soup, sour cream, light salt and pepper to taste (optional).

4 servings
1 fat gram per serving

Rich Ravioli Casserole

This is so quick and easy that it is almost embarrassing. As I mentioned in a previous recipe, one of the most popular national brands of cheese ravioli is now fat-free. As long as the public continues to demand it, companies will continue to reduce the fat in popular commercially prepared foods. That is a real blessing to those of us who love to eat but don't want the fat.

2 15-ounce cans fat-free cheese ravioli
No-stick cooking spray
2 cups fat-free cottage cheese
¼ cup fat-free Parmesan cheese, grated
1 cup fat-free mozzarella
¼ cup fat-free egg substitute
1 10-ounce package frozen spinach, cooked and
   squeezed dry
Light salt and pepper to taste (optional)

Layer 1 can of the cheese ravioli in a baking dish that has been coated with no-stick cooking spray. Combine the cottage cheese, Parmesan cheese, mozzarella cheese, egg substitute, spinach, light salt and pepper. Spread over the ravioli. Spoon the contents of the remaining can of ravioli over the cheese layer. Cover tightly with aluminum foil and bake for 30 minutes at 350 degrees. Uncover and bake for 10 more minutes. Allow to stand for about 10 minutes before serving. Sprinkle with additional fat-free Parmesan cheese if desired.

4 servings
0 fat grams per serving

Shortcut Lasagna

With this easy recipe, the noodles don't have to be boiled. Homemade lasagna can be ready for the oven in minutes.

1 large onion, chopped
No-stick cooking spray
1 tablespoon garlic powder, divided
2 15-ounce cans tomato sauce
1 cup water
1 15-ounce can sliced mushrooms, drained
1 tablespoon dried oregano
2 cups fat-free cottage cheese
1 cup fat-free mozzarella shredded
¼ cup fat-free Parmesan cheese, grated
¼ cup fat-free egg substitute
Light salt and pepper to taste
8-ounce package lasagna noodles, uncooked

Sauté the onion in a saucepan that has been coated with no-stick cooking spray. Add 2 teaspoons of the garlic powder, the tomato sauce, water, mushrooms and the oregano. In a mixing bowl, combine the remaining 1 teaspoon garlic powder, the cottage cheese, mozzarella, Parmesan cheese and the egg substitute. Add light salt and pepper to taste (optional).

In a 9" x 11" baking dish that has been coated with no-stick cooking spray, spread 1 cup of the sauce. Top with three uncooked noodles followed by half of the cheese mixture. Spread 1 cup sauce on top of the cheese mixture. Add three more noodles, followed by the remaining cheese mixture, 1 cup sauce, the remaining three noodles and the remaining sauce. Sprinkle with additional grated Parmesan if desired. Cover tightly with foil and bake for 45 minutes at 350 degrees. Uncover and bake for 15 additional minutes. Allow to stand for 10-15 minutes.

8 servings, 1 fat gram per serving

South Of The Border Baked Tacos

These are tacos without the mess. Since the tacos are baked in a casserole, they are eaten with a fork. Therefore, the filling ends up in our mouths instead of our laps! Add a bit of low-fat browned ground round or chopped chicken breast to the filling if you wish.

12 fat-free corn tortillas
1 15-ounce can fat-free or low-fat refried beans
2 cups fat-free Cheddar cheese, shredded
2 cups fat-free cottage cheese
1 medium onion, finely chopped
2 15-ounce cans chunky taco sauce

Toppings:
Finely shredded lettuce
Fat-free shredded Cheddar cheese
Fat-free sour cream
Hot or mild taco sauce
Finely chopped onion

Soften the tortillas by puncturing the package and microwaving them for 30 seconds. Spread about 2 tablespoons of the refried beans down the center of each tortilla. Combine the Cheddar cheese, cottage cheese and chopped onion. Place a generous amount down the center of each tortilla. Enclose the filling by folding both sides of the tortilla to the center. Spread a thin layer of taco sauce in a 9" x 13" baking dish that has been coated with no-stick cooking spray. Lay each stuffed tortilla seam side down in the baking dish. Pour the remaining sauce over the tacos. Cover tightly with aluminum foil and bake for 30 minutes at 350 degrees. Just before serving add the toppings or allow each person to add their own at the table.

4 servings 0 fat grams per taco

Terrific Enchiladas

Don't laugh! Potatoes make a hearty and rich filling for enchiladas. I give potatoes a lot of the credit for my weight loss. I love them any way they are prepared. Being able to enjoy a hot baked potato, oven fries or a rich potato casserole prepared with low-fat ingredients is so satisfying. It is definitely not deprivation.

12 fat-free corn tortillas (1 package)
2 cups fat-free mashed potatoes (see recipe index)
1½ cups fat-free Cheddar cheese, divided
½ cup fat-free cottage cheese
1 medium onion, chopped
¼ cup fat-free egg substitute
Light salt and pepper to taste (optional)
2 15-ounce cans chunky Mexican-style tomato sauce
No-stick cooking spray

Punch several holes in the tortilla package and microwave 30 seconds to soften them. Combine the mashed potatoes, 1 cup of the Cheddar cheese, the cottage cheese, onion, egg substitute, light salt and pepper. Spread a thin layer of the tomato sauce in a 9" x 13" baking dish that has been coated with no-stick cooking spray. Remove a warm tortilla from the package and place several tablespoons of the mashed potato filling down the center of each tortilla. Fold both sides to the middle. Place seam side down in the baking dish. Continue filling all of the tortillas. Cover the filled tortillas with the tomato sauce. Cover tightly with foil and bake for 30 minutes at 350 degrees. Allow to stand several minutes before serving. Just before serving, top with the remaining ½ cup cheese.

4 servings
0 fat grams per serving

BREADS

Apple Fritters

Fritters are a beloved staple of the American kitchen. Unfortunately, they are also fried, so they are loaded with fat. A fritter can absorb up to a tablespoon of oil in the frying process. So, we simply bake our fritters instead of frying them. "But isn't that just a muffin?" you ask. No, a fritter has a heavier, chewier texture than a muffin. That's part of what makes it so satisfying.

¼ cup egg substitute
1 cup skim milk
¼ cup unsweetened applesauce
2 tablespoons sugar and 3 packets sugar substitute
¼ teaspoon light salt
3 cups all-purpose flour
2 teaspoons baking powder
¼ teaspoon nutmeg
¼ teaspoon cinnamon
1½ cups apple, peeled and coarsely chopped
No-stick cooking spray

Combine the egg substitute, skim milk, and applesauce. Add the sugar, salt, flour, baking powder, nutmeg and cinnamon. Stir just until the ingredients are combined, then fold in the chopped apple. Spoon into miniature muffin tins that have been coated with no-stick cooking spray. Bake for 20 minutes at 350 degrees. For an added treat, serve with apple butter.

24 fritters
0 fat grams per fritter

Baked Banana Fritters

Here is another baked fritter recipe. I used to love to dine at luau-style restaurants. They might have been hokey to the sophistocated crowd, but I thought they were loads of fun. Many of them served only a few desserts and one of them was usually fried bananas. They were actually batter dipped chunks of fruit that resembled fritters. There aren't many of these restaurants around now but I can make my own version of those fritters at home.

¼ cup egg substitute
1 cup skim milk
¼ cup fat-free sour cream
¼ cup sugar
¼ teaspoon light salt
3 cups all-purpose flour
2 teaspoons baking powder
¼ teaspoon nutmeg
¼ teaspoon cinnamon
2 medium bananas, very coarsely chopped
No-stick cooking spray

Combine the egg substitute and skim milk. Add the sour cream, sugar, salt, flour, baking powder, nutmeg and cinnamon. Stir just until all ingredients are combined. Add the chopped bananas and stir them into the batter. Spoon into miniature muffin tins that have been coated with no-stick cooking spray. Bake for 25 minutes at 350 degrees.

24 fritters
0 fat grams per fritter

Blueberry Bran Muffins

It is widely recognized that wheat bran is very good for you. It can also be very tasty when added to muffins or other breads. This is a delicious way to add fiber to your food.

1½ cups bran cereal
½ cup boiling water
1⅓ cups whole wheat flour
1¼ teaspoons baking soda
⅓ cup sugar or ¼ cup sugar and 2 packets sugar substitute
½ teaspoon cinnamon
¼ teaspoon nutmeg
¼ cup fat-free egg substitute
½ cup fat-free sour cream
¾ cup fresh or frozen blueberries
No-stick cooking spray

Combine the bran cereal and boiling water and let stand 15 minutes. Combine the flour, baking soda, sugar and spices. Add the cereal, then the egg substitute, and sour cream. Stir just until ingredients are combined. Fold in the blueberries. Spoon into muffin tins that have been coated with no-stick cooking spray. Bake for 25 minutes at 350 degrees.

12 muffins
0 fat grams per muffin

Classic Corn Fritters

1 15-ounce can creamed corn
3 tablespoons finely minced onion
½ cup fat-free egg substitute
1 cup self-rising flour
½ teaspoon light salt
No-stick cooking spray

Combine the corn, onion and egg substitute. Gradually add the flour and salt. Spoon into muffin tins that have been coated with no-stick cooking spray. Bake for 30 minutes at 350 degrees.

24 fritters
0 fat grams per fritter

Classic Muffins

2 cups all-purpose flour
2 tablespoons sugar and 3 packets sugar substitute
¼ cup fat-free egg substitute
1½ cups skim milk
3 tablespoons applesauce
No-stick cooking spray

Combine the dry ingredients. Add the egg substitute, milk and applesauce. Stir until the ingredients are just combined. Spoon into muffin tins that have been coated with no-stick cooking spray. Bake for 25 minutes at 375 degrees. Variation: Add ½ cup blueberries or finely chopped apple.

12 muffins
0 fat grams per muffin

Comforting Cornbread

This recipe makes a moist, delicious cornbread. I love cornbread because it is filling and goes so well with soups and the homestyle dishes that we eat at our house. It is one of my comfort foods. I think that it is important to learn how to prepare our favorite comfort foods in a low-fat way. The foods that we have emotional ties to are those that we often turn to when we are stressed or tired or just plain hungry. They make us feel better. Having to give up some of my comfort foods is one of the reasons diets never worked for me. Thank goodness I finally learned that I really didn't have to give them up to lose.

1 cup self-rising cornmeal
1½ cups water
½ cup fat-free egg substitute
No-stick cooking spray

Preheat your oven to 400 degrees. Combine the dry ingredients. Slowly add the water while stirring constantly. Add the egg substitute. Pour the mixture into an 8" iron skillet or 8" square baking pan that has been coated with no-stick cooking spray. Bake for 30 minutes or until brown.

Variation: Add 2 tablespoons imitation bacon bits, 2 tablespoons minced dried onion and ½ cup shredded fat-free Cheddar cheese. Finely minced hot pepper or red pepper flakes may be added.

4 servings
1 fat gram per serving

Kind Of Donuts

These morsels are reminiscent of one of my favorite good-ies–cake donuts. They are close enough in taste to satisfy that donut craving, without the fat!

1½ cups all-purpose flour
1½ teaspoons baking powder
⅓ cup sugar
¼ teaspoon light salt
¼ teaspoon nutmeg
½ cup skim milk
¼ cup fat-free egg substitute
No-stick cooking spray
10 packets aspartame-based sugar substitute
1 teaspoon cinnamon

Combine the flour, baking powder, sugar, salt and nutmeg. Gradually add the milk and the egg substitute. Spoon the mixture into mini-muffin tins that have been coated with no-stick cooking spray. Bake for 20 minutes at 350 degrees. When they are done, turn out onto a plate to cool. When they are cool, spray each muffin lightly with no-stick cooking spray. Combine the sugar substitute and cinnamon. Place the mixture in a zip-top plastic bag. Place the muffins in the bag and toss to coat with the mixture.

24 muffins
0 fat grams per muffin

Lazy Day Apple Muffins

This recipe is so easy that it is almost not a recipe at all! Try it when you are in a real hurry–or on those days when you want something warm and comforting to eat, but can't face more than a few minutes in the kitchen.

1 box low-fat yellow cake mix
½ cup fat-free egg substitute
1 cup water
1 15-ounce can unsweetened sliced apples, coarsely chopped
1 teaspoon nutmeg
No-stick cooking spray

Combine the cake mix, egg substitute and water. Fold in the apples and nutmeg. Spoon into muffin tins that have been coated with no-stick cooking spray. Bake for 30 minutes at 350 degrees.

12 muffins
1 fat gram per muffin

Mom's Yeast Cornbread

Another cornbread variation that is nice for a change. The yeast adds volume, as well as a lovely aroma and taste. I can never smell yeast without becoming ravenously hungry.

1½ cups plain cornmeal
¾ cup flour
1½ teaspoons baking powder
1 teaspoon salt
½ teaspoon baking soda
1 tablespoon sugar
1 package dry yeast
¾ cup fat-free egg substitute
2 cups low-fat buttermilk
No-stick cooking spray

Combine the dry ingredients. Add the egg substitute and the buttermilk. Pour into an iron skillet or baking pan that has been coated with no-stick cooking spray. Bake for 30 minutes at 425 degrees.

6 servings
1 fat gram per serving

Onion Flatbread

I love cooked onions. There is something so elemental, yet luxurious about them. Even when sautéed without oil, they become caramelized and develop a richness that we usually associate with cooking in lots of butter or oil. Combine that flavor with the wonderful taste of yeast bread and you have a really great treat.

2 large onions, thinly sliced
Butter-flavored no-stick cooking spray
¼ teaspoon garlic powder
Light salt and pepper to taste
1 loaf frozen white bread dough, thawed

Sauté the onions in a skillet that has been coated with no-stick cooking spray. When they become a rich caramel brown, add the garlic powder and light salt and pepper to taste. Meanwhile, press the thawed bread dough into a 9" x 13" baking dish that has been coated with no-stick cooking spray. Spread the onions over the dough. Lightly coat the surface with the no-stick cooking spray. Bake for 30 minutes at 350 degrees.

12 servings
0 fat grams per serving

Poor Folks' Pizza

This isn't really pizza, of course. I just jokingly call it that because it sort of resembles slices of pizza. My husband, Ken and I love cornbread and eat it often. We eat it so often, in fact, that one night I decided to serve it a little differently, for variety. I split each wedge in half horizontally and topped each piece with liquid fat-free margarine, finely chopped mild onion and shredded fat-free Cheddar cheese.

1 cup self-rising cornmeal mix
1 cup water
¼ cup fat-free egg substitute
2 tablespoons fat-free sour cream
No-stick cooking spray

Toppings:
Liquid fat-free margarine or ketchup
Finely chopped mild onion
Fat-free Cheddar cheese, shredded

Slowly add the water to the cornmeal mix. Add the egg substitute and sour cream. Pour into an 8" iron skillet or baking pan that has been coated with no-stick cooking spray. Bake for 30 minutes at 400 degrees or until brown and crusty. Cut into 6 pie-shaped wedges. Cut each wedge in half horizontally. Top with margarine or ketchup, followed by finely chopped onion and cheese. Serve immediately.

4 servings
1 fat gram per serving

Quick Apple-Cinnamon Muffins

¾ cup low-fat baking mix
1 envelope instant apple cinnamon oatmeal
½ cup skim milk
¼ cup fat-free egg substitute
No-stick cooking spray

Combine the baking mix and instant oatmeal. Add the skim milk and egg substitute. Spoon into 6 muffin cups that have been coated with no-stick cooking spray. Bake for 15 minutes at 375 degrees.

6 muffins
0 fat grams per muffin

Sweet Potato Muffins

½ cup fat-free egg substitute
1 cup skim milk
1 cup cooked, mashed sweet potatoes (fresh or canned)
⅓ cup unsweetened applesauce
1½ cups all-purpose flour
1 tablespoon sugar
5 teaspoons baking powder
½ teaspoon salt
½ teaspoon nutmeg
No-stick cooking spray

Combine the egg substitute, skim milk, sweet potatoes and applesauce. Mix until smooth. In a separate bowl, combine the dry ingredients. Add the dry ingredients to the potato mixture and stir just until combined. Spoon into muffin tins that have been coated with no-stick cooking spray. Each muffin cup should be ⅔ full. Bake for 30 minutes at 375 degrees.

12 muffins
0 fat grams per muffin

Vegetables

Coffee Baked Beans

2 15-ounce cans fat-free baked beans, drained
1 medium onion, finely minced
2 tablespoons ketchup
2 teaspoons prepared mustard
1 tablespoon Worcestershire sauce
3 packets sugar substitute
1 teaspoon instant coffee granules

Combine the beans, onion, ketchup, mustard, Worcestershire sauce, sugar substitute and coffee granules in a microwave-proof baking dish. Mix well. Cover and microwave on medium power for 10 minutes. Stir before serving.

8 servings
0 fat grams per serving

My Mom's Broccoli Casserole

2 10-ounce packages frozen broccoli, cooked and drained
I medium onion, finely minced
1 cup fat-free mayonnaise
½ cup fat-free egg substitute
4 tablespoons fat-free liquid margarine
1 can 97% fat-free cream of mushroom soup
1 cup fat-free Cheddar cheese, shredded
Light salt and pepper to taste (optional)
No-stick cooking spray

Combine all of the ingredients. Pour into a casserole dish that has been coated with no-stick cooking spray. Bake for 30 minutes at 350 degrees.

8 servings
1 fat gram per serving

Sautéed Broccoli Oriental

3 large stalks broccoli
No-stick cooking spray
2 tablespoons low-sodium soy sauce
1 teaspoon garlic powder

Wash the broccoli, peel the tough lower stems and chop into bite-sized pieces. Sauté the broccoli in a skillet that has been coated with no-stick cooking spray. When it is tender-crisp, add the soy sauce and garlic powder. Cover and steam for 2-3 minutes.

4 servings
0 fat grams per serving

The Best Brussels Sprouts

Brussels sprouts have long been considered bad news by children and by some adults too. Like spinach, they suffer from undeserved jokes about their taste. They are really good.

2 10-ounce packages frozen Brussels sprouts
2 tablespoons liquid fat-free margarine
1 tablespoon lemon juice
1 teaspoon Worcestershire sauce
Light salt and pepper to taste (optional)

In a saucepan over medium heat, bring 5 cups water to a boil. Add the sprouts and cook for approximately 10 minutes, or until tender. Drain the water and add the margarine, lemon juice and Worcestershire sauce. Add light salt and pepper to taste if desired.

4 servings
0 fat grams per serving

Skillet Cabbage Supreme

1 medium head cabbage, coarsely chopped
1 medium onion, coarsely chopped
1 medium bell pepper, coarsely chopped
2 stalks celery, coarsely chopped
No-stick cooking spray
1 tablespoon imitation bacon bits
1 15-ounce can tomato sauce
2 packets sugar substitute

Sauté the cabbage, onion, bell pepper and celery until tender in a skillet that has been coated with no-stick cooking spray. When tender, add the bacon bits, tomato sauce and sugar substitute.

6 servings
Less than 1 fat gram per serving

Snappy Cabbage

1 medium cabbage, coarsely chopped
No-stick cooking spray
3 tablespoons liquid fat-free margarine
3 tablespoons prepared mustard
Light salt and pepper to taste (optional)

Sauté the cabbage in a skillet that has been coated with no-stick cooking spray until it is tender-crisp and slightly browned. Combine the margarine, mustard, light salt and pepper. Add the sauce to the cabbage, cover and cook 5 additional minutes.

6 servings
0 fat grams per serving

Tender-Crisp Cabbage

1 head green cabbage, chopped
No-stick cooking spray
4 tablespoons liquid fat-free margarine
1 packet sugar substitute

Using only the water that clings to it after washing, place the cabbage in a skillet that has been coated with no-stick cooking spray. Sauté over medium heat until the cabbage is tender-crisp and slightly browned. Add the margarine and sugar substitute.

8 servings
0 fat grams per serving

Double Corn Pudding

1 7-ounce package low-fat cornbread mix
1 cup fat-free sour cream
¾ cup fat-free egg substitute
1 15-ounce can whole kernel corn
1 medium onion, finely chopped
1 cup fat-free Cheddar cheese, shredded
Light salt and pepper to taste (optional)
No-stick cooking spray

Combine the cornbread mix, sour cream, egg substitute corn, onion, cheese , light salt and pepper. Place the mixture in a baking dish that has been coated with no-stick cooking spray. Bake for 45 minutes at 350 degrees.

6 servings
3 fat grams per serving

Mexican Corn Casserole

The surprise zip of jalapeno peppers make this casserole different and very good.

1 medium onion, chopped
1 bell pepper, chopped
2 stalks celery, chopped
No-stick cooking spray.
2 cups cooked rice
2 15-ounce cans cream-style corn
1 cup fat-free Cheddar cheese
2 tablespoons fat-free sour cream
1-2 tablespoons chopped jalapeno pepper, depending on
    the degree of hot pepper taste desired
Light salt and pepper to taste (optional)

Sauté the onion, bell pepper and celery in a skillet that has been coated with no-stick cooking spray. When the vegetables are tender, combine them with the remaining ingredients in a casserole dish that has also been coated with no-stick cooking spray. Bake for 30 minutes at 350 degrees.

6 servings
1 fat gram pre serving

Skillet Creole Eggplant

If you like eggplant, you will love this spicy dish. Even if you don't like eggplant, give it a try. Eggplant is a vegetable that is versatile, tasty and good for you.

1 large eggplant, unpeeled
1 medium onion, chopped
1 bell pepper, chopped
No-stick cooking spray
1 15-ounce can tomato sauce
1 teaspoon garlic powder
1 teaspoon dried oregano
Light salt and pepper to taste (optional)
Louisiana hot sauce to taste

Sauté the eggplant, onion and pepper in a skillet that has been coated with no-stick cooking spray. When the vegetables are tender, add the tomato sauce, garlic powder, oregano, light salt, pepper and hot sauce. Cover and simmer for 5 minutes.

6 servings
0 fat grams per serving

Chinese-Style Green Bean Casserole

2 15-ounce cans French-style green beans
1 8-ounce can sliced water chestnuts, drained
1 8-ounce can sliced mushrooms, drained
1 15-ounce can bean sprouts, drained
1 8-ounce can bamboo shoots, drained
1 medium onion, finely minced
1 10¾-ounce can 97% fat-free cream of mushroom soup
Light salt and pepper to taste (optional)
No-stick cooking spray

Combine the green beans, water chestnuts, mushrooms, bean sprouts, bamboo shoots, onions, soup, light salt and pepper. Place the mixture in a baking dish that has been coated with no-stick cooking spray. Bake for 30 minutes at 350 degrees.

8 servings
1 fat gram per serving

Quick And Tasty Green Beans

2 15-ounce cans green beans or 2 10-ounce packages
    frozen green beans, cooked and drained
½ cup fat-free sour cream
2 tablespoons dehydrated onion flakes
Light salt and pepper to taste (optional)

Combine all of the ingredients in a saucepan over medium heat. Cook for 5 minutes or until heated through.

8 servings
0 fat grams per serving

Onions! Onions! Onions!

I guess you can tell that I love onions since I use them in lots of recipes. This rich-tasting casserole is about as oniony as you can get!

4 medium onions, coarsely chopped
6 green onions, chopped, including green tops
No-stick cooking spray
1 1-ounce package dehydrated onion soup mix
1 cup skim milk
2 tablespoons all-purpose flour
3 tablespoons liquid fat-free margarine
1 cup fat-free mozzarella cheese, shredded
1 cup low-fat seasoned commercially prepared croutons
Light salt and pepper to taste (optional)

Sauté the onions in a skillet that has been coated with no-stick cooking spray. When they are tender, add the onion soup mix and blend well. Remove from the heat. In a saucepan over medium heat, combine the milk, flour and fat-free liquid margarine. Stir constantly until thickened. Add to the onions and blend well. Add the mozzarella cheese and light salt and pepper to taste. Place the mixture in a baking dish that has been coated with no-stick cooking spray. Sprinkle the croutons on top. Bake for 30 minutes at 350 degrees.

8 servings
Less than 1 fat gram per serving

Mediterranean-Style English Peas

1 medium onion, chopped
No-stick cooking spray
1 cup cracker crumbs, made from fat-free saltines
1 15-ounce can Italian-style chunky tomato sauce
2 15-ounce cans English peas, drained
1 15-ounce can sliced mushrooms, drained
½ cup fat-free Parmesan cheese, grated

Sauté the onions in a skillet that has been coated with no-stick cooking spray until they are tender. Add the cracker crumbs, tomato sauce, English peas, mushrooms and half of the grated Parmesan cheese. Place the mixture in a baking dish that has been coated with no-stick cooking spray. Bake for 30 minutes at 350 degrees. Top with the remaining Parmesan cheese.

8 servings
0 fat grams per serving

Sour Cream Peas

2 15-ounce cans tiny green peas, drained
1 8-ounce can sliced mushrooms, drained
1 cup fat-free sour cream
¼ cup liquid fat-free margarine
Light salt and pepper to taste (optional)

Combine the green peas, mushrooms, sour cream, margarine, light salt and pepper. Place the mixture in a microwave-proof casserole dish and cook on medium for 5 minutes, or place in a saucepan over medium heat on the stovetop and cook until thoroughly warmed.

8 servings
0 fat grams per serving

Hot And Spicy Black-Eyed Peas

1 pound black-eyed peas, soaked overnight and drained
6 cups water
1 medium onion, chopped
1 bell pepper, chopped
2 jalapeno peppers, sliced
1 packet ham or chicken bouillon

In a slow cooker combine the peas, water, onion, peppers and bouillon. Cook on low for 8-10 hours. May also be cooked in a saucepan on the stovetop on medium heat for approximately 1 hour, or until tender.

6 servings
0 fat grams per serving

Barbecued Potatoes

Everyone knows about eating ketchup with French fries, but ketchup and its cousin, barbecue sauce, are terrific with potatoes any way they are cooked.

4 large potatoes, peeled and diced
1 medium onion, chopped
No-stick cooking spray
1 cup fat-free barbecue sauce
1 teaspoon Louisiana-style hot sauce

Sauté the potatoes and onions in a skillet that has been coated with no-stick cooking spray. When they are tender, add the barbecue sauce and hot sauce. Cover and simmer for 5 minutes.

6 servings
0 fat grams per serving

"Butter-Fried" Potatoes

Butter-flavored no-stick cooking spray
5 large baking potatoes, peeled
Butter flavored granules to taste
Liquid fat-free margarine
Louisiana-style hot sauce to taste

Spray a large cookie sheet with low sides with butter-flavored no-stick cooking spray. Cut the potatoes into thin matchsticks or larger-size French fries, depending on preference. Place the potatoes in a single layer on the baking sheet. Very lightly spray the potatoes with butter-flavored no-stick cooking spray. Bake at 425 degrees for 30 minutes, depending upon how brown you like the potatoes. After removing the potatoes from the oven, spray lightly again with the butter-flavored no-stick cooking spray. Sprinkle the potatoes with fat-free, butter-flavored granules to taste. Serve with liquid fat-free margarine combined with a few drops of Louisiana-style hot sauce for dipping.

4 servings
0 fat grams per serving

Fat-Free Mashed Potatoes

This recipe originally appeared in *Live! Don't Diet!* as Mom's Mashed Potatoes. I am repeating it here because several recipes in this book call for prepared fat-free mashed potatoes.

6 medium potatoes, peeled and cut into large chunks
1 ½-ounce package butter-flavored granules
3 tablespoons nonfat dry milk powder
3 tablespoons fat-free sour cream
Light salt and pepper to taste (optional)

Cover the potatoes with water and boil until tender. Drain the potatoes, reserving the cooking liquid. Mash the potatoes, adding the butter-flavored granules, dry milk powder and sour cream. Return as much cooking liquid as needed to achieve desired consistency.

6 servings
0 fat grams per serving

Meal In One Stuffed Potatoes

These make a great side dish but could also serve as an entree with the addition of a little diced low-fat ham or chicken breast.

4 large potatoes, baked 2 tablespoons skim milk
1 10-ounce package frozen chopped broccoli, cooked
    and drained
$\frac{1}{2}$ cup fat-free cottage cheese
$\frac{1}{2}$ cup fat-free sour cream
1 cup fat-free Cheddar cheese, shredded
4 green onions, chopped, including green tops
4 tablespoons liquid fat-free margarine
Light salt and pepper to taste (optional)
2 tablespoons fat-free Parmesan cheese, grated

Cut the baked potatoes in half horizontally. Scoop the flesh out of each potato half, leaving the skin intact. Mash the potatoes with the milk. Add the broccoli, cottage cheese, sour cream, Cheddar cheese, green onions, liquid margarine and light salt and pepper to taste. The mixture should be firm but not dry. Add additional milk if needed. Stuff the potato skins with the mashed potato mixture. Top with the Parmesan cheese. Bake for 30 minutes at 350 degrees.

8 servings
0 fat grams per serving

Old Country Potato Stuffing

1 medium onion, finely chopped
1 cup celery, finely chopped
No-stick cooking spray
2 cups prepared fat-free mashed potatoes (see recipe index)
1 cup dry bread crumbs
2 tablespoons fat-free liquid margarine
¼ teaspoon sage
¼ cup fat-free egg substitute
Light salt and pepper to taste (optional)

Sauté the onion and celery in a skillet that has been coated with no-stick cooking spray until the vegetables are tender. Combine the sautéed vegetables with the mashed potatoes, bread crumbs, margarine, sage and egg substitute. Add light salt and pepper to taste (optional). Place the mixture in a casserole dish that has been coated with no-stick cooking spray. Bake for 30 minutes at 350 degrees.

4 servings
1 fat gram per serving

My Favorite Sweet Potatoes

4 medium sweet potatoes, peeled, sliced and boiled
½ cup water or skim milk
3 packets sugar substitute
Liquid fat-free margarine

In a mixing bowl, use a potato masher to mash the cooked potatoes until no lumps remain. Add the water or milk and the sugar substitute. Top portions with liquid fat-free margarine to taste.

4 servings
0 fat grams per serving

Sweet Potatoes To Die For

4 large sweet potatoes
Butter-flavored no-stick cooking spray
Fat-free liquid margarine to taste
Cinnamon to taste
Aspartame-based granulated sugar substitute to taste

Lightly coat the potato skins with butter-flavored no-stick cooking spray and place them on a baking pan that has been covered with foil. Bake at 350 degrees for about 2 hours, or until the potatoes are very tender. The actual baking time will depend on the size and shape on the potatoes. Before serving, cut each potato almost in half lengthwise. Squeeze gently to slightly mash the flesh. Add a liberal amount of fat-free liquid margarine to each potato, followed by cinnamon and granulated sugar substitute to taste. Serve immediately.

4 servings
0 fat grams per serving

Easy Baked Rice

1 cup uncooked white rice
1 15-ounce can low-sodium chicken broth
¼ cup water
2 tablespoons Worcestershire sauce
1 package dehydrated onion soup mix
No-stick cooking spray

Combine the rice, chicken broth, water, Worcestershire sauce and onion soup mix in a casserole dish that has been coated with no-stick cooking spray. Cover and bake for 1½ hours at 350 degrees.

4 servings
2 fat grams per serving

Autumn Harvest Fruited Rice

1 medium onion, finely chopped
No-stick cooking spray
1 cup uncooked white rice
1 15-ounce can low-sodium, fat-free chicken broth
½ cup plus 2 tablespoons water
½ cup dried apricots, finely chopped
2 tablespoons raisins

In a saucepan that has been coated with no-stick cooking spray, sauté the onion until slightly wilted. Add the rice, chicken broth, water, apricots and raisins. Bring the mixture to a boil, cover and simmer 20 minutes, or until the rice is tender.

4 servings
1 fat gram per serving

Cheesy Spinach Bake

1 cup fat-free egg substitute
1 cup skim milk
1 cup soft breadcrumbs, made from reduced-calorie bread
1 10-ounce package frozen chopped spinach, cooked
    and drained
4 green onions, chopped
¼ cup fat-free Parmesan cheese, grated
1 cup fat-free mozzarella, shredded
Light salt and pepper to taste (optional)
No-stick cooking spray

Combine the egg substitute, milk and breadcrumbs. Let the mixture stand for 5 minutes to moisten the crumbs thoroughly. Add the spinach, onions, Parmesan cheese, mozzarella, light salt and pepper. Place the mixture in a baking dish that has been coated with no-stick cooking spray. Bake for 30 minutes at 350 degrees.

4 servings
Less than 1 fat gram per serving

Deluxe Squash Casserole

1 pound yellow summer squash, boiled, mashed and drained
1 medium onion, finely chopped
10 fat-free saltine crackers, crushed into coarse crumbs
1 cup fat-free Cheddar cheese, shredded
2 tablespoons fat-free sour cream
$\frac{1}{2}$ cup fat-free egg substitute
No-stick cooking spray

Combine the squash, onion, cracker crumbs, cheese, sour cream and egg substitute. Place the mixture in a baking dish that has been coated with no-stick cooking spray. Bake for 30 minutes at 350 degrees.

4 servings
0 fat grams per serving

Old-Fashioned Squash Dressing

1 pound yellow summer squash
1 medium onion, finely minced
1 box herb-seasoned stuffing mix prepared according to
    package directions, omitting the margarine
2 tablespoons fat-free sour cream
No-stick cooking spray

Place the squash and onion in a saucepan. Cover with water and simmer until tender. Drain, then mash the squash. Combine all of the ingredients. Place the mixture in a casserole dish that has also been coated with no-stick cooking spray. Bake for 30 minutes at 350 degrees.

6 servings
0 fat grams per serving

Summer Squash Italian-Style

4 yellow summer squash, sliced
4 zucchini, sliced
1 medium onion, sliced
No-stick cooking spray
1 cup fat-free spaghetti sauce
1 tablespoon Parmesan cheese, grated

Sauté the yellow summer squash, zucchini and onion in a skillet that has been coated with no-stick cooking spray. When the vegetables are tender, add the spaghetti sauce. Serve topped with Parmesan cheese.

4 servings
0 fat grams per serving

Skillet-Baked Tomatoes

4 large, firm, ripe tomatoes, halved
No-stick cooking spray
4 tablespoons fat-free Italian salad dressing

Sauté the tomatoes, cut side down in a skillet that has been coated with no-stick cooking spray. When they are slightly brown, turn and spoon 1 tablespoon Italian dressing over the cut side of the tomato halves. Cover and continue cooking for several minutes until warmed through.

8 servings
0 fat grams per serving

Condiments

Barbecue Rub

Many true connoisseurs of barbecue like to coat meat or chicken with a dry marinade before cooking. The traditional tomato-based sauce is added only at the last minute.

¼ cup paprika
¼ cup black pepper, coarsely ground
¼ cup chili powder
2 tablespoons garlic powder
1 tablespoon light salt
2 tablespoons granulated sugar substitute

Combine all ingredients. Store in a tightly covered jar.

1 cup
0 fat grams in the recipe

Bread And Butter Pickles In Minutes

I love bread and butter pickles. They are great with sandwiches or chopped and added to chicken or ham salad. They are also good all by themselves. I like making my own because I can control the amount of salt in them.

¾ cup cider vinegar
1 tablespoon mixed pickling spice
¾ teaspoon light salt
Sugar substitute to equal ⅓ cup sugar
6 cucumbers, preferably unwaxed, sliced
2 medium onions, sliced

Combine the vinegar, the pickling spice and the light salt in a saucepan. Bring to a boil over medium heat. Remove from the heat and add the sugar substitute. Place the vegetables in pint canning jars or in a glass bowl. Pour the vinegar over the vegetables. Store in the refrigerator.

3 pints
0 fat grams in the recipe

Cajun-Style Mayonnaise

Cajun seasoning adds the flair and sparkle that are important in low-fat dishes. This spicy mayonnaise is really good on sandwiches, salads, cold meats or as a dip.

1 cup fat-free mayonnaise
1 tablespoon Cajun seasoning, commercially prepared or
   homemade (see recipe index)
1 tablespoon lemon juice
1 teaspoon garlic powder

Combine the mayonnaise, Cajun seasoning, lemon juice, and garlic powder. Serve chilled.

1 cup
0 fat grams in the recipe

Cajun-Style Seasoning

Popular Cajun-style seasoning is available in most grocery stores. However, it is easily made at home from spices you probably already have on hand.

1 tablespoon light salt
1 tablespoon ground black pepper
2 teaspoons ground red pepper
1 tablespoon dry mustard powder
1 teaspoon garlic powder

Combine the salt, black pepper, red pepper, dry mustard and garlic powder. Store in a tightly capped jar.

4 tablespoons
0 fat grams in the recipe

Country-Style Apple Butter

2 pounds cooking apples, peeled and chopped
½ cup cider vinegar
Juice of 1 lemon
1 tablespoon ground cinnamon
1 teaspoon ground cloves
Aspartame-based sugar substitute to equal 2 cups sugar

Combine the apples, vinegar, lemon juice and spices in a saucepan. Cook until the apples are very tender. If there are any whole pieces of apple remaining, puree or mash them until the mixture is smooth. When cool, add the sugar substitute. Store in the refrigerator.

3-4 pints
0 fat grams in the recipe

Dill Sauce For Fish

This recipe is terrific with either fish or shellfish. It is also great as a dressing for potato salad.

¾ cup fat-free mayonnaise
3 tablespoons fat-free sour cream
1 tablespoons skim milk
1 tablespoon dillweed
Light salt to taste

Combine the mayonnaise, sour cream, skim milk, dillweed and light salt. Serve chilled.

1 cup
0 fat grams in the recipe

Extra-Spicy Barbecue Sauce

1 cup ketchup
½ cup cider vinegar
1 tablespoon lemon juice
¼ cup Worcestershire sauce
1 teaspoon garlic powder
1 teaspoon black pepper
1 tablespoon Cajun-style seasoning, commercially
    prepared or homemade (see recipe index)
1 tablespoon liquid smoke
Sugar substitute to equal 2 tablespoons sugar

Combine the ketchup, vinegar, lemon juice, Worcestershire sauce, spices and liquid smoke in a saucepan. Simmer over medium heat for 15 minutes. Remove from the heat and when cool, add the sugar substitute.

2 cups
0 fat grams in the recipe

Guilt-Free Strawberry Preserves

These preserves are really terrific. While perhaps not as thick as sugary, calorie-laden preserves, they have more intense and wonderful strawberry flavor. A drop or two of red food coloring may be added to deepen the red color. This can double as a great strawberry sauce with angel food cake or fat-free ice cream.

6 cups fresh or frozen strawberries, slightly mashed
1 package pectin made for low-sugar preserves
Aspartame-based sugar substitute to taste

Combine the strawberries and the pectin. Allow to stand 10 minutes. Place in the microwave oven in a deep, microwave-safe bowl. Microwave 5 minutes or until the mixture comes to a boil. Stir, then microwave 4 additional minutes. Stir once again, then microwave 4 more minutes. Allow to cool, then add sugar substitute to taste. Pour into canning jars or plastic freezer containers. Store in the refrigerator or freezer.

3 pints
0 fat grams in the recipe

Homemade Crispy Coating For Chicken

This is a homemade version of the coating mixes sold for oven-frying chicken. It is also good as a coating for oven-fried vegetables. Just spray the chicken or vegetables with no-stick cooking spray and dip in the coating mix. Spray the coated pieces again lightly with the no-stick cooking spray and bake at 425 degrees.

2 cups fine, dry breadcrumbs
½ cup all-purpose flour
2 teaspoons light salt
1 tablespoon poultry seasoning
1 teaspoon black pepper
2 teaspoons garlic powder

Combine the breadcrumbs, flour, light salt, poultry seasoning, black pepper and garlic powder. Store in a tightly covered jar.

2³/₄ cups
0 fat grams in the recipe

Honey Mustard Sauce

This makes a really good dip, salad dressing, sandwich spread or sauce for grilled chicken. This recipe is a really terrific one–it has only three inexpensive ingredients, can be made in seconds and can be used a number of ways. You can't ask for more than that!

½ cup Dijon-style mustard
½ cup fat-free mayonnaise
2 tablespoons honey

Combine the Dijon mustard, mayonnaise and honey. Can be served chilled or warm.

4 servings
0 fat grams per serving

Peach Pie Preserves

I had a basket of fresh peaches on hand last summer that had gotten very ripe. I am a terribly lazy cook. Rather than get my act together and peel those peaches, I decided to experiment by leaving the peels on. If my experiment hadn't worked, I guess I would have had to change the name of the recipe to Fuzzy Peach Preserves. However, they really turned out great. There was no sign of peach fuzz and the peels on the peaches were not even noticeable.

12-15 very ripe peaches, chopped
1 box pectin made for low-sugar preserves
Aspartame-based sugar substitute to taste
Nutmeg to taste
Cinnamon to taste

Slightly mash the peaches. Combine them with the pectin and allow to stand for 10 minutes. Bring to a boil over medium heat. Lower the heat and allow to simmer 10 minutes. Remove from the heat. When the preserves have cooled slightly, add the sugar substitute and spices to taste. Pour into canning jars or plastic freezer containers. Store in the refrigerator or freezer.

3 pints
0 fat grams in the recipe

Piquant Beet Relish

I happen to like beets but even those who don't may like this relish. It is good with dried beans.

3 15-ounce cans sliced beets, chopped
1 medium onion, chopped
½ medium green cabbage, chopped
½ teaspoon light salt (optional)
1½ cups cider vinegar
Sugar substitute to equal ¾ cup sugar

Combine the beets, onion, cabbage, salt and vinegar in a medium saucepan. Bring to a boil, then simmer 10 minutes. Remove from the heat and when cool, add the sugar substitute. Store in canning jars or a covered glass dish in the refrigerator.

3 pints
0 fat grams in the recipe

Zippy Mayonnaise

Even if you don't care for fat-free mayonnaise, you will like this spicy version. It is good as a sandwich spread or as a dressing for green salads, pasta salads, or potato salad.

1 cup fat-free mayonnaise
3 tablespoons prepared mustard
2 teaspoons lemon juice
1 teaspoon Louisiana-style hot sauce

Combine the mayonnaise, mustard, lemon juice and hot sauce. Serve chilled.

1¼ cups
0 fat grams in the recipe

DESSERTS

Angel's Wing Cake

This cake is so light and delicious I could eat it all by myself. It makes a nice fat-free birthday cake since it is very pretty.

1 8-ounce container fat-free whipped topping, thawed
1 small (4 serving-size) box vanilla fat-free, sugar-free
    pudding mix
1 8-ounce can juice-packed crushed pineapple, drained
1 commercially prepared angel food cake

In a mixing bowl, combine the whipped topping, the dry pudding mix and the fruit. Fold the ingredients together gently. Slice the cake horizontally into 3 equal layers. Frost the top and sides of one layer with the whipped topping mixture. Add the second layer, then the third, frosting the top and sides of each.

12 servings
0 fat grams per serving

Autumn Fruit Bake

This is a wonderful dessert for cool weather, I guess because the dried fruit seems like fall or winter. It is good topped with fat-free whipped topping or ice cream. Leave off the cookie topping and it could be served as a fruit compote with ham or turkey.

1 15-ounce can juice-packed pear halves, drained
    and chopped (reserve juice)
1 15-ounce can juice-packed peaches, drained and
    chopped (reserve juice)
1 cup mixed dried fruit (prunes, apples and apricots)
1 15-ounce can light cherry pie filling
4 fat-free or low-fat oatmeal cookies, crumbled
No-stick cooking spray

Combine the reserved juice with the dried fruit. Cover and microwave for 5 minutes. Drain and discard any remaining liquid. Combine the pears, peaches, dried fruit and cherry pie filling. Top with the crumbled cookies. Spray the cookies lightly with no-stick cooking spray. Bake for 30 minutes at 350 degrees.

8 servings
0 fat grams per serving,
if fat-free cookies are used

Banana Pudding In A Cone

Thank goodness for ice cream cones. They make ice cream a portable treat. Now they do the same thing for another favorite dessert–banana pudding. An old-fashioned ice cream cone has only a trace of fat and only 20 calories. They can be used in a variety of creative ways that appeal to kids, as well as the kid in all of us. Sundaes in cones (fat-free frozen yogurt, low-fat sundae topping and fat-free whipped topping), pudding in cones or even cupcakes in cones (light cake mix baked in flat-bottomed cones) are just some of the possibilities.

1 small (4 serving-size) box fat-free, sugar-free banana-flavored pudding mix
2 cups skim milk
1 medium banana, thinly sliced
4 old-fashioned, flat-bottomed ice cream cones
4 tablespoons fat-free whipped topping

Combine the pudding mix and milk. Blend well. When it has thickened, layer pudding and banana slices in each cone. Top with a tablespoon of fat-free whipped topping.

4 servings
Less than 1 fat gram per serving

Banana Shortcake

Light cake mixes are now available in many flavors. They have substantially less fat than conventional cake mixes and taste just as good. You will never notice that this tasty short-cake is missing anything, especially since it tastes so rich and creamy. It couldn't be any better.

1 light white or yellow cake mix
½ cup fat-free egg substitute
1 large (8 serving-size) box fat-free, sugar-free
   vanilla pudding mix
4½ cups skim milk
2 medium-size ripe bananas

Prepare the cake mix according to package directions, using fat-free egg substitute instead of eggs. Bake in a 9" x 13" baking dish that has been coated with no-stick cooking spray. Baking time will depend on package directions. Meanwhile, combine the pudding and the skim milk. The pudding should be the consistency of a custard sauce. Add additional milk if needed to achieve desired consistency. Shortly before serving, thinly slice the bananas. Cut the cake into twelve equal squares. For each serving, place one cake square on an individual serving plate. Top with a portion of the sauce and banana slices.

12 servings
Less than 2 fat grams per serving

Cheesecake Truffles

8 ounces fat-free cream cheese softened
½ teaspoon vanilla, coconut, orange or almond extract
12 packets aspartame-based sugar substitute
¼ cup graham cracker crumbs
Dash cinnamon

Combine the softened cream cheese with the extract and 10 packets of sugar substitute. Taste and add more sugar substitute or extract if desired. Chill the mixture until firm. Meanwhile, combine the graham cracker crumbs, 2 packets of sugar substitute and a dash of cinnamon. Shape the cream cheese mixture into small balls and roll each ball in the graham cracker crumbs. Store in the refrigerator.

24 candies, 0 fat grams per candy

Cherry Cobbler Cake

This is a tasty combination–the fruity filling of cobbler topped by the moist tenderness of cake. For all its simplicity, this is a big hit when I take it to potluck dinners.

2 15-ounce cans light cherry pie filling
No-stick cooking spray
1 light yellow or white cake mix
½ cup fat-free egg substitute

Pour the cherry pie filling into a 9" x 13" baking dish that has been coated with no-stick cooking spray. Prepare the cake mix according to package directions, using egg substitute instead of eggs. Pour the prepared cake batter over the fruit filling. Bake for 30 minutes at 350 degrees.

12 servings
2 fat grams per serving

Cherry Cream Cheese Pie

Commercially prepared pie crusts can be fairly low in fat if you read labels carefully and choose the right brand. Pastry crusts average 8 fat grams per serving if you divide your pie into eight servings. Graham cracker crusts average 6 grams for the same size serving. Lower-fat prepared graham cracker crusts are now in grocery stores. They have only 3 fat grams per serving.

1 small (4 serving-size) box fat-free, sugar-free vanilla
    pudding mix
1½ cups skim milk
1 8-ounce package fat-free cream cheese, softened
¼ teaspoon vanilla extract
6 packets aspartame-based sugar substitute
1 lower-fat graham cracker pie crust
1 15-ounce can light cherry pie filling

In a mixing bowl, combine the pudding mix and skim milk. Blend until the pudding mix is dissolved. Set aside. In a separate mixing bowl, combine the cream cheese, vanilla extract and sugar substitute. Gently fold the pudding and cream cheese together. When thoroughly combined, pour the mixture into the graham cracker pie crust. Spread the cherry pie filling over the cream cheese layer. Chill for several hours.

8 servings
3 fat grams per serving

Chocolate Decadence

Never leave me alone with this dessert. There won't be any left if I get my hands on it.

1 large (8 serving-size) box fat-free, sugar-free chocolate
   fudge pudding mix
4 cup cold skim milk
1 light cake mix, chocolate or chocolate fudge flavor
½ cup fat-free egg substitute
No-stick cooking spray
6 fat-free or low-fat chocolate cream-filled cookies
1 cup fat-free whipped topping

Combine the pudding mix and skim milk. Stir well. Refrigerate until needed. Meanwhile prepare the cake mix according to package directions, using the egg substitute instead of eggs. Bake the cake in a 9" x 13" pan that has been coated with no-stick cooking spray. The baking time will depend on package directions. When the cake has cooled, cut into 1" wide slices. Chop the cookies into coarse crumbs. In a large serving dish, preferably clear glass, place a layer of cake slices, followed by a layer of pudding. Sprinkle the pudding with chopped cookie crumbs. Repeat the layers until all of the cake and pudding has been used. Reserve some cookie crumbs for the top of the dessert. After all of the cake and pudding has been used, spread the whipped topping over the top. Sprinkle with the reserved cookie crumbs.

12 servings
2 fat grams per serving

Cranberry Upside Down Cake

The surprise ingredient in this delicious recipe is the cranberry sauce. It develops a mellow richness in the cooking process. Few people would even guess that it's just good old cranberry sauce in disguise.

2 15-ounce cans whole berry cranberry sauce
1 15-ounce can juice-packed crushed pineapple, undrained
1 light yellow or white cake mix
½ cup fat-free egg substitute
No-stick cooking spray

Combine the cranberry sauce and the crushed pineapple. Spread the mixture into a 9" x 13" baking dish that has been coated with no-stick cooking spray. Prepare the cake mix according to package directions, using the egg substitute instead of the eggs called for in the recipe. Pour the cake mix over the cranberry layer. Bake for 30 minutes at 350 degrees.

12 servings
Less than 2 fat grams per serving

Desperation Pie In An Instant

Here's another taste-alike. This is what I often make when I have a craving for apple pie and there is no low-fat apple pie around. It's a pretty effective way to satisfy that sweet tooth in a quick and healthy manner. You get crunch from the rice cake and the delicious taste of apples and cinnamon–the same taste sensations that make real apple pie so wonderful.

For each "pie":
1 caramel rice cake
2 tablespoons unsweetened applesauce
Cinnamon to taste
Granulated aspartame-based sugar substitute

Spread the applesauce on the rice cake. Sprinkle with the cinnamon and sugar substitute to taste. Can be topped with fat-free vanilla frozen yogurt if desired. Serve immediately.

1 serving
0 fat grams per serving

Fabulous Tropical Frozen Yogurt

Isn't it great that ice cream and frozen yogurt are now available in a fat-free, sugar-free form? It is fun to experiment by using your own favorite extras to create a personalized frozen treat. The possibilities are limitless.

½ gallon fat-free, sugar-free, vanilla-flavored frozen
   yogurt, softened
2 teaspoons coconut extract (or more, according to taste)
1 15-ounce can juice-packed crushed pineapple, drained
1 8-ounce can juice-packed mandarin oranges, drained

In a mixing bowl, combine the softened frozen yogurt, coconut extract, pineapple and mandarin oranges. Place the mixture in a freezer-proof storage container with a sealable lid and refreeze. Let stand at room temperature for 5 minutes before serving.

16 servings
0 fat grams per serving

Fat-Free, Sugar-Free Fudge Truffles

Truffles are a favorite of candy lovers. Unfortunately, they are loaded with sugar and fat. Never fear! Here are two recipes for truffles that can satisfy your your sweet tooth and your healthy lifesyle. To be fancy, place in ruffled paper candy cups.

3-4 tablespoons cocoa powder
10-12 packets aspartame-based sugar substitute
8 ounces fat-free cream cheese, softened

Gradually add the cocoa powder and sugar substitute to the softened cream cheese. Taste after adding three tablespoons of cocoa. At this point the candies will have the taste of bittersweet chocolate. Add additional cocoa powder and/or sugar substitute if you wish. Chill until firm. Shape the mixture into small balls, then roll in additional cocoa powder mixed with an equal amount of sugar substitute. Store in the refrigerator.

24 candies, 0 fat grams per candy

Guilt-Free No-Bake Cheesecake

One of the world's most beloved desserts is unfortunately one of the most fat-laden. There are many recipes for low-fat cheesecake around but they often still contain heaps of sugar. Here is the recipe that has no fat, no sugar and as an added bonus, does not have to be baked.

3 tablespoons cornflake crumbs combined with 1 packet
    sugar substitute and ¼ teaspoon cinnamon
4 8-ounce packages fat-free cream cheese, softened
Aspartame-based sugar substitute to equal 1 cup sugar
1 packet unflavored gelatin
1¼ cups water, divided
1 teaspoon each vanilla, butter, coconut and orange extract

Coat an 8 inch or 9 inch springform pan with no-stick cooking spray. Sprinkle with the cornflake crumb mixture and shake the pan to coat the bottom and sides evenly. Reserve a bit of the mixture to top the cheesecake if desired. Add the sugar substitute to the softened creamed cheese. In a measuring cup, combine the unflavored gelatin with ¼ cup cold water. Allow it to stand for 2 minutes, then microwave for 1 minute. Make sure the gelatin is completely dissolved. Add the gelatin to the cream cheese mixture, followed by the remaining 1 cup of water and the extract. Blend well, preferably with a hand mixer or whisk. Chill until firm.

6 servings
0 fat grams per serving

Heavenly Ambrosia

2 15-ounce cans juice-packed pineapple tidbits, drained
4 medium oranges, peeled, seeded and sectioned
2 medium bananas, thinly sliced
1 cup miniature marshmallows
1 cup fat-free vanilla-flavored yogurt
1 small (4-serving-size) box fat-free, sugar-free vanilla
   pudding mix
1 cup skim milk

In a serving bowl, combine the pineapple, oranges, bananas and marshmallows. In a separate bowl, combine the yogurt, pudding mix and milk. Blend well. Combine the yogurt mixture with the fruit mixture and serve immediately. Serve alone in stemmed glasses or over fat-free pound cake or angel food cake.

8 servings
0 fat grams per serving

Kind Of Pie

When I want pie, I often make a taste-alike version that will make me happy without having a whole pie around to tempt me. My very favorite pie is lemon icebox. I like the smooth creamy tartness of the filling and the crunchy texture of the graham cracker crust. While this recipe is for a lemon icebox taste-alike, this parfait can satisfy your desire for almost kind of pie. Just substitute your own favorite filling. The real appeal of pie is the sweetness of a fruit or cream filling combined with crunch. You get that here, along with a simplicity of preparation that can't be beat.

1 small (4 serving-size) box fat-free, sugar-free vanilla
   pudding mix
1¾ cups skim milk
2 tablespoons lemon juice
Sugar substitute to taste
½ cup graham cracker crumbs
4 tablespoons fat-free whipped topping

Combine the pudding mix and milk. Add the lemon juice and sugar substitute to taste. For each serving, layer the pudding mixture and graham cracker crumbs in individual parfaits or serving dishes. Top with the whipped topping.

4 servings
0 fat grams per serving

Light And Fruity Orange Sherbet

This is also great made with other fruit juices. Try pineappple juice, grape juice or combined juices, like orange-pineapple.

2 cups unsweetened orange juice
$\frac{1}{3}$ cup non-fat dry milk powder
3 packets aspartame-based artificial sweetener

Combine the orange juice, milk powder and sweetener. Blend thoroughly. Pour the mixture into a baking pan and freeze until slightly firm. Remove from the freezer and beat until smooth and creamy. Return to the freezer. Allow to stand a few minutes at room temperature before serving.

4 servings
0 fat grams per serving

Old-Fashioned Peach Dumplings

Dumplings lend themselves to all kinds of delicious adaptations, including dessert. They are also a terrific comfort food. Fat-free, sugar-free vanilla frozen yogurt is great served on top of individual servings.

2 15-ounce cans sliced juice-packed peaches, juice reserved
4 cups water
1 13.5-ounce package fat-free flour tortillas, cut
   into 1" squares
8 packets aspartame-based sugar substitute
1 tablespoon cinnamon

Combine the reserved peach juice and water in a saucepan. Bring to a boil over medium heat. Gradually add the tortilla squares, stirring frequently, so that they won't stick together. Cook for 10 minutes or until the dumplings lose their doughy consistency. Add the peaches, 6 packets sugar substitute and a dash of cinnamon. In a separate bowl, combine the remaining sugar substitute and cinnamon. Place the dumplings in individual serving bowls and top with a bit of the cinnamon mixture. Serve immediately,

8 servings
0 fat grams per serving

Pancake Cake

While not exactly a company dessert, this a distant cousin of the elaborate gourmet treat Crepes Suzette. Low-fat packaged pancake mix or frozen pancakes can be used if you prefer.

2¼ cups all-purpose flour
4 teaspoons baking powder
1 teaspoon light salt
2 cups skim milk
¼ cup fat-free egg substitute
4 tablespoons fat-free cottage cheese
Butter-flavored no-stick cooking spray
1 cup low-sugar orange marmalade

Orange Sauce:
1 cup orange juice
1 tablespoon cornstarch
3 packets aspartame-based sugar substitute

Combine the flour, baking powder, salt, skim milk and egg substitute. On a griddle that has been coated with no-stick cooking spray, pour enough batter to form an 8" pancake. When bubbles form on the uncooked side, turn and cook for 2 additional minutes. Repeat until all of the pancake batter has been used. Spread each layer with a generous coating of orange marmalade, then stack them to resemble a cake. To make the sauce, combine the orange juice and cornstarch. Bring to a boil over medium heat until the mixture thickens. Add the sugar substitute. Top with the warm orange sauce.

4 servings
0 fat grams per serving

Punchbowl Cake

This is another flexible dessert recipe that is popular around our house. You can use low-fat yellow or white cake or angel food cake and just about any fruit that suits your fancy. I like to use purchased angel food cake for several reasons. It is fat-free, delicious, and best of all, I don't have to bake it! This is very pretty when served in a glass punchbowl or serving dish.

1 large (8 serving-size) box fat-free, sugar-free vanilla pudding mix
4 cups skim milk
1 large commercially prepared angel food cake ring, torn into bite-size pieces
1 15-ounce can juice-packed sliced peaches, drained and chopped
1 8-ounce can juice-packed crushed pineapple, drained
3 large ripe bananas, thinly sliced
1 15-ounce can light cherry pie filling
1 cup fat-free whipped topping

Combine the pudding mix and milk. Set aside to thicken. In a large glass serving bowl, place ¼ of the cake pieces, followed by the peaches, then ¼ of the pudding. Repeat the layers, using the pineapple. Repeat again, using the sliced bananas. Top the bananas with the last layer of cake, followed by pudding, then the cherry pie filling. Garnish with dollops of whipped topping.

12 servings
Less than 1 fat-gram per serving

Rich And Creamy Cheesecake

Here is another tasty no-bake cheesecake without fat or sugar. Use any type crushed fat-free cereal to make the crust and any flavor fat-free pudding mix.

6 tablespoons fat-free nutty nugget-type cereal
Dash cinnamon
15 packets aspartame-based sugar substitute, divided
No-stick cooking spray
¼ cup boiling water
1 packet unflavored gelatin
1 small (4 serving-size) box fat-free, sugar-free vanilla
   pudding mix
1 ½ cups skim milk
3 8-ounce packages fat-free cream cheese, softened
1 teaspoon vanilla extract

Combine the cereal, cinnamon and 3 packets sugar substitute. Coat an 8" or 9" springform pan or pie plate with no-stick cooking spray. Pour the cereal mixture into the pan and shake the pan gently to coat the bottom and sides with the cereal mixture. In a measuring cup, combine the boiling water and gelatin. Stir well to dissolve the gelatin. Allow to cool to room temperature. In a mixing bowl, combine the pudding mix and milk. Add the cooled gelatin mixture and blend well. Gently fold the pudding mixture into the softened cream cheese. Add 12 packets sugar substitute and the vanilla extract. Pour the cream cheese mixture over the crust. Cover and chill for at least 4 hours.

8 servings
0 fat grams per serving

Taste-Alike Instant Dutch Apple Cobbler

I am a sucker for Dutch apple pie. Lots of us are. While it is usually made with hefty amounts of butter and sugar, we don't have to do without it just because we are eating healthy. We can make a taste-alike. Let's analyze the taste we love in Dutch apple pie. There is the taste of apples, cinnamon and sugar combined with the sweet crunch of streusel. All we have to do is use sugar substitute for the sugar, while low-fat granola cereal makes a dandy substitute for the streusel.

    2 15-ounce cans sliced, unsweetened apples
    Sugar substitute to taste
    1 teaspoon apple pie spice
    4 tablespoons low-fat granola cereal

Combine the apples, the sugar substitute and apple pie spice in a microwave-safe baking dish. Cover loosely with plastic wrap and microwave on high power for 5 minutes. Remove and evenly sprinkle the granola over the fruit. Return to the microwave for 30 seconds on high power. Serve plain or topped with fat-free, sugar-free frozen yogurt.

Variation: Use canned, sliced peaches or low-sugar commercially prepared fruit pie filling.

4 servings
1 fat gram per serving

40 New Recipes

Hawaiian Appetizer Wieners

Small cocktail wieners are popular for parties and snacks. However, just 8 of the tasty little morsels can have a mind-boggling 16 grams of fat. The solution is to use fat-free wieners cut into bite-size portions. The taste is still there without the fat.

No-stick cooking spray
1 pound fat-free wieners
2 tablespoons dehydrated minced onion
1 cup low-sugar grape jelly
$\frac{1}{3}$ cup mustard
1 15-ounce can juice-packed pineapple chunks, drained
Sugar substitute to equal 3 tablespoons sugar

Sauté the wieners in a skillet coated with no-stick cooking spray until they are lightly browned. Add the dehydrated onion, jelly, mustard, and pineapple. Heat until the sauce is warm. Add the sugar substitute and mix well. Serve with cocktail picks.

8 servings
0 fat grams per serving

Zesty Pickles

I like to keep pickles like these in the refrigerator. A few bites often will satisfy hunger. I like to make my own pickles rather than eat the commercially prepared variety. They can be made in minutes and I can control the amount of salt in them. They are still good and I can eat as many as I want without looking like a balloon the next day.

3 large cucumbers, preferably not waxed, sliced
3 medium onions, sliced
2 large red or green bell peppers, sliced
4 large carrots, peeled and sliced
1 medium cauliflower, separated into florets
2 tablespoons salt
2½ cups cider vinegar
1 tablespoon mustard seeds
1 teaspoon celery seeds
½ teaspoon ground cloves
Sugar substitute to taste

Layer the vegetables with the salt in a colander to draw liquid from them. Place the colander in the sink, since liquid will drain from the vegetables. Cover the vegetables with plastic wrap and place a heavy object on top of them. Allow to stand 2 hours. This will help the liquid to drain.

Rinse the vegetables to remove the salt. In a saucepan, bring the vinegar, mustard seeds, and celery seeds to a boil. Remove from the heat, and when sufficiently cool, add sugar substitute to taste. Place the vegetables in canning jars or plastic freezer containers and pour the vinegar mixture over the vegetables. Store in the refrigerator or freezer.

5 pints
0 fat grams per serving

Antipasto Pickles

Here's another pickle recipe. Because they contain the classic Italian seasonings oregano, basil, and garlic, I call them Antipasto Pickles. They make a nice addition to an antipasto platter served before an Italian dinner, along with some fat-free mozzarella cheese and perhaps some fat-free ham or turkey cut into strips. You can add just about any vegetables you wish to these pickles.

4 cups cider vinegar
1½ cups water
1 teaspoon whole peppercorns
2 teaspoons dried oregano
2 teaspoons dried basil
3 cloves garlic, minced
1 teaspoon light salt (optional)
3 bell peppers, sliced
3–4 small zucchini, sliced
3 medium onions, sliced
4–5 carrots, sliced
4 stalks celery, sliced
2 cups fresh mushrooms, sliced

Combine the vinegar, water, peppercorns, oregano, basil, garlic, and salt. Bring to a boil over medium heat. Lower the heat, then add the rest of the ingredients. Simmer 4 minutes. Store in the refrigerator in canning jars or plastic freezer containers.

5 pints
0 fat grams per serving

Southern Salad

Black-eyed peas are a Southern staple and so is rice. Put them together and you have that Southern classic, Hopping John, which is traditionally served on New Year's Day for good luck in the coming year. Add a few additional ingredients and you have a new twist on Hopping John. I call it Southern Salad.

2 15-ounce cans black-eyed peas, drained
2 cups cooked white rice
1 medium onion, finely chopped
1 green pepper, finely chopped
1 2-ounce jar chopped pimento, drained
1 8-ounce bottle fat-free zesty Italian salad dressing

Combine the black-eyed peas, rice, onion, green pepper, and pimento. Add the salad dressing and mix well. Chill well before serving.

12 servings
0 fat grams per serving

Unique Broccoli Salad

If you're always trying to think of new ways to entice your family to eat more green vegetables, this salad is worth a try.

3 large stalks broccoli, chopped
   (if also using stems, peel first)
1 medium onion, finely chopped
3 tablespoons raisins
1 cup fat-free mayonnaise
2 tablespoons cider vinegar
2 packets aspartame-based sugar substitute
   or 1 tablespoon sugar

Combine the broccoli, onion, and raisins. In a separate bowl, combine the mayonnaise, vinegar, and sugar substitute or sugar. Add the mayonnaise mixture to the broccoli mixture. Chill until ready to serve.

4 servings
0 fat grams per serving

Garden Delight Salad

If this salad seems to contain almost every vegetable in the garden, that's because it just about does!

1 15-ounce can small lima beans, drained
1 15-ounce can green beans, drained
1 15-ounce can small English peas, drained
1 15-ounce can whole-kernel corn, drained
1 medium onion, minced
1 medium green pepper, minced
1 stalk celery, finely minced
1 cup cider vinegar
2 tablespoons water
Sugar substitute to equal 1 cup sugar

Combine the lima beans, green beans, English peas, corn, onion, green pepper, and celery. In a separate bowl, combine the vinegar, water, and sugar substitute. Add the dressing to the vegetables and toss. Chill until ready to serve.

12 servings
0 fat grams per serving

Fruited Chicken Salad

This versatile recipe is a real treat. It is delicious and very pretty served as a salad with wedges of melon, apple, pear, and perhaps a few grapes arranged on the plate. It is also good served in a sandwich. Fat-free mayonnaise has really come a long way. It is now almost as good as the real thing, which makes it possible to enjoy the mayonnaise-laden salads that used to be a real no-no in a healthy lifestyle.

5 cups skinless chicken breast, cooked and chopped
1 cup fat-free mayonnaise or salad dressing
1 teaspoon lemon juice
1 cup seedless green grapes
1 red apple, cubed
1 green apple, cubed
2 stalks celery, minced

Combine the chicken, mayonnaise, lemon juice, grapes, apples, and celery. Chill until ready to serve.

8 servings
6 fat grams per serving

Creamy Strawberry Salad

When I asked my mom for the recipe after eating this salad at her house, I was surprised to find that one of the ingredients is buttermilk. I would have never guessed it. With a name like buttermilk, it is interesting that most of the buttermilk available in stores is very low in fat. Since it is a common ingredient in everything from corn bread to ranch salad dressing, that is a real plus.

1 20-ounce can juice-packed, crushed pineapple
1 large package sugar-free, fat-free strawberry gelatin
2 cups low-fat buttermilk
1 16-ounce container fat-free whipped topping, thawed

Bring the crushed pineapple and its juice to a boil. Add the gelatin and stir until it is completely dissolved. Add the buttermilk. Allow the mixture to cool to room temperature, then gently fold in the whipped topping. Pour into a serving dish and refrigerate until firm.

Variation: Use orange, cherry, or lime gelatin.

12 servings
1 fat gram per serving

Tuna Pasta Salad

It is just a few simple steps from tuna casserole to tuna pasta salad, but your family will enjoy the difference, especially in warm weather.

1 7-ounce can water-packed white chunk tuna,
    drained and flaked
1 12-ounce package rotini pasta (pasta twists), cooked
    according to package directions
1 8-ounce can sliced water chestnuts
1 medium onion, minced
1 10-ounce package frozen green peas, thawed
1 cup fat-free mayonnaise
3 tablespoons fat-free sour cream
3 tablespoons sweet or dill pickle relish
Light salt and pepper to taste

Combine the tuna, pasta, water chestnuts, onion, and peas. In a separate bowl, combine the mayonnaise, sour cream, pickle relish, and seasonings. Add the mayonnaise mixture to the tuna mixture. Chill until ready to serve.

8 servings
1 fat gram per serving

Zippy Baked Steak

1 pound round steak, all visible fat removed
No-stick cooking spray
1 medium onion, sliced
1 green pepper, coarsely chopped
1 16-ounce can stewed tomatoes
2 tablespoons ketchup
1 tablespoon Worcestershire sauce
Light salt and pepper (optional)

Cut the steak into 4 equal pieces. Place the meat in a baking dish that has been coated with no-stick cooking spray. Top the meat with the onion and green pepper. In a mixing bowl, combine the tomatoes, ketchup, and Worcestershire sauce. Add light salt and pepper if desired. Tightly cover the baking dish with aluminum foil. Bake for 1 1/2 hours at 350° or until the meat and vegetables are tender.

4 servings
5 fat grams per serving

Zesty Skillet Pork Chops

One-skillet dishes are nice since they often include all the elements of a healthy meal–meat, rice or potatoes, and other vegetables. A salad and bread will be the only additions needed. An added bonus–reduced clean-up time since there's only one skillet to wash.

4 4-ounce slices pork tenderloin
No-stick cooking spray
3 cups water
1 8-ounce can tomato paste
1 cup uncooked long-grain rice
1 medium onion, chopped
1 green or red pepper, chopped
1 8-ounce can sliced mushrooms, drained
2 teaspoons garlic powder
Light salt and pepper to taste

Place the pork tenderloin slices between two sheets of plastic wrap or waxed paper and flatten with a meat mallet or another heavy object. Place the meat in a skillet that has been coated with no-stick cooking spray and sauté until lightly browned on both sides. Combine the water and tomato paste, then add them to the skillet. Add the rice, onion, green or red pepper, mushrooms, tomato paste, garlic powder, light salt and pepper. Bring to a boil, cover, and simmer on low for 1 hour until the rice is tender. Check every 15 minutes since cooking time may vary slightly.

4 servings
5 fat grams per serving

The Corn Boil
A Country-Style Indoor/Outdoor Dinner

In the South, a popular way of entertaining in the season of fresh corn is a "Corn Boil," an outdoor affair similar to the New England shore dinner. However, instead of steaming lobsters, clams, potatoes, and corn by the seashore, we take advantage of locally grown fresh corn and other fixings to cook a down-home dinner for a crowd. This recipe can be increased or decreased to suit the number of diners, from two to two hundred. This is a pared-down indoor version for the family. For a large crowd, it's fun to do it outdoors and serve it picnic-style.

6 medium-sized potatoes, with skins
6 onions, peeled
10 carrots, peeled
2 pounds low-fat smoked sausage cut into 6 pieces
3 tablespoons liquid shrimp- or crab-boiling spices
1 tablespoon garlic powder
6 ears freshly picked corn, shucked
Fat-free liquid margarine

In a very large cooking pot or Dutch oven, layer the potatoes, onions, carrots, and smoked sausage. Add enough water to cover by at least 4 inches, and stir in the liquid boiling spices and garlic powder. Cover the pot with a lid placed slightly ajar to allow steam to escape, or cover loosely with foil. Bring to a boil, then reduce to a simmer. Simmer for 1 hour or until the vegetables are almost tender. Add the corn and continue cooking 10 additional minutes. Before serving, drizzle the vegetables and sausage with fat-free liquid margarine.

6 servings
5 fat grams per serving

Crunchy Ranch Chicken

1 cup cornflake crumbs
1 .4-ounce package dry ranch salad dressing mix
¼ cup fat-free egg substitute mixed
   with 3 tablespoons water
6 4-ounce boneless, skinless chicken breasts
No-stick cooking spray

Combine the cornflake crumbs and salad dressing mix. Dip each chicken breast into the egg-water mixture, then into the crumb mixture. Coat the chicken completely with the crumbs on both sides. Place the chicken in a baking pan that has been sprayed with no-stick cooking spray. Spray the chicken lightly with the cooking spray. Bake at 400° for 20 minutes or until the chicken is well done.

6 servings
4 fat grams per serving

Sweet And Sour Cabbage

This is good served with ham or with low-fat smoked sausage and potatoes, especially when the weather is getting a little chilly.

1 large head red cabbage, coarsely chopped or shredded
1 large red onion, chopped
2 tablespoons red wine vinegar
1 cup water
1 tablespoon lemon juice
No-stick cooking spray
Aspartame-based sugar substitute to equal
3 tablespoons sugar

Place the cabbage, onion, vinegar, water, and lemon juice in a skillet that has been coated with no-stick cooking spray. Cover and cook over low heat until the vegetables are tender. Remove from the heat and add the sugar substitute.

8 servings
0 fat grams per serving

Cheesy Chili Surprise

8 ounces extra-lean ground round, cooked, rinsed,
   and patted dry to remove excess grease
3 15-ounce cans red kidney beans, drained
1 medium onion, chopped
2 teaspoons garlic powder
3 tablespoons chili powder
2 6-ounce cans tomato paste
1 15-ounce can crushed tomatoes
2 cups water (can be adjusted to reach your preferred
   consistency)
8 tablespoons fat-free cheddar cheese, shredded
8 tablespoons fat-free sour cream
4 teaspoons green onion, chopped

Combine the ground round, kidney beans, onion, garlic powder, chili powder, tomato paste, crushed tomatoes, and water. Simmer for 20 minutes over medium heat until the onions are tender. Place 2 tablespoons cheese, a tablespoon of sour cream, and a teaspoon of green onion in the bottom of each of 4 soup bowls. Top with a serving of chili.

4 servings
6 fat grams per serving

French Country-Style Chicken Casserole

This is similar to the famous French country-style dish, cassoulet. I imagine that French chefs would faint if they saw this version. Not only does it contain less fat than the original, but it also is made with canned beans! Serve with salad and hot French bread.

1 medium onion, coarsely chopped
1 bell pepper, chopped
½ pound 97% fat-free smoked sausage, sliced
No-stick cooking spray
1 cup boneless, skinless chicken breasts,
    cooked and chopped
3 15-ounce cans navy beans, rinsed and drained
    to remove excess salt
1 teaspoon garlic powder
1 15-ounce can chunky tomato sauce

Sauté the onion, bell pepper, and smoked sausage in a skillet that has been coated with no-stick cooking spray. When the onions and sausage are lightly browned, add the chicken, beans, garlic powder, and tomato sauce. Simmer 15 minutes. Place the mixture in a baking dish that has been coated with no-stick cooking spray. Bake for 20 minutes at 325°.

6 servings
4 fat grams per serving

Rich Rice Casserole

1/4 cup fat-free egg substitute
1 cup skim milk
1 onion, chopped
2 cups cooked white rice
1/2 cup fat-free cheddar cheese, shredded
Light salt and pepper to taste (optional)
No-stick cooking spray

Combine the egg substitute, skim milk, onion, rice, cheese, and salt and pepper to taste (optional). Pour the mixture into a casserole dish coated with no-stick cooking spray. Bake for 30 minutes at 350°.

4 servings
0 fat grams per serving

Elegant Spinach-Rice Soufflé

2 cups cooked rice
1 10-ounce package frozen spinach, cooked
   and squeezed dry
1 cup skim milk
1 package dehydrated vegetable soup mix
1/2 cup fat-free egg substitute
1 cup fat-free sour cream
Light salt and pepper to taste (optional)
No-stick cooking spray

Combine the rice and spinach. In a separate mixing bowl, combine the milk, dry soup mix, egg substitute, sour cream, and light salt and pepper. Combine with the rice mixture and place in a baking dish coated with no-stick cooking spray. Bake for 30 minutes at 350°.

4 servings
0 fat grams per serving

Summer Squash and Onion Sauté

My family is from the country, and when we had squash cooked this way we called it simply "fried squash." But, just as what we used to call noodles or spaghetti is now known as pasta, some things we used to call "fried" are now more commonly referred to as sautéed.

No-stick cooking spray
6 yellow summer squash, thinly sliced
1 large onion, chopped
Light salt and pepper to taste

In a skillet coated with no-stick cooking spray, layer the squash and onion. Cook, covered, over medium heat until the vegetables are tender. Allow the bottom layer to brown, then turn with a spatula to develop a brown crust. Add light salt and pepper to taste.

4 servings
0 fat grams per serving

Onion Baked Rice

1 cup white rice
2 cups water
1 1-ounce package dehydrated onion soup mix
1 medium onion, finely chopped
4 green onions, including green tops, chopped
No-stick cooking spray
¼ cup fat-free liquid margarine

Combine the rice, water, onion soup mix, chopped onion, and green onions in a casserole dish coated with no-stick cooking spray. Bake for 1 hour at 350°. Stir in the liquid margarine before serving.

4 servings
1 fat gram per serving

Delicious Oven Browned Potatoes

5 tablespoons Dijon mustard
1 tablespoon oil
1 teaspoon garlic powder
1 teaspoon Italian seasoning
2 pounds small, red-skinned new potatoes, quartered

Combine the mustard, oil, garlic powder, Italian seasoning, and potatoes. Place in a single layer in a baking dish that has been coated with no-stick cooking spray. Bake at 400° for 30 minutes or until tender and lightly browned.

4 servings
4 fat grams per serving

Yummy Potato Puffs

2 cups fat-free prepared mashed potatoes (see recipe index)
1 cup soft bread crumbs, made from low-fat, reduced-
  calorie bread
1 small onion, finely minced
1 tablespoon fat-free liquid margarine
Light salt and pepper to taste (optional)
No-stick cooking spray

Combine the mashed potatoes, bread crumbs, onion, margarine, and light salt and pepper. Chill for 15 minutes. Shape the mixture into 1-inch balls and place them on a baking sheet coated with no-stick cooking spray. Lightly spray each potato puff with cooking spray. Bake for 20 minutes at 425°.

8 servings
0 fat grams per serving

Sweet Potato Croquettes

2 cups sweet potatoes, cooked and mashed
¼ cup fat-free egg substitute
6 packets sugar substitute
1 teaspoon nutmeg
1 teaspoon cinnamon
1 cup cornflake crumbs
No-stick cooking spray

Combine the sweet potatoes, egg substitute, sugar substitute, and spices. Allow to chill for about 15 minutes, then roll into 2-inch-long logs. Spray the logs lightly with no-stick cooking spray then coat with the cornflake crumbs. Place the croquettes on a baking sheet coated with no-stick cooking spray. Coat the croquettes lightly with the cooking spray. Bake for 20 minutes at 400°.

4 servings
Less than 1 fat gram per serving

Squash Hush Puppies

A cross between hush puppies and squash fritters, these are an interesting taste treat as a bread or as a vegetable side dish.

6 yellow summer squash, boiled, drained, and mashed
1 small onion, finely minced
1 cup cornmeal mix
$\frac{1}{4}$ cup fat-free egg substitute
$\frac{3}{4}$ cup low-fat buttermilk
$\frac{1}{4}$ cup fat-free Cheddar cheese, shredded
No-stick cooking spray

Combine all of the ingredients. Spoon into mini-muffin tins that have been coated with no-stick cooking spray. Bake for 20 minutes at 350°.

24 mini-muffins
0 fat grams per muffin

Cheddar-Rice Corn Bread

At our house we love corn bread and rice in any form or fashion, so this recipe is a big hit.

1 cup self-rising cornmeal
½ cup self-rising flour
1 teaspoon light salt
1¼ cups skim milk
¼ cup fat-free egg substitute
1 cup cooked rice, cooled
1 cup fat-free cheddar cheese, shredded
1 small onion, finely minced
No-stick cooking spray

Combine the cornmeal, flour, and salt. Add the milk and egg substitute, then the rice, cheese, and onion. Place the mixture in either a 10" iron skillet or 8" square baking pan that has been coated with no-stick cooking spray. Bake for 30 minutes at 350°.

6 servings
1 fat gram per serving

Creamy Corn Bread

This recipe makes a moist, delicious corn bread that is rather like a cross between corn bread and that old southern favorite, spoon bread. It will be a unique addition to your corn bread recipe collection.

1 cup yellow cornmeal
¼ cup all-purpose flour
1 teaspoon baking powder
½ teaspoon salt
1 cups skim milk
¼ cup fat-free egg substitute
No-stick cooking spray

Preheat your oven to 400°. Combine the dry ingredients. Add 1 cup of the skim milk, then the egg substitute. Pour the mixture into an 8" square baking pan that has been coated with no-stick cooking spray. Evenly pour the remaining cup skim milk over the top. Do not stir. Bake for 30 minutes.

4 servings
1 fat gram per serving

Pizza Breadsticks

These breadsticks are very quick and very simple because they are made with refrigerated pizza dough. They are good with any pasta meal or even as a nice alternative to crackers with a salad. They are also good served as a snack or appetizer with a little spaghetti sauce or pizza sauce on the side for dipping.

1 10-ounce can refrigerated pizza-crust dough
Butter-flavored or olive-oil flavored no-stick cooking spray
Garlic powder to taste
Dried Italian seasoning or oregano to taste
Fat-free Parmesan cheese to taste
Light salt to taste

Open the can of refrigerated pizza dough as directed on the label. Unroll the dough and place on a cutting board. Cut the dough into strips about 1" wide. Place the strips of dough on a baking sheet that has been coated with no-stick cooking spray. The strips should be at least 1 inch apart. Lightly spray the dough with no-stick cooking spray. Sprinkle with the garlic powder, Italian seasoning, Parmesan cheese, and light salt to taste. Bake for 20 minutes at 350° or until lightly browned.

4 servings
2 fat grams per serving

Tempting Batter Bread

This is a very simple version of homemade white bread. You get a lot of taste, not to mention the terrific aroma, without much work. The trade-off: The texture of the bread is rather coarse because the dough is not kneaded.

2 packages dry yeast
1 tablespoon salt
2 tablespoons sugar
2 cups very warm water
⅔ cup dry skim-milk powder
4½ cups all-purpose flour
No-stick cooking spray

Combine the yeast, salt, sugar, water, and skim milk powder. Gradually add the flour. Spoon the dough into two loaf pans coated with no-stick cooking spray. Lightly spray the tops of the loaves with no-stick cooking spray. Cover loosely with plastic wrap. Allow the bread to rise in a warm, draft-free place for 20 minutes, or until it fills about ⅔ of the pan. While the dough is rising, preheat the oven to 250°. When the dough has risen, remove the plastic wrap and place the pans in the oven. Bake for 10 minutes at 250°. Then increase the oven temperature to 375°. Bake the bread for approximately 30 additional minutes or until the bread sounds hollow when tapped.

6 servings per loaf
0 fat grams per serving

Golden Cheese Sticks

These can also be shaped into patties and served as an entree. Either way, a little spaghetti sauce makes a good topping.

1 cup fat-free cheddar cheese
2 cups fat-free cottage cheese
1 cup saltine cracker crumbs
2 tablespoons dehydrated minced onion
Light salt and pepper to taste
½ cup fat-free egg substitute
Additional cracker crumbs for coating

Combine the cheddar cheese, cottage cheese, cracker crumbs, minced onion, salt, and pepper. Blend in the egg substitute. Chill the mixture for 1 hour. Shape into 2"-long sticks or into patties. Roll in cracker crumbs and place on a baking sheet that has been coated with no-stick cooking spray. Bake for 30 minutes at 400°.

Variation: Add ¼ cup each finely minced celery, green pepper, and ham if serving as an entree.

4 servings
0 fat grams per serving

Ranch Fries

You may notice I use dry ranch dressing mix as an ingredient in several recipes. That's because it provides lots of terrific, zesty flavor with no fat!

3 pounds russet potatoes, peeled
No-stick cooking spray
1 .4-ounce packet dry ranch salad dressing mix
Commercially prepared fat-free ranch salad dressing

Preheat the oven to 420°. Cut the potatoes into your favorite French fry style–regular, shoestring, steak fries, etc. Lightly spray the potatoes with no-stick cooking spray. Place the dry ranch dressing mix in a zip-top plastic bag. Add the potatoes a few at a time and shake until they are all coated with the dry mix.

Cover a cookie sheet with aluminum foil and spray with no-stick cooking spray. Place the coated potatoes in a single layer on the cookie sheet. Bake at 420° for about 30 minutes or until the fries are browned. Serve with commercially prepared ranch dressing (or more dry ranch dressing mix blended with fat-free mayonnaise and skim milk to your preferred consistency) as a dipping sauce.

4 servings
0 fat grams per serving

Turkey Wrap it Up!

The following three recipes are for a popular trend in sandwiches: wraps. They are very simple—just center your favorite sandwich ingredients on a flour tortilla and roll. This turkey wrap has an interesting and tasty surprise ingredient—cranberry sauce. After all, it's a classic accompaniment for turkey dinners. Why not on a turkey sandwich? Try it—you'll like it.

For each sandwich:
1 large fat-free flour tortilla
2 tablespoons fat-free mayonnaise
1 tablespoon whole-berry cranberry sauce
3 slices deli-sliced fat-free turkey
2 tablespoons fat-free cheddar cheese, shredded
Shredded lettuce

Warm the tortilla for 10 seconds on high power in a microwave oven to soften. Spread the warm tortilla with the fat-free mayonnaise, followed by the cranberry sauce. Center the turkey slices on the tortilla followed by the cheese and lettuce. If the tortilla has cooled, warm again briefly. Roll the sandwich as tightly as possible. Secure with a toothpick or wrap in plastic wrap until serving time.

1 serving
0 fat grams per serving

Mexican Wrap

For each sandwich:
1 large fat-free flour tortilla
3 tablespoons fat-free refried beans
2 tablespoons fat-free sour cream
2 tablespoons commercially prepared chunky salsa
3 slices deli-sliced fat-free turkey
2 tablespoons fat-free cheddar cheese, shredded
Shredded lettuce
Finely minced onion

Warm the tortilla for 10 seconds on high power in a microwave oven to soften. Spread the warm tortilla with the fat-free sour cream, followed by the refried beans and the salsa. Center the turkey slices on the tortilla followed by the cheese, lettuce, and onion. If the tortilla has cooled, warm again briefly. Roll the sandwich as tightly as possible. Secure with a toothpick or wrap in plastic wrap until serving time.

1 serving
0 fat grams per serving

Mediterranean Wrap

For each sandwich:
1 large fat-free flour tortilla
2 tablespoons fat-free mayonnaise or plain yogurt
1 teaspoon garlic powder
3 slices deli-sliced low-fat roast beef
Finely chopped cucumber
Finely chopped tomato
2 tablespoons fat-free mozzarella, shredded
Shredded lettuce
Finely chopped onion

Warm the tortilla for 10 seconds on high power in a microwave oven to soften. Spread the warm tortilla with the fat-free mayonnaise or yogurt. Sprinkle with the garlic powder. Center the roast beef slices on the tortilla followed by the cucumber, tomato, cheese, lettuce and onion. If the tortilla has cooled, warm again briefly. Roll the sandwich as tightly as possible. Secure with a toothpick or wrap in plastic wrap until serving time.

1 serving
2 fat grams per serving

Fruit Salad in a Flash
1 16-ounce can peach pie filling
2 15-ounce cans juice-packed pineapple tidbits, drained
2 15-ounce cans mandarin oranges, drained
1 cup miniature marshmallows
3 medium bananas, sliced

Combine the pie filling, pineapple tidbits, and mandarin oranges. Stir gently to avoid breaking the orange segments. Chill until serving time. Just before serving add the marshmallows and sliced bananas.

Optional: For color add a few maraschino cherries, halved.

14 servings
0 fat grams per serving

Strawberries Melba

This recipe may be sacrilegious to those of you who live in areas where fresh raspberries are king, but down South they are relatively rare and expensive. Even frozen raspberries are not always found in grocery stores. Therefore, I adapted that classic dessert, peach Melba, to the berries we Southerners cherish: strawberries. This is very pretty served in a stemmed glass.

1 pint fat-free, sugar-free vanilla ice cream or
   frozen yogurt
1 15-ounce can juice-packed peach slices, drained
   and chopped
1 pint fresh or frozen strawberries, puréed
Sugar substitute to equal 3 tablespoons sugar

Combine the puréed strawberries and sugar substitute. Place ½ cup ice cream in a stemmed glass. Top with several table-spoons peaches, then with the puréed strawberries.

4 servings
0 fat grams per serving

Gingerbread Muffins

We love gingerbread at our house. I used to serve it mainly as a dessert, usually with lemon sauce, but it also makes wonderful muffins. This recipe has the added benefit of providing bran for extra fiber.

1¼ cups all-purpose flour
1 tablespoon baking powder
1 teaspoon ground ginger
½ teaspoon cinnamon
½ teaspoon ground cloves
1¼ cups fat-free bran cereal
1½ cups skim milk
¼ cup molasses
¼ cup fat-free egg substitute
2 tablespoons fat-free sour cream
No-stick cooking spray

Combine the flour, baking powder, ginger, cinnamon, and cloves. In a separate bowl, combine the cereal and skim milk. Let stand for 5 minutes. Add the molasses, egg substitute, and sour cream to the cereal mixture. Combine the dry ingredients and the milk mixture. Stir until the ingredients are thoroughly combined. Spoon into muffin tins coated with no-stick cooking spray. Bake for 25 minutes at 350°.

12 muffins
0 fat grams per muffin

Éclair Cake

Who doesn't love chocolate éclairs? The creamy custard enclosed in a cream puff and topped with chocolate glaze is a sweet lover's dream and a weight watcher's nightmare. Here's a simple and much healthier version that is close enough to the real thing to satisfy your desire for one without sabotaging your healthy eating plans.

    1 low-fat yellow cake mix
    No-stick cooking spray
    1 small box fat-free, sugar-free vanilla instant pudding mix
    1 small box fat-free, sugar-free chocolate instant
        pudding mix
    4 cups skim milk, divided

Prepare the cake mix according to package directions, or for an extra-low-fat cake, omit any oil and use egg substitute in place of eggs. Bake in a 9" x 13" baking dish that has been coated with no-stick cooking spray.

Meanwhile, prepare the vanilla pudding mix using 2 cups of the skim milk. Using the remaining 2 cups of skim milk, prepare the chocolate pudding.

When the cake is done, allow it to cool completely in the baking dish, then cut into 1-inch slices. Place a layer of the cake slices, cut-side up, in another 9" x 13" baking dish. Spread the vanilla pudding over the cake layer. Top with another layer of cake. Spread with the chocolate pudding. Chill until ready to serve.

12 servings
5 fat grams per serving using oil and eggs
as called for in cake-mix directions
1 fat gram per serving omitting oil
and using fat-free egg substitute

Pineapple Cheese Pie

1 15-ounce can juice-packed crushed pineapple
2 tablespoons cornstarch
2 tablespoons water
Sugar substitute to equal 3/4 cup sugar, divided
1 reduced-fat frozen pie crust
1 8-ounce package fat-free cream cheese
Sugar substitute to equal 1/4 cup sugar
1 teaspoon vanilla
¾ cup fat-free egg substitute

Combine the crushed pineapple, cornstarch, and water in a saucepan over medium heat. Bring to a boil, stirring frequently. When thick, add sugar substitute to equal ½ cup sugar. Let cool and pour into the pie shell. In a mixing bowl, beat the softened cream cheese, remaining sugar substitute, vanilla, and egg substitute until smooth. Pour the cream cheese mixture over the pineapple mixture. Bake at 350° for 40 minutes or until a knife inserted into the cream cheese layer comes out clean.

8 servings
6 fat grams per serving

Fresh Strawberry Pie

When I was a teenager a popular restaurant chain intro-
duced fresh strawberry pie. It was a sight to behold, those huge,
fresh strawberries coated with glistening strawberry glaze,
heaped like rubies in a crisp crust. And it was available year-
round, which then was a real miracle since we were used to
enjoying fresh strawberries only in season. Of course, that was
eons ago. Now we think nothing of having the most exotic
fruits and vegetables any time of year.

1 .3 ounce package sugar-free strawberry gelatin
3 tablespoons cornstarch
1 cup water
3 cups fresh, whole strawberries, stems removed
1 low-fat commercially prepared frozen pie shell, baked
Fat-free whipped topping

Combine the gelatin, cornstarch, and water. Bring to a boil
over medium heat, stirring constantly. When the mixture is
thick enough to coat a spoon, remove it from the heat and add it
to the strawberries. Toss gently to coat the berries. Arrange the
strawberries in the pie shell. Chill until ready to serve. Top each
serving with a dollop of whipped topping.

6 servings
5 fat grams per serving

Cool And Creamy Tropical Pie

This pie couldn't be easier. It makes a delicious, refreshing dessert.

2 pints fat-free, sugar-free vanilla ice cream or
    frozen yogurt, softened
1 small container orange juice concentrate, thawed
1 15-ounce can mandarin orange sections, drained
1 15-ounce can juice-packed crushed pineapple, drained
1 commercially prepared low-fat graham cracker crust

Combine the ice cream, orange juice concentrate, mandarin oranges, and pineapple. Blend well and pour into the pie shell. Place in the freezer until ready to serve. Allow to stand 3–5 minutes at room temperature before serving.

8 servings
3 fat grams per serving

Index